Also by Greg Knight

Westminster Words (with Stephen Parker)
Honourable Insults
Parliamentary Sauce
Right Honourable Insults
The Ultimate Book of Naughty Graffiti

DISHONOURABLE INSULTS
A Cantankerous Collection of Political Invective

Greg Knight

The Robson Press

First published in Great Britain in 2011 by
The Robson Press
Westminster Tower
3 Albert Embankment
London
SE1 7SP

Copyright © Greg Knight 2011

Greg Knight has asserted his right under the Copyright, Designs and Patents Act
1988 to be identified as the author of this work.

Note: In the course of preparation of this book there may well have been a number
of changes in Members' positions in the Houses of Parliament. While every effort
has been made to keep the text up to date, it may not have been possible where a
change has taken place between the completion of the manuscript and publication.
Some quotes and insults published here have appeared in an earlier compilation by
Greg Knight. They have been retained in this book either to give continuity to the
text or where new contributions from other politicians have made their inclusion
desirable.

ISBN 978-1-84954-161-9

10 9 8 7 6 5 4 3 2 1

A CIP catalogue record for this book is available from the British Library.

Set in Sabon by Namkwan Cho
Printed and bound in Great Britain by
CPI Group (UK) Ltd, Croydon, CR0 4YY

For the memory of Eric Forth

CONTENTS

ACKNOWLEDGEMENTS

The author wishes to thank the following for their help, advice, suggestions and assistance:

Nicholas Bennett, the late Dr John Blackburn MP, Sir Sydney Chapman, Lord Coe, Rt Hon. David Davis MP, the late Sir Nicholas Fairbairn QC MP, the late Rt Hon. Eric Forth MP, Rt Hon. Andrew Mackay, Rt Hon. Andrew Mitchell MP, Rt Hon. John Redwood MP, Rt Hon. Lord Ryder of Wensum, Rev. Martin Smyth MP, the late Sir John Stradling-Thomas MP and Matthew Thomas Esq.

The following books contain some excellent political stories, a few of which are recalled here and are acknowledged with grateful thanks:

An American Life by Ronald Reagan (Hutchinson); *The View from Number 11* by Nigel Lawson, (Bantam Press); *Glittering Prizes* by William Camp (Macgibbon and Kee); *The Making of a Prime Minister* by Harold Wilson (Weidenfeld and Nicholson); *Speaking My Mind* by Dr Rhodes Boyson (Peter Owen); *Upwardly Mobile* by Norman Tebbit (Weidenfeld and Nicholson).

INTRODUCTION

The title of this book is not meant to be disrespectful to my parliamentary colleagues or unduly critical of them. An insult which might at first seem disrespectful or even 'dishonourable' is often no such thing. Indeed, the parliamentary insult is as old as the game of democratic politics itself.

Anyone who has studied democratic politics will know that one of the regular activities of our elected representatives over the centuries has been insulting each other. Even during a constructive debate, a politician will often take time out to be abusive to his or her opponent – and sometimes even a colleague too.

Vitriol, insult, impudence and audacity are all part of a good debater's armoury. The crescendo of emotion, the torrent of abuse and the flash of bad temper are the ingredients which can make a good political speech *great*. Anyone who heard the late Aneurin Bevan on his feet will realise how effective the use of ridicule during a speech can be. And anyone who has been captivated by an oration by the late Lord Hailsham will know that the occasional use of passion and even rage can be both compelling and devastating. It can guarantee that the attention of the audience is firmly held by the speaker, a necessary prerequisite of a great speech.

Politicians also sometimes use unwarranted abuse to enliven what they know is a dull brief. They are aware that the barb helps them to hold the floor and thereby get their message across.

There is also another explanation for the frequency of the political insult. In the chamber of either House the 'audience' is not an impartial gathering, waiting to be convinced by rational argument and reasoned discussion. Unlike a jury in court, those listening *are* partial and do have a vested interest in the outcome of the debate, regardless of the strength of argument for either side. In the present House of Commons, all MPs except one belong to a political party. Therefore, when a government minister is forced to defend some policy or initiative, Conservative and (usually) Lib Dem MPs will give their support, even if the opposition have set out a good argument why the policy is wrong or should be changed. In this scenario, where the outcome depends more on party whipping than on the facts placed before the House, no wonder one of the weapons – frequently deployed by all sides – is the parliamentary insult.

This is not a twenty-first century phenomenon. Politicians have been spewing vitriol at each other through the centuries and, even though the trend is somewhat diminished, it shows no signs of abating. It has, however, ebbed somewhat from the heady days of Gladstone and Disraeli. The reason for this is undoubtedly the advent of the broadcasting of parliamentary proceedings, initially on radio and, since the 1980s, on television. Democratic politicians always have an eye on the electorate. They have to. And it did not take MPs long to realise that the public do not like to see arm-waving, ranting and gratuitous abuse emanating from the TV set in their own front room.

These days, therefore, party leaders are more circumspect than their forebears. They have learned from the late President Ronald Reagan, one of the most effective political communicators of the television age, that a message conveyed with a reassuring smile and some gentle self-deprecation can be devastatingly effective – and also popular with the voters. Being acerbic on television *can* work, but there is a real danger that the lasting impression left with the viewer will not be one of the mocked victim of the abuse but a negative image of the perpetrator, who appears as mean and unpleasant.

But while some of the catcalling at Westminster is considered routine, other remarks – at first perhaps seemingly innocuous – incur the wrath of the Speaker and must be withdrawn.

Accusations of lying are always blocked by the Speaker and, unless withdrawn, can mean expulsion from the Chamber. Former Labour MP Tam Dalyell was twice ejected for calling Margaret Thatcher a liar. On one occasion, after describing her as 'a sustained brazen deceiver', he went further, adding: 'She is a bounder, a liar, a deceiver, a cheat and a crook.'

On one occasion, however, Winston Churchill got away referring to a lie as a 'terminological inexactitude'.

One unexpected ruling during the 1980s was by Speaker Bernard Weatherill. He surprised many MPs by ruling the word 'poppycock' to be unparliamentary because the original meaning in Dutch is rude.

The word 'twerp' has had a chequered history. When used in 1956, the then Speaker ruled it in order because, I have been told, he wrongly assumed 'it was a sort of technical term of the aviation industry'. But when years later the late anti-monarchist Labour MP Willie Hamilton described Prince Charles as 'that young twerp', he was instantly ordered to withdraw the soubriquet.

Even the word 'Tory', still commonly used today by the media to describe Conservatives, originated as an insult; it meant 'an Irish outlaw'.

In 1896, the parliamentary description 'Tory skunk' was ruled admissible and yet the term 'political skunk' was ruled out of order a century later.

Oddly, 'political weasel and guttersnipe' have passed previous Speaker's censorship, but the term 'rat' has a chequered career, sometimes being in order and sometimes not, depending on who was in the chair at the time.

One Labour MP was once called to order for saying that a Tory was a member of the SS. As he withdrew the term, he pretended he thought the letters stood for 'silly sod'.

Ex-Labour MP Paul (now Lord) Boateng was once brought to book for using the term 'Sweet FA' because the authorities wrongly thought it was a way of using the 'F-word'. In fact, it is nineteenth-century naval slang for packed mutton. It refers to Fanny Adams, who was murdered in 1867, cut into pieces and thrown into a river down in Hampshire.

Michael Foot did not get into political hot water for calling Norman Tebbit a 'semi-house-trained polecat'. Indeed, Tebbit was so proud of the description that he used a polecat in his coat-of-arms when he later was appointed to the House of Lords.

The late Sir Nicholas Fairbairn escaped rebuke, but not disdain, by describing women MPs as 'mostly hideous – they have no fragrance and I dislike women who deny their femininity. They are just cagmags, scrub heaps, old tattles.'

The advent of universal suffrage, party selection committees and tabloid newspapers have destroyed most of the vitriol formerly found in politicians' correspondence. Over the years MPs have moderated their response to criticisms from the voters, although many still get annoyed when a voter writes to *demand* that the MP vote in a particular way.

The one class of person who is normally safe from the vitriol of an MP is the constituent. I emphasise *constituent*, rather than the general public, because it is the possession by a person of the power to vote, for or against the MP, which makes all the difference. Votes do matter to our elected representatives and they know that a sharp rebuke or apparent unsympathetic ear can cost them electoral support. However, even the most forbearing Member can occasionally lose his composure when faced with a stubborn or silly elector.

However, it is not surprising that the confrontational approach of democratic politicians does not promote respect from the public. If members of all parties abuse one another, it is hardly surprising that the public sometimes end up doing likewise!

Occasionally, parliamentary anger is vented in response to an abusive letter the MP has received. One response that has been used from time to time by MPs of all parties is the reply:

'Dear Sir, Today I received an abusive and insulting letter from some crackpot who has signed the letter in your name. I thought you should know at once about this.'

This is mild compared to what used to be written. Anthony Henry, who was an MP at the beginning of the eighteenth century, was once asked by a group of his constituents to vote against the Budget of 1714. Angered that they should have the temerity to write to try to influence his voting intentions, he replied: 'Gentlemen, I have received your letter about the excise, and I am surprised at your insolence at writing to me at all. You know, and I know, that I bought this constituency. You know, and I know, that I am now determined to sell it, and you know what you think I don't know that you are now looking out for another buyer, and I know, what you certainly don't know, that I have now found another constituency to buy.'

As Henry's letter continued, he became more abusive, adding for good measure: 'About what you said about the excise, may God's curse light upon you all, and may it make your homes as open and as free to the excise officers as your wives and daughters have always been to me while I have represented your rascally constituency.'

Generally, today's elected representatives are more careful about what they say in public and how they say it. They behave in a more responsible manner and as a consequence they can be dull and boring.

But not always! Detailed between the covers of this book are those occasions when politicians have thrown caution to the wind and sparks have flown. The book covers most political caustic gems uttered on both sides of the Atlantic over the past one hundred years, right up to the present day. Looking at the insults contained within, one can easily agree with George Bernard Shaw's view of a general election, which he described as: 'A moral horror, as bad as a battleground except for the blood; a mud bath for every soul concerned with it.'

Benjamin Disraeli once commented: 'The wisdom of the wise and the experience of the ages are perpetuated by quotations.'

He could have added: 'and insults too'.

The Rt Hon. Greg Knight MP
House of Commons, 2011

GONE WITH THE WIND

Diarist and Tory, Doctor Samuel Johnson took a keen interest in the politics of his day and was actually responsible for inventing many of the speeches of contemporary politicians during the eighteenth century.

Because it was against the law at the time to print transcriptions of British parliamentary proceedings, *The Gentleman's Magazine* hired someone to attend debates and surreptitiously write down notes, which Johnson transformed into 'Debates in the Senate of Lilliput'. The skimpy nature of the notes handed to him meant that Johnson had to imagine what the speakers actually said. Johnson used names which the average Briton could decode into their British counterparts.

He therefore largely wrote the speeches himself, which meant in many cases that the reported speeches were far better than what had actually been delivered. The series was very successful, and considerably boosted the magazine's circulation.

When one politician boasted of his patriotism, Johnson's uttered perhaps his most famous retort: 'Patriotism is the last refuge of a scoundrel.'

He had a low opinion of Tory Prime Minister Lord North, of whom he dismissively said: 'He fills a chair.'

On newcomers he opined: 'We are inclined to believe those whom we do not know because they have never deceived us.'

He had no time for the sport of angling, which led to the utterance of perhaps his second most famous retort. He defined the practice as 'a stick and a piece of string with a worm on one end and a fool at the other'.

He accurately summed up his fellow countrymen: 'When two Englishman meet, their first talk is of the weather.'

⧗

LORD FALKLAND is today largely forgotten, apart from one quip which has stood the test of time. His political maxim was: 'When it is not necessary to change, it is necessary not to change.'

⧗

POLITICIAN EDMUND BURKE in 1774 neatly summed up the duties of our elected representatives, after some of his own constituents had demanded that he vote for a particular cause. Whilst addressing his electors in Bristol he told them: '[A constituent's] wishes ought to have great weight with [their MP]... It is his duty to... prefer their interest to his own. But his unbiased opinion, his mature judgement, his enlightened conscience, he ought not to sacrifice to you, to any man, or to any set of men living... Your representative owes you, not his industry only, but his judgement; and he betrays, instead of serving you, if he sacrifices it to your opinion... government and legislation are matters of reason and judgement, and not of inclination.' An accurate exposition but also a brave one: Burke lost his seat!

Speaking of his political opponents: 'They defend their errors as if they were defending their inheritance.'

And on our revenue collection system: 'To tax and to please, no more than to love and be wise, is not given to men.'

And on being in government: 'Those who have been once intoxicated with power, and have derived any kind of emolument from it, even though but for one year, can never willingly abandon it.'

And his views on the attitude of politicians to their colleagues: 'I am convinced that we have a degree of delight in the real misfortunes of others.'

Clever he was, but those with the most brains are not always the most interesting or stimulating orators. Burke was so dull and boring when addressing the Commons that he earned the nickname 'The Dinner Bell'. As soon as he rose to his feet, the majority of MPs decided it was time to leave and take some refreshment in the Members' Dining Room.

☒

THE DUKE of Wellington was one of the rudest men of his day. He was Prime Minister for nearly three years from January 1828 to November 1830, returning for a mere three weeks in 1834.

He always spoke his mind and certainly did not suffer fools at all: two traits that on their own would certainly bar him from office today. He was completely out of touch with the electorate and had no knowledge whatsoever of trade or commerce. He admitted he did not know how to flatter and when this was put to him by a colleague who praised Sir Robert Peel, he retorted 'I may have no small talk but Robert Peel has no manners.'

When at a reception two French marshals, still smarting over their battlefield defeat, turned their backs on him, he remarked loudly: 'It doesn't bother me, I have seen their backs before!'

He was, however, even-handed in dispensing insults, frequently insulting his own troops. Of the then British cavalry, he said: 'The only thing that they can be relied on to do is to gallop too far and too fast.'

He later opined: 'There is nothing on earth so stupid as a gallant officer.'

☒

WILLIAM COBBETT was not a popular MP. In the early nineteenth century, his insults caused great offence to many of his colleagues. He became a hate figure for many in authority because of his invective. Indeed, he was so vitriolic in his utterances that he actually spent two years in Newgate Gaol for treasonable libel!

It was Cobbett who founded the first regular journal of parliamentary debates, a publication which he later sold out to one Luke Hansard, whose name is now synonymous with the parliamentary Official Report.

Unusually in those times, he spoke up for the oppressed and regularly criticised those in authority for the way they treated junior soldiers.

Of Prime Minister Henry Addington he snapped: 'A pompous chanticleer crowing upon his own dunghill.'

On Benjamin Franklin: 'A crafty and lecherous old hypocrite.'

On universities, his comment might strike a chord with some today: 'They are dens of dunces.'

Of Tory William Pitt he was basic: 'That great snorting bawler.'

As language is a living, changing thing, some of his insults have today lost their edge. Of Thomas Malthus, a 'left-wing' vicar of his time he said: 'He is a *Parson*.' (At the time this meant a Borough-monger's tool.)

Of the landed gentry of the day he opined: 'Incomparable cowards, wretched, dirty creatures who call themselves country gentlemen ... there is a foul and stinking baseness of these fellows.'

Despite all his rage and wrath, Cobbett was actually a political moderate!

⌛

IN 1874 Lord Morley coined a phrase which many dictators today would do well to remember. He said: 'You have not converted a man because you have silenced him.'

He started his political life as the Liberal MP John Morley, being first elected to the House of Commons in 1883. He was ennobled as Viscount Morley of Blackburn in 1908, whilst serving as Secretary of State for India. He was Lord President of the Council between 1910 and 1914.

Of his other comments, the following are worthy of note:

'It is more true to say that our opinions depend upon our

lives and habits, than to say that our lives and habits depend on our opinions.'

'Three things matter in a speech: who says it, how he says it, and what he says, and of the three, the last matters the least.'

'Where it is a duty to worship the sun it is pretty sure to be a crime to examine the laws of heat.'

'It is not enough to do good – one must do it the right way.'

Towards the end of his life he predicted, wrongly, that Lord Birkenhead (F. E. Smith) would become Prime Minister in the Lords with Winston Churchill leading the Commons. He said: 'They will make a formidable pair. Birkenhead has the best brain in England.' Perhaps at the time he was forgetting one of his own aphorisms which could easily have applied to Smith: 'No man can climb out beyond the limitations of his own character.'

⧗

LORD MACAULAY, formerly Thomas Babington Macaulay, served as Secretary of State for War between 1839 and 1841 and was Paymaster General between 1846 and 1848.

This Liberal politician frequently enlivened nineteenth-century debate in the House of Lords. He once snapped at a colleague: 'It is possible to be below flattery as well as above it.'

Commenting on Socrates, he said: 'The more I read him, the less I wonder that they poisoned him.'

On the arts, he opined: 'Perhaps no person can be a poet, or even enjoy poetry, without a certain unsoundness of mind.'

On a fellow politician: 'His imagination resembled the wings of an ostrich. It enabled him to run, though not to soar.'

Among his other quips, the following are worthy of note:

'The measure of a man's real character is what he would do if he knew he would never be found out.'

'I would rather be poor in a cottage full of books than a king without the desire to read.'

'The object of oratory alone is not truth, but persuasion.'

'I know of no spectacle so ridiculous as the British public in one of its periodical fits of morality.'

'Nothing is so useless as a general maxim.'

⌛

FIERY ORATOR Daniel O'Connell was an extremely colourful character. On several occasions he was unwise enough to gripe to the press about his speeches not being given sufficient prominence. He also complained about what he called 'press misreporting'.

In the 1830s he complained again, on this occasion to *The Times*, saying: 'Your reporting is scandalous. I made a speech yesterday which was more cheered than any, I believe, I ever made. The report is contained in a few insignificant lines.' He went on to complain that those 'insignificant lines' were also incorrect. On this occasion, the journalist responsible unwisely tried to calm O'Connell by insisting that his notebook had got wet in the rain on the way back to his office and washed most of the words away. At this O'Connell erupted: 'That was the most extraordinary shower of rain I ever heard of, for it not only washed out details of the speech I made from your notebook, but it also washed in another and an entirely different one!'

O'Connell's frequent rantings were counter-productive because the sensitive press corps at the time imposed a ban on his speeches as a result of his impudence, with one journalist explaining that it was 'to repel with the utmost scorn and indignation the false and calumnious charges brought against us.'

⌛

ROBERT ARTHUR TALBOT GASCOYNE-CECIL, the third Marquess of Salisbury, was a Conservative politician who was thrice Prime Minister, serving for a total of over thirteen years. He was the first British Prime Minister of the twentieth century and the last Prime Minister to head his full administration from the House of Lords.

He was first elected to the House of Commons in 1854 and had a laid-back view of British politics. He said: 'English policy is to float lazily downstream, occasionally putting out a diplomatic boathook to avoid collisions.'

Commenting on life, he once said: 'If you believe the doctors, nothing is wholesome; if you believe the theologians, nothing is innocent; if you believe the military, nothing is safe.'

And, his view of politicians: 'Many who think they are workers in politics are really merely tools.'

Salisbury was offered a dukedom by Queen Victoria but declined, citing the prohibitive cost of the lifestyle dukes were expected to maintain as his reason for refusal. He died in 1903.

⧗

TORY LEADER Arthur Balfour, who was Prime Minister between 1902 and 1905, could have been talking about today's newspapers when musing over whether politicians should read them line by line. He concluded, 'I have never put myself to the trouble of rummaging through an immense rubbish heap on the problematical chance of discovering a cigar-end.'

He also could have been talking about the Conservative Party in recent years when he said 'It is not the principle of the Tory party to stab its leaders in the back but I must confess it often appears to be a practice.'

Amongst his utterances, the following are the best:

'It is unfortunate, considering that enthusiasm moves the world, that so few enthusiasts can be trusted to speak the truth.'

'Biography should be written by an acute enemy.'

On Winston Churchill: 'I thought he was a young man of promise but it turns out he was only a young man of promises.'

And on himself: 'I never forgive but I always forget.'

⧗

BENJAMIN DISRAELI, who died in 1881, was something of an enigma. Born of Jewish parentage, he was an opportunist and brilliant orator who was rarely dull. He also knew the importance of language in politics, once commenting: 'with words we govern men'.

He first entered Parliament in 1837 and his maiden speech was a disaster. However, by sheer brilliance he worked his way up the ranks of the Conservative Party, becoming Chancellor of the Exchequer before finally reaching the top.

Disraeli reserved most of his venom for his chief political opponent, the Liberal William Gladstone, once famously saying: 'He has not one single redeeming defect.'

Some of Disraeli's other most memorable comments on Gladstone are:

'A sophisticated rhetorician, inebriated with the exuberance of his own verbosity, and gifted with an egotistical imagination that can at all times command an interminable and inconsistent series of arguments to malign an opponent and to glorify himself.'

Explaining the difference between a misfortune and a calamity: 'If Gladstone fell into the Thames, it would be a misfortune. But if someone pulled him out, it would be a calamity.'

Commenting on Robert Peel: 'The right honourable gentleman is reminiscent of a poker. The only difference is that a poker gives off the occasional signs of warmth.'

Also on Peel: 'He is a great parliamentary middleman. It is well known what a middleman is; he is a man who bamboozles one party and plunders the other.'

And on Peel again: 'The right honourable gentleman's smile is like the silver fittings of a coffin.'

Of himself, he opined: 'To talk well is a rare gift – quite as rare as singing; and yet everyone is expected to talk well and very few to be able to sing.'

And: 'When I want to read a novel I write one.'

On the House of Lords: 'Nobody wants a second chamber except a few disreputable individuals.'

Amongst his other writings and sayings, the following are the most memorable:

'The palace is not safe when the cottage is not happy.'

'Never trust a gentleman by halves.'

'Youth is a blunder; Manhood a struggle; Old Age a regret.'

'Men moralise among ruins.'

'The disappointed are always young.'

'Increased means and increased leisure are the two civilisers of man.'

'Eloquence is the child of Knowledge.'

'Every man has a right to be conceited until he is successful.'

'The very phrase "foreign affairs" makes an Englishman convinced that I am about to talk on a subject with which he has no concern.'

'To be conscious that you are ignorant is a great step to knowledge.'

'London is a nation not a city; with a population greater than some kingdoms and districts as different as if they were under different governments and spoke different languages.'

When Viscount Palmerston, as a 79-year-old man, was cited as a co-respondent in a divorce petition having formed a relationship with a Mrs O'Kane, Disraeli quipped: 'She was Kane but was he Able?'

However, Disraeli soon realised the political implications of an affair involving a 79-year-old politician and lamented that it had become public knowledge because he feared it would mean that Palmerston's popularity would soar and he would sweep the country at the next General Election. Disraeli was right – Palmerston did just that.

⌛

LORD BIRKETT was an excellent advocate but the lengths of his speeches were always unpredictable and he often spoke for longer than his audiences expected. This led him on one occasion to jest: 'I do not object to people looking at their watches when I am speaking but I strongly object when they start shaking them to make certain that they are still going.'

❖

LORD DEWAR, who died in 1930, was a Scottish whisky distiller who built his family label Dewars into a very successful company. He also served in the Commons as a Conservative MP before entering the Lords.

He coined quite a few *bon mots*. Amongst his best are the following:

'The road to success is filled with women pushing their husbands along.'

'Four-fifths of the perjury in the world is expended on tombstones, women and competitors.'

'Lions of society are tigers for publicity.'

'Judge a man not by his clothes, but by his wife's clothes.'

'Love is an ocean of emotions, entirely surrounded by expenses.'

'A husband should tell his wife everything that he is sure she will find out, and before anyone else does.'

'Minds are like parachutes: they only function when open.'

'It is only the people with push who have a pull.'

'Confessions may be good for the soul but they are bad for the reputation.'

❖

DAVID LLOYD GEORGE, who was Britain's Prime Minister during the First World War, held public office for over seventeen years. This impressive record has been recognised by politicians of all parties and Lloyd George is one of the few British statesmen who, along with Winston Churchill and Margaret Thatcher, have a statue erected in his honour in the Members' Lobby of the House of Commons. He was a superb orator – an ability he retained right to the end of his life.

He once said of a colleague he disliked: 'He is like the North Pole: often explored and never found.'

In a similar vein, he said of Lord Derby: He is like a cushion. He always bears the impression of the last man who sat on him.'

After listening to a fellow politician ranting at a public meeting he remarked 'It's easy to settle the problems of the world on a soap box.'

When a Cabinet colleague suggested caution, he snapped: Don't be afraid to take a big step if one is needed. You cannot cross a chasm in two small jumps.'

On Winston Churchill: 'He spoilt himself by reading about Napoleon.'

On Tory Neville Chamberlain: 'A retail mind in a wholesale business.'

On hereditary peers in the House of Lords: 'Five hundred men chosen at random from the ranks of the unemployed.'

His comments on Tory MP Bonar Law also revealed something about his own make up: 'He was honest to the verge of simplicity.'

Commenting on Lord Bridgeman, who cut an extremely portly figure, he was by today's standards very un-PC when he said of him: 'In his anger he is very rude. Lord Bridgeman is a comfortable, rather heavy gentleman, but we all know that when fat catches fire it is very unpleasant – and so was he.'

His view on what constituted our class system: 'Aristocracy is like a cheese: the older it is, the higher it becomes.'

His view of life as Prime Minister: 'There can be no friendship at the top.'

⌛

FREDERICK EDWIN SMITH, who later became the first Earl of Birkenhead, entered Parliament in 1906. Helped by the fact that on his election the Conservative benches were much depleted by the Liberal landslide, he made full use of his powers of oratory in speeches laced with sarcasm and wit. His career took off from the moment he made his maiden speech which, contrary to tradition, was highly political and partisan.

His rise thereafter through the Tory party ranks was meteoric, but he made what some regard as a bad career move by accepting the post of Lord Chancellor. Although this post carried a seat in the Cabinet and was one of the great offices of state, it then necessitated the office bearer sitting in the House of Lords. On becoming Lord Chancellor, therefore, Smith effectively kissed goodbye to any chance he had of becoming Prime Minister.

Lord Beaverbrook summed up the widely held view of Smith's contemporaries when he said: 'His chief enemy has always been his own biting and witty tongue, which spares no man.'

When, during his first election campaign in 1906, 'F.E.'[*] was accused of always appearing in court for the licensed trade, 'particularly if the licensees belonged to the Tory Party', he angrily rejected the criticism of his professional integrity. He was particularly irked by the local Liberal leader, Edward Evans, of whom he said: 'Mr Evans, I understand, purveys amongst other things pills. I have not the slightest doubt that he sells pills to Conservatives and Liberals alike. He sells pills and I sell brains and I claim the same right in my profession to choose my customers by the same standards as Mr Evans claims in his.'

At this riposte, Evans said that it was F.E.'s selling of his brains that was just what he complained of, adding that F.E. 'did not appear to have any left' and 'empty vessels make the most noise'.

---

[*]   Even after he was ennobled as the first Earl of Birkenhead, right up to his death in 1930 he was still widely known as 'F.E.'.

Another Liberal candidate, who clashed with F.E. on the subject of the trade figures, told F.E. not to be 'pessimistic' about the future. Smith snapped back: 'The only pessimism of which I am conscious at the moment is that which is occasioned by seeing the blind pretentiously putting themselves forward as guides to the blind.' This was a brave response as the Liberal candidate was no other than one A. P. Thomas, who was a professor of commercial law at Liverpool University!

Referring to Liberal dirty tricks in the 1906 election, he said: 'I do not in the least mind being cheated at cards – but I find it a trifle nauseating if my opponent then proceeds to ascribe his success to the favour of the Most High.'

During his maiden speech he took a vicious swipe at Austin Taylor, a fellow Liverpool MP who, within weeks of being re-elected unopposed as a Conservative, had crossed the floor of the House to become a Liberal. F.E., alluding to the Liberal's landslide of 1906, said of Taylor: 'He has entered the House, not like his new colleagues on the crest of a wave, but rather by means of an opportune dive.'

During the same speech, he audaciously lashed out at Winston Churchill, who had also crossed the floor of the House to join the Liberals before undertaking a number of speaking engagements around Britain. Smith referred to an argument put forward by Winston with the barb: 'The House will recognise the peroration – I rather think it has been at the disposal of both parties in the House before undertaking a provincial tour.'

For a few years after his election he continued to practise at the Bar and there is a cornucopia of stories of his impudence in court. To one judge who told him that, having read F.E.'s pleadings, he was no wiser than when he started, F.E. snapped back: Possibly not my Lord, but you are far better informed.'

To another judge who said that he did not think much of F.E.'s case, he responded: 'I am sorry to hear that my Lord, but your Lordship will find that the more you hear of it, the more it will grow on you.'

One of the most famous incidents in court occurred when F.E. demolished a boy's claim for damages after an accident. He started very sympathetically and asked the young lad to show the court how high he could lift his injured arm. With extreme effort the boy raised it to the level of his shoulder. F.E. continued: 'Thank you very much. Will you now show us how high you could raise it before the accident?' Innocently, the boy shot his arm high in the air – and lost the case.

On the British constitution Smith remarked: 'Britain is the only country in the world which has at once an uncontrolled constitution and an ineffective second chamber... we have a constitution at the mercy of a momentary gust of parliamentary opinion; and secondly... we have no second chamber equipped with the political and constitutional power to resist such a gust.'

When he was attending a dinner at which he was scheduled to make the final speech he became extremely irritated by the other speakers who were all long-winded and overran their time considerably. When F.E.'s turn came, he rose to his feet and said: 'Ladies and gentlemen, I have prepared two speeches for this evening. One of them is a long speech and the other a short speech. In view of the lateness of the hour, I now intend to deliver them both.'

On another occasion, when he was again the last speaker on the card, Smith was once more kept waiting an inordinate length of time. The toastmaster finally called upon F.E. to give his address, at which point he rose to his feet, said '32 Grosvenor Gardens' and left.

Once he was invited to breakfast by the young undergraduate Bob Boothby. He arrived and sat in silence for several minutes before finally remarking: 'Except for one melancholy occasion at 10 Downing Street, this is the first time I have breakfasted in company for twenty years – and I hope to God it is the last.'

In 1919 King George V was informed of an intended reshuffle in the coalition government led by Lloyd George and there was one appointment which he tried, at first, to block. The PM announced that he wished to promote Sir Frederick Smith, the Attorney-General, to the position of Lord Chancellor. The King's secretary, Lord Stamfordham, protested, firstly on the grounds of Smith's age (forty-six) adding, 'His Majesty feels the appointment will come as somewhat of a surprise to the legal profession... His Majesty does not feel that Sir Frederick has established such a reputation in men's minds as to ensure the country will welcome him to the second highest post which can be occupied by a subject of the crown.'

Lloyd George, however, held out, the King eventually gave way and Smith took his seat on the Woolsack as the first Lord Birkenhead. To the surprise of many, including the King, Smith disliked tempering justice with levity and, when sitting as a Lord of Appeal, he prided himself that no observation he ever made was followed by laughter in court.

However, once out of legal robes, he was just as insulting, rude and flippant as he had ever been. Shortly after his elevation as Lord Chancellor, he was invited on board the Royal Yacht *Britannia* at Cowes. Having dined rather well he started to puff smoke from a huge cigar into the Queen's face until a courtier eventually persuaded him to go on deck to see the stars.

Later, when being entertained by Lord Beaverbrook, someone inquired as to the vintage of the claret they were drinking and wanted to know what vineyard it was from. 'One can tell straight away by its distinctive taste', Smith intervened, 'that it is from the local grocer's'.

Jimmy Thomas, the railwaymen's leader who had been elected as an MP in 1910, was often the butt of F.E.'s insults. Rather surprisingly the two became friends, although this did not prevent Smith from continuing to needle Thomas who was notorious for not pronouncing his aitches. When Thomas complained of 'an 'orrible 'eadache', Smith replied: 'What you need, my dear chap, is a couple of aspirates.'

Whilst attending a luncheon in Swansea to mark the opening of the new Town Hall, he found himself sitting next to the Prince of Wales. They both had to sit through a very long-winded speech by the Mayor and the Prince uttered to Smith: 'One wishes there was some way of stopping this dreadful bore.' At this, F.E. picked up the menu card, wrote a few words on the back and asked the toastmaster to give it to the speaker. Shortly after he had done this, the Mayor made some very brief closing remarks and sat down. The Prince was amazed that F.E.'s note had done the trick and asked him what he had written. 'Oh nothing much,' Smith replied, 'I just told him his fly buttons were undone.'

Among his best-remembered barbs are the following:

On Austen Chamberlain: 'He always played the game – and he always lost.'

Commenting on the Cabinet of Conservative Prime Minister Andrew Bonar Law (of which he was not a member): 'He tried to confront first-class problems with a team of second-class brains.'

On politics: 'To say what is not is the road to success.'

His view of the Liberal Party: 'Political Rip Van Winkles.'

And of a speech by Hilaire Belloc: 'The more often I hear it, the more I like it.'

Commenting on a political opponent, who was not known for his good looks: 'The arguments he produces in his election address will win no more votes than his photograph on the front cover.'

His gibe to the Liverpool Liberal leader Edward Evans: 'He is the greatest asset his opponents enjoy and I for one wish him many more years of pretentious pompousness and fussy failure.'

On democracy: 'Votes are to swords exactly what bank notes are to gold. The one is effective only because the other is believed to lie behind it.'

On Churchill (before he and F.E. became friends): 'He has been hungering and thirsting for office and will take anything he is offered.'

On Stanley Baldwin and his first Cabinet (before he and

F.E. became friends): 'It is, of course, a tragedy that so great an army should have so uninspiring a commander-in-chief.'

And, again on his own party leader, Stanley Baldwin: 'A jellied bulwark of the Conservative Party.'

On the 1925 coal dispute: 'I should have thought that the miners' leaders were the stupidest men in the kingdom – if I had not met the owners.'

Referring to the lavish entertaining undertaken by the Marquis of Londonderry before his promotion to high government office, F.E. caustically observed that Londonderry had 'catered his way to the Cabinet'.

Commenting on the breaking off of diplomatic relations with the USSR in 1927: 'I am delighted. We have got rid of the hypocrisy of pretending to have friendly relations with this gang of murderers, revolutionaries and thieves. I breathe quite differently now we have purged our capital of the unclean and treacherous elements.'

And in response to those who were arguing for a cut in Britain's armed forces he said: 'Is the ownership of the world to be stereotyped by perpetual tenure in the hands of those who possess the different territories today? The world continues to offer glittering prizes to those who have stout arms and sharp swords, and it is therefore extremely improbable that the experience of future nations will differ in any material respect from that which has happened since the dawn of the human race.'

Commenting on Lloyd George, (before he and F.E. became friends): 'He is a nimble demagogue and someone who would ruin a prime minister if he could supplant him. His speeches are fustian and clap-trap.'

The fact that Lloyd George was prepared to forget these insults when he indeed did become Prime Minister, by appointing F.E. Attorney-General, shows the admiration and respect he had for Smith.

Right to the end of his life F.E. had quite a good head of hair. On one occasion a few years before he died he went for a haircut and the barber, who was totally bald, made the unwise observation: 'Getting a little thin at the back, sir.' F.E. snapped: 'I do not think that a man of your limited resources is in a position to comment.' Then, when asked how he would like his hair to be cut, he retorted: 'In silence.'

When his local postman one day told Smith: 'My Missus is expecting her ninth child.' Smith told him: 'It would be a blessing for us all if in future *you* were confined more and your wife less.'

On the comments of a peer whose speech he did not think much of: 'A collection of imbecilic maunderings.'

On Woodrow Wilson: 'He has a mania for vague generalisations. A loose thinker.'

On one occasion during a dinner there was a lull in the conversation and someone asked Lord Birkenhead what were the three great milestones in his life. F.E. remained silent for a few moments and then said: 'The first when I heard that I'd got a double first at Oxford. I suppose the second was when I was made a K.C. and the third was when I became Lord Chancellor.'

His wife who was sitting nearby interrupted and said: 'But darling, what about the day we got married?'

Without a moment's hesitation, Lord Birkenhead replied: 'My dear, I think you must have misheard. We are talking about milestones – not millstones.'

Once, an English High Court judge presiding in a sodomy case sought advice on sentencing from Lord Birkenhead. 'Could you tell me,' he asked, 'what do you think one ought to give a man who allows himself to be buggered?'

Birkenhead replied without hesitation: 'Oh, thirty shillings or two pounds; whatever you happen to have on you.'

Amongst his other remarks the following are the best:

'Meet success like a gentleman and disaster like a man.'

On socialism: 'Nature has no cure for this sort of madness, though I have known a legacy from a rich relative to work wonders.'

'We have the highest authority for believing that the meek shall inherit the earth; though I have never found any particular corroboration of this aphorism in the records of Somerset House.'

On his reluctance to use flattery: 'I have not found the language of idle compliment a useful coinage, except in the company of very foolish men.'

On Liberal MP Augustine Birrell (for which he was censured): 'That type of man who would still be fiddling if all his colleagues were burning.'

During the summer of 1930 Smith fell seriously ill with bronchial pneumonia and died on 30 September that year at the tragically young age of fifty-eight.

After his death, Labour politician Richard Crossman described F.E. as 'one of only three geniuses in British politics during the twentieth century'.

But former Labour Party Chairman Harold Laski was less charitable, saying of Smith, 'He shot across politics like a meteor and his disappearance from the sky leaves it unchanged.'

This swipe is untrue. During his tenure as Lord Chancellor he made substantial and sweeping changes to the law of property in England and Wales which have survived up to the present day.

Despite his achievements, looking back over Smith's career one cannot help feeling a sense of waste. Towards the end he became bored with power and the responsibility that went with it. His epitaph is perhaps best summed up by the words of Geoffrey Chaucer, who over five hundred years earlier remarked: 'When a man has an over-great wit, often he will misuse it.'

⟨⟩

TORY PRIME MINISTER Stanley Baldwin never expected to achieve the highest office in politics, nor did many of his contemporaries. However, from the moment he entered Number 10 in

1923 until he quit active politics in 1937, he was a dominating influence in Britain.

His impressive booming voice and down to earth approach, made him, for a while, very popular with the public, although many of his Tory colleagues were irritated by his constant references to his humble origins and his pig farming.

Baldwin never liked or trusted Liberal politician Lloyd George. When the latter was Chancellor of the Exchequer, he said of him: 'He is a mere shadow of his former self, wandering in a sort of Celtic twilight, his only intention being to rob hen roosts.'

And he later gave his own summary of Lloyd George's career: 'He spent his whole life in plastering together the true and the false and therefrom manufacturing the plausible.'

In 1933, Winston Churchill, then a backbencher, was seeking to reverse the British government's policy on India and this set him on a collision course with Baldwin. Their previous relationship, although not cordial, was at least amicable enough. Now, as a result of Churchill's campaigning, the two men no longer spoke to one another. One day, after leaving the chamber of the House of Commons, Churchill entered a small lavatory reserved for MPs which had only enough room for two men to relieve themselves at the same time. He saw, to his embarrassment, that one of the 'pissoirs' was occupied by Baldwin. As Baldwin had noticed him entering, Churchill felt it was too late to retreat. Baldwin remained silent for a moment, then, as he did up his trousers, he turned to Churchill and snapped: 'I am glad that there is one common platform upon which we can still meet,' and walked off!

He later said of Churchill: 'He is a military adventurer who would sell his sword to anyone. He has his sentimental side but he lacks soul.'

However, he made his most effective swipe at Churchill in a public speech when he said: 'When Winston was born, lots of fairies swooped down on his cradle and gave him gifts – imagination, eloquence, industry and ability. Then came the fairy who said 'No one person has a right to so many gifts,' picked him up and gave him a shake and a twist and despite all these gifts, he was denied judgement and wisdom. And that is why, while we delight to listen to him in the House, we do not take his advice.'

On leading his party: 'Leading the Conservative Party is like driving pigs to market.'

On socialism: 'No gospel founded on hate will ever be the gospel of our people.'

Some of his other best-remembered quips are the following:

'The intelligent are to the intelligentsia what a gentleman is to the gents.'

'A platitude is simply a truth repeated until people get tired of hearing it.'

'You will find in politics that you are much exposed to the attribution of false motive. Never complain and never explain.'

'There are three groups that no British prime minister should provoke: the Vatican, the Treasury and the miners.'

Commenting on the 1922 General Election, won by the Conservatives led by Bonar Law and which saw Lloyd George resign as PM, Baldwin said: 'The election was won on six words of Lloyd George, who had complained that the Conservative Bonar Law was "honest to the verge of simplicity". The public had said, "By God! That is what we have been waiting for," and voted for us.'

On his opponents: 'I often wonder if my silent contempt irritates them more than if I were to speak out.'

When he left office, Baldwin's popularity was as high as ever but the clouds of war gathering over Europe soon led to a change of public mood. From 1940 onwards until his death Baldwin was reviled for his earlier policy of appeasement towards Hitler.

On his last day in office he did, however, make a remark to a passing journalist which even today is good advice for any retiring politician. He was asked whether, after leaving office, he would be available to give his successor the benefit of his opinions. He responded firmly: 'No. Once I leave, I leave. I am not going to speak to the man on the bridge and I am not going to spit on the deck.'

⧗

ANDREW BONAR LAW became Prime Minister in 1922, a year before his death. He was frank about his own limitations: 'If I am a great man then a good many great men of history are frauds.'

And equally frank about his own party: 'I must follow them. I am their leader.'

⧗

LORD CURZON was a talented but arrogant politician who, even in his day, was regarded as somewhat out of touch. In an age when politicians were treated with deference by the press, he very nearly became Prime Minister. In the event, he lost out to Stanley Baldwin and he never quite came to terms with the fact.

Despite his disappointment, he agreed to serve as Baldwin's Foreign Secretary but showed little gratitude to his boss, of whom he remarked: 'It is heart-breaking serving under such a man. He is guilty of... a mixture of innocence, ignorance, honesty and stupidity – fatal gifts in a statesman when wholly disassociated from imagination, vision or *savoir faire*. He is a man of the utmost insignificance.'

On the Cabinet of which he was a member: 'They secretly grumble. Baldwin's evil geniuses are the whippersnappers of the Cabinet, Amery and Neville Chamberlain. They buzz about him day and night and he is lamentably weak.'

⧗

LORD HALIFAX, who was Foreign Secretary at the beginning of the Second World War, on the troubles facing Europe: 'I often think how much easier the World would have been to manage if Herr Hitler and Signor Mussolini had been at Oxford.'

⧗

FORMER LABOUR PREMIER Clement Attlee was a diminutive figure who lacked charisma and had an extremely terse style. When he was made a junior minister in 1924, few would have predicted that he would go on to lead the Labour Party and become Britain's first post war premier.

He once shocked a TV news reporter, to whom he had agreed to give an interview, with his extremely laconic manner. The hapless reporter waited for his television colleagues to set up the early recording equipment, the lights and the boom microphone and then began his great interview, for which fifteen minutes of air time had been allocated. 'Would the Prime Minister like to share with the viewers his plans for the forthcoming General Election?' he asked. Attlee puffed on his pipe. 'No,' he replied. 'Next question.'

It was said by one of Attlee's contemporaries that he 'gave away' India in twenty minutes. This led one wag to question why it took so long. The truth is that unlike most politicians of today, Attlee felt that he could get his point across more effectively if he was succinct.

He had a dim view of television, later describing it as 'an idiot's lantern'.

On our political system, he opined: 'Democracy means government by discussion, but it is only effective if you can stop people talking.'

His view of Winston Churchill: 'Fifty per cent genius, fifty per cent bloody fool.'

And, again on Churchill: 'The trouble with Winston is he nails his trousers to the mast and can't climb down.'

On fellow Labour politician Hugh Dalton: 'A perfect ass.'

On Communism: 'The illegitimate child of Karl Marx and Catherine the Great.'

In 1952, when he faced a hostile meeting of the Parliamentary Labour Party, his laconic style helped save his skin. He rose to his feet and announced: 'King dead. Meeting adjourned.'

After he quit the Commons, he took his seat in the House of Lords, as by custom most prime ministers do. He soon noticed the different atmosphere saying: 'The House of Lords is like a glass of champagne that has stood for five days.'

And, on his own style, which could not be more different from today's spin-obsessed party machines: 'I have none of the qualities which create publicity.'

Commenting accurately on Attlee's brusque style, Douglas Jay, who was President of the Board of Trade under Harold Wilson, said: 'He never used one syllable where none would do.' Echoing this, *The Economist* wrote: 'Mr Attlee touches nothing that he does not dehydrate.'

George Orwell was more vicious, saying: 'Attlee reminds me of a dead fish before it has had time to stiffen.'

Attlee himself summed up what he thought of this criticism with a few lines of doggerel on himself:

Few thought he was even a starter,
There were many who thought themselves smarter,
But he became PM,
CH and OM,
An Earl and a Knight of the Garter.

Tony Blair was rather fond of referendums but not so the Labour Party under Attlee: 'I could not consent to the introduction into our national life of a device so alien to all our traditions as the referendum, which has only too often been the instrument of Nazism and Fascism.'

Praise for Attlee has however been forthcoming from a most unexpected quarter. Lady Thatcher has said of him: 'Contrary to many politicians of today, Attlee was all substance and no show.'

☒

SIR WINSTON CHURCHILL, one of only five recent Premiers not to take a seat in the House of Lords,[*] was the master of the political insult. During sixty-two years in the House of Commons, his humour and wit enlivened many a debate and his sharp tongue put down many an opponent.

After his capture in the Boer War, he joined the South African Light Horse and grew a moustache. A friend of his mother said she neither cared for his politics nor his moustache. Churchill replied 'Madam, I see no earthly reason why you should come into contact with either.'

It is well known that it is out of order for one MP to call another 'a liar' in the House of Commons. Churchill cleverly managed to do so, within the rules of order, by referring to the remarks of an opponent as being a 'terminological inexactitude'.

Commenting on Clement Attlee, then the Labour Party leader, he said: 'An empty taxi cab drew up at the House of Commons and Clement Attlee got out.'

On Labour Prime Minister Ramsay MacDonald: 'He has, more than any other man, the gift of compressing the largest number of words into the smallest amount of thought.'

And on Bonar Law, then leader of the Conservative Party, while Churchill was still a Liberal: 'The raw and rowdy Under-Secretary[†] whom the nakedness of the land, and the jealousies of his betters, have promoted to the leadership of the Tory Party!'

On the qualities required for political office: 'In my belief, you cannot deal with the most serious things in the world unless you also understand the most amusing.'

---

[*]   The others are Sir Edward Heath MP, Prime Minister 1970–74; Sir John Major, Prime Minister 1990–97; Tony Blair, Prime Minister 1997–2007 and Gordon Brown, Prime Minister 2007–2010.

[†]   Bonar Law, although leader of the Tories in opposition had never been more than a junior minister when the party was in office.

On Sir William Joynson-Hicks MP, former Home Secretary: 'The worst that can be said of him is that he runs the risk of being most humorous when he wishes to be most serious.'

On Communist Russia: 'I cannot forecast to you the action of Russia. It is a riddle wrapped in a mystery inside an enigma.'

On the Labour government's foreign policy: 'Dreaming all night of giving away bits of the British Empire, and spending all day doing it!'

On William Gladstone: 'They told me how he read Homer for fun, which I thought served him right.'

On his definition of a prisoner of war: 'Someone who tries to kill you, fails and then asks you not to kill him.'

On Sir Redvers Buller, former Commander-in-Chief of the British forces: 'He was a characteristic British personality. He looked stolid. He said little and what he said was obscure. He was a man of considerable scale. He plodded on from blunder to blunder and from one disaster to another, without losing either the regard of his country or the trust of his troops, to whose feeding as well as his own he paid serious attention.'

And, on the Sudanese soldier: 'At once slovenly and uxorious, he detested his drills and loved his wives with equal earnestness.'

When a cabbage was thrown at him whilst speaking at a public meeting, he showed his ready wit with the riposte: 'I asked for the gentleman's ears, not his head.'

Although he insulted many, including some women, he expressed his philosophy on the opposite sex: 'It is hard, if not impossible, to snub a beautiful woman; they remain beautiful and the snub rebounds.'

On an official report he received from Admiral Pound, who Churchill did not rate, he wrote in the margin: 'Pennywise'.

On fellow Tory Stanley Baldwin: 'An epileptic corpse. Occasionally he stumbled over the truth, but hastily picked himself up and hurried on as if nothing had happened.'

On F. E. Smith MP, before they became friends: 'No one has

succeeded in manufacturing a greater amount of heroism with a smaller consumption of the raw material of danger.'

After an election defeat he said: 'I returned with feelings of deflation which a bottle of champagne represents when it is half-emptied and left uncorked for a night.'

Later, after Adolf Hitler had militarised the Rhineland, he attacked Premier Baldwin's unpreparedness: 'The Government simply cannot make up their minds, or they cannot get the Prime Minister to make up his mind. So they go on in strange paradox, decided only to be undecided, resolved to be irresolute, adamant for drift, solid for fluidity, all powerful to be impotent.'

During the Second World War, a senior naval officer complained that his service's role in the conflict was not in accordance with its great traditions. 'Well, Admiral, have you ever asked yourself what the traditions of the Royal Navy are?' Churchill responded. 'I will tell you in three words: rum, sodomy and the lash.'

As he first became Prime Minister during the Second World War, it is not surprising that a number of Churchill's barbs were directed at Adolf Hitler. On Hitler's tactics, Churchill said: 'When a snake wants to eat his victims he first covers them with saliva.'

On Prime Minister Neville Chamberlain's attempts to agree peace with Hitler: 'You were given the choice between war and dishonour. You chose dishonour and you will have war.'

On dictators generally he said: 'Dictators ride to and fro upon tigers which they dare not dismount.'

When Germany invaded Czechoslovakia after the Munich Agreement, Prime Minister Neville Chamberlain complained that he could not imagine anyone lying to him, claiming he had been betrayed by Hitler. Churchill opined: 'This high belief in the perfection of man is appropriate in a man of the cloth, but not in a Prime Minister.'

His comment on the policies of Lenin: 'Christianity with a tomahawk.'

On one occasion when President Roosevelt visited Number 10, he was directed to the bathroom door as Winston was mid-way through having his bath. 'Come on in Mr President,' Winston boomed, 'Britain has nothing to hide from her allies.'

When it was announced that Tom Driberg, the left-wing Labour MP, was to marry, quite a few eyebrows were raised. Driberg's homosexuality was well known at Westminster and when a photograph of the MP with his extremely plain fiancée appeared in one of the daily papers, Churchill was heard to say: 'Ah well, buggers can't be choosers.' On hearing this, a fellow MP added: 'Poor woman – she won't know which way to turn.'

On Lord Charles Beresford: 'He can best be described as one of those orators who, before they get up, do not know what they are going to say; when they are speaking, do not know what they are saying; and when they have sat down, do not know what they have said.'

On Lord Roseberry: 'He outlived his future by ten years and his past by more than twenty.'

On the House of Lords: 'The House of Lords is not a national institution but a party dodge.'

On political policies: 'However beautiful you think the strategy is, you should occasionally look at the results.'

Unintentionally upsetting the electorate in a marginal seat, he said: 'I like pigs. Dogs look up to us. Cats look down on us. Pigs treat us as equals.'

To George Wyndham MP, in a debate in the Commons: 'I like the martial and commanding air with which the Right Honourable Gentleman treats facts. He stands no nonsense from them.'

On a former Conservative MP seeking to stand as a Liberal 'The only instance of a rat swimming towards a sinking ship.'[*]

He frequently railed against the BBC saying it was an

---

[*]   This barb was reused very successfully over thirty years later by Nigel
       Lawson, who said of the announcement by the Liberals in the 1970s

organisation that was 'honeycombed with socialists – probably with Communists'. And on one memorable occasion he exploded when the BBC Director-General John (later Lord) Reith insisted that broadcasts during the General Strike of 1926 had to be 'impartial'. He considered this outrageous and told Reith: 'You have no right to be impartial between the fire and the fire brigade.'

And, once, after being attacked by his opponents, he replied with gusto: 'Nothing in life is more exhilarating than to be shot at without result.'

His view of politics generally: 'A politician is asked to stand, he wants to sit and he is expected to lie.'

In reply to criticism that he was scaring the public with his speeches about the dangers of the Nazi regime: 'It is much better to be frightened now than to be killed hereafter.'

Brushing aside an attack by Ulster MP James Craig: 'If I valued his opinion I might get angry.'

When a young MP told a rather vulgar joke in his presence, Churchill quipped: 'Young man, I predict you will go far – in the wrong direction.'

Upon being told that an arrest had been made in Hyde Park involving a semi-naked MP who had been making sexual advances to another in sub-zero weather, his reaction was: 'Naked and below zero! Makes you proud to be British.'

Amongst his other aphorisms, the following are amongst his best:

'Never prophesy unless you know.'

'Too often the strong, silent man is silent because he does not know what to say.'

'Never be afraid to eat your words. On the whole I have found them to be a most wholesome diet.'

'The longer you can look back, the farther you can look forward.'

---

that they were to form the Lib–Lab pact with the then Labour government: 'The only time in history that rats have joined a sinking ship.'

'It would be an inconvenient rule if nothing could be done until everything can be done.'

On the French: 'The Almighty, in his infinite wisdom, did not see fit to create Frenchmen in the image of Englishmen.'

On political leaders: 'If a prime minister trips, he must be sustained. If he makes mistakes, they must be covered. If he sleeps, he must not be disturbed. If he is no good, he must be pole-axed.'

On the decision to go to war: 'Never, never, never believe any war will be smooth and easy, or that anyone who embarks on the strange voyage can measure the tides and hurricanes he will encounter. The statesman who yields to war fever must realise that once the signal is given, he is no longer the master of policy but the slave of unforeseeable and uncontrollable events.'

Churchill was widely known as a heavy drinker. Once, when the Chief Mormon met him he observed: 'Mr Churchill, the reason I do not drink is that alcohol combines the kick of the antelope with the bite of the viper.' Churchill replied instantly: 'All my life, I have been searching for a drink like that.'

In his later years, Churchill continued to be unfazed by his reputation as a drinker, saying: 'Always remember that I have taken more out of alcohol than alcohol has taken out of me.'

At a time when the press were more respectful of politicians, over-consumption of alcohol was not usually mentioned. At worst, it sometimes led to the description 'heavy drinker'. Churchill was not the only PM to like a tot. Prime Minister Herbert Asquith, nicknamed 'Squiffy', used to sway on his feet when speaking in the House. He even became the subject of a popular song during the First World War, when the words 'Mr Asquith says in a manner sweet and calm; another little drink won't do us any harm' were frequently heard in the music halls.

Former Conservative Chancellor Reginald Maudling's death was apparently hastened by his excessive drinking. On his first visit to Northern Ireland as Home Secretary, Maudling is said to have declared: 'For God's sake bring me a large Scotch. What a bloody awful country.'

Former Deputy Prime Minister George Brown was also known for being 'tired and emotional' in office.

Former Chancellor Lord Healey commented: 'I had to work with him because I was Defence Secretary at the time when he was Foreign Secretary and we arranged that we would meet once a week for an hour. I found I had to have the meetings before twelve in the morning because otherwise there was the risk that George would be the worse for drink. It was a very, very serious problem with him.'

However, while many MPs have, over the years, sat in the Chamber whilst under the influence, the Chancellor of the Exchequer is the only member of the House officially permitted to consume alcohol whilst in the Commons. A drink is allowed during the delivery of the Budget speech, though not all have taken advantage of the rule. Geoffrey Howe had his gin and tonic and Ken Clarke drank Scotch whisky but John Major only drank mineral water – as did Gordon Brown. No one has yet worked out whether the presence of alcohol makes for a better Budget!

Whether in drink or not, Winston was widely admired for his speech-making abilities. He once declared: 'A good speech is the result of the art of making deep sounds from the stomach sound like important messages from the brain.'

On the USA: 'You can always trust the Americans. In the end they will do the right thing, after they've eliminated all the other possibilities.'

Reflecting on his life in politics he said: 'In war you can only be killed once but in politics you can be killed many times.'

And, in a similar vein: 'The trouble with committing political suicide is that you live to regret it.'

On himself: 'Megalomania is the only form of sanity.'

Finally, his advice to his ministerial colleagues: 'When you are going through hell, don't stop.'

NANCY ASTOR, elected to the House of Commons in 1919, was Britain's first sitting female MP. She had a well-known love-hate relationship with Churchill. Once, when Winston was due to attend a fancy dress ball, he asked her what costume he should wear. 'If you want to come in a disguise,' Astor replied, 'Why not come sober?'

Indeed, many of the most oft-reported quotes are insulting exchanges between Lady Astor and Winston. One example was an occasion when Churchill told Lady Astor that having a woman in Parliament was like having one intrude on him in the bathroom. She retorted, 'Winston, you are not handsome enough to have such fears.'

Possibly the most famous retort of all was when Lady Astor said to Churchill, 'If you were my husband, I'd poison your tea.' To which Churchill responded, 'Madam, if you were my wife, I'd drink it!'

Amongst her other barbs, the following are the most memorable:

'One reason why I don't drink is because I wish to know when I am having a good time.'

'Pioneers may be picturesque figures, but they are often rather lonely ones.'

'The only thing I like about rich people is their money.'

'The penalty for success is to be bored by the people who used to snub you.'

'The main dangers in this life are the people who want to change everything... or nothing.

And, describing herself: 'I am the kind of woman I would run from.'

She retired from active politics in 1945.

⧗

IN NOVEMBER 1945, the first Constituent Assembly of France unanimously elected Charles de Gaulle as head of the French government. He held the post until resigning in January 1946.

He returned to power in 1958 when he was elected President of France. Following student riots against his government in 1968 and negative results in a referendum, de Gaulle finally resigned from office in April 1969. He is widely considered to be one of the most influential leaders in the history of France.

Of leadership, of which he had much experience, both as a soldier and as a politician, he said: 'A true leader always keeps an element of surprise up his sleeve, which others cannot grasp but which keeps his public excited and breathless.'

Amongst the many quotes, quips and insults made during his long career, the following are the most worthy of note:

'Church is the only place where someone speaks to me and I do not have to answer back.'

'A great country worthy of the name does not have any friends.'

'Authority doesn't work without prestige, or prestige without distance.'

'Don't ask me who's influenced me. A lion is made up of the lambs he's digested.'

'Greatness is a road leading towards the unknown.'

On his own duties as leader: 'How can anyone govern a nation that has two hundred and forty-six different kinds of cheese?'

'Diplomats are useful only in fair weather. As soon as it rains they drown in every drop.'

His view of politicians: 'Since a politician never believes what he says, he is surprised when others believe him.'

'I have come to the conclusion that politics are too serious a matter to be left to the politicians.'

'I have tried to lift France out of the mud. But she will return to her errors and vomiting. I cannot prevent the French from being French.'

'The better I get to know men, the more I find myself loving dogs.'

'The graveyards are full of indispensable men.'

'The leader must aim high, see big, judge widely, thus setting himself apart from ordinary people who debate in narrow confines.'

'The true statesman is the one who is willing to take risks.'

'There can be no prestige without mystery, for familiarity breeds contempt.'

'To govern is always to choose among disadvantages.'

'Treaties are like roses and young girls. They last while they last.'

'When I want to know what France thinks, I ask myself.'

'I respect only those who resist me, but I cannot tolerate them.'

'In order to become the master, the politician poses as the servant.'

'Never relinquish the initiative.'

'No country without an atom bomb could properly consider itself independent.'

'No nation has friends, only interests.'

'Old age is a shipwreck.'

'One cannot govern with "buts".'

'Patriotism is when love of your own people comes first; nationalism, when hate for people other than your own comes first.'

To a dissenting colleague: 'I have heard your views. They do not harmonise with mine. The decision is taken unanimously.'

On British Prime Minister Winston Churchill: 'When I am right, I get angry. Churchill gets angry when he is wrong. So we were very often angry at each other.'

Charles de Gaulle died in 1970.

THE LATE Labour heavyweight Aneurin Bevan was once asked by a new MP, 'How do you choose your friends in the House of Commons?' He replied: 'You don't have to worry about choosing your friends here – it is choosing your enemies that matters.'

Bevan was one of the most effective Labour debaters of his day. During and just after the Second World War, no one could match his great gift of oratory. However, his weakness was his acerbic tongue and he would often cross the line between robust argument and unacceptable invective.

In the 1940s he caused uproar when he said: 'No amount of cajolery and no attempt at ethical and social seduction, can eradicate from my heart a deep burning hatred for the Tory Party... in so far as I am concerned, they are lower than vermin.'

This over-the-top rant badly backfired with the public and the press. It also led to a number of right-wing Conservatives proudly launching a new dining group called the 'Vermin Club', complete with an engraved brass badge displaying a rodent, for members to display on their car bumper!

Again, attacking the Conservatives: 'The Tories always hold the view that the state is an apparatus for the protection of the swag of the property owners... Christ drove the money changers out of the temple, but you inscribe their title deed on the altar cloth.'

And: 'Whenever you scratch a Tory you find a Fascist.'

On his own party leader, Hugh Gaitskell: 'A desiccated calculating machine.'

On Conservative PM Neville Chamberlain: 'Listening to a speech by Neville Chamberlain is like paying a visit to Woolworths; everything in its place and nothing above sixpence.'

On leadership: 'The first function of a political leader is advocacy. It is he who must make articulate the wants, the frustrations and the aspiration of the masses.'

On Winston Churchill: 'His only answer to a difficult situation is to send a gun-boat.'

And again on Churchill: 'His ear is so sensitively attuned to the bugle note of history that he is often deaf to the more raucous clamour of modern life.'

And on Fleet Street: 'I read the newspaper avidly – it is my one form of continuous fiction.'

Of his own party leader, Clement Attlee: 'He seems determined to make a trumpet sound like a tin whistle. He brings
to the fierce struggle of politics the tepid enthusiasm of a lazy
summer afternoon at a cricket match.'

Bevan died at the age of sixty-two in 1960 whilst he was
the Deputy Leader of the Labour Party.

⌛

MAURICE HAROLD MACMILLAN, who later became the first Earl of
Stockton, was Conservative Prime Minister from January 1957
until he resigned, allegedly for health reasons, in October 1963.

When, as PM, Macmillan sacked a number of his ministers in a reshuffle, one of those he dismissed, Lord Kilmuir,
complained that 'a cook would have been given more notice
of his dismissal.' Macmillan retorted: 'Ah, but good cooks are
hard to find.'

Commenting on a colleague: 'He is forever poised between
a cliché and an indiscretion.'

Macmillan summed up much of parliamentary bandage
when he said: 'I have never found, in a long experience of politics, that criticism is ever inhibited by ignorance.'

On the Profumo scandal: 'These people live in a raffish,
theatrical, bohemian society where no one really knows
anyone and everyone is "darling". John Profumo MP does not
seem to have realised that we have – in public life – to observe
different standards from those prevalent in many circles.'

On the then Labour leader, Hugh Gaitskell: 'A contemptible creature; a cold-blooded Wykehamist.'

On the French: 'Notable for their spiritual arrogance and
shameless disregard of truth and honour.'

Commenting on the younger generation:'People with cynical and satirical values.'

On a new MP called Margaret Thatcher: 'A clever
young woman.'

On the Liberal manifesto: 'As usual, the Liberals offer a

mixture of sound and original ideas. Unfortunately, none of the sound ideas are original, and none of the original ideas are sound.'

Once when asked what represented the greatest challenge for a statesman, Macmillan replied: 'Events, my dear boy, events.'

Showing signs of irritation in the early 1960s when the then leader of the Labour Party, Harold Wilson, claimed to the Press that when he was a boy his family were too poor to afford to buy him any boots, Macmillan snapped: 'If Harold Wilson ever went to school without any boots, it was merely because he was too big for them.'

Macmillan lived out a long retirement but was just as trenchant a critic of his successors in old age as he was of his predecessors in his youth. He died on 29 December 1986, aged ninety-two.

RICHARD AUSTEN BUTLER, known universally as 'RAB', twice almost became Prime Minister, but was regarded as too left-wing by many mainstream Conservatives, some of whom openly referred to him as 'a milk and water socialist'.

His critics also claimed that he behaved more like a civil servant than a politician. What was beyond dispute was his undoubted talent for organising and management. What were often questioned were his vision and his willingness to stand up to civil servants and political opponents.

He generally preferred to make out a good case for what he was doing, preferring to ignore the political barb and insult. The result was usually that his speeches were well-argued but lacked punch.

Despite his generally quiet manner, he did sometimes resort to the discomforting comment and even occasionally he 'put the boot in'. When a right-wing Conservative showed he was unconcerned about the effects of economic deflation, he retorted: 'Those like you who talk about creating pools of unemployment should be thrown into them and made to swim.'

His view of Lord Beaverbrook was succinct: 'I found him green and apish.'

On Labour Premier Harold Wilson: 'He was adept at using the smear as a political weapon.'

On Sir Samuel Hoare MP, former Secretary of State for India: 'I was amazed by his ambitions; I admired his imagination, I stood in awe of his intellectual capacity, but I was never touched by his humanity. He was the coldest fish with whom I ever had to deal.'

On former Prime Minister Sir Alec Douglas-Home, who became leader of the Conservative Party in 1963, when many thought RAB would be chosen: 'An amiable enough creature – however, I am afraid he doesn't understand economics or even education at all.'

Later, taking a further swipe at Sir Alec, with just a hint of bitterness, he added: 'I may never have known much about ferrets or flower arranging, but one thing I did know is how to govern the people of this country.'

When he was invited to attend the retirement dinner of Lord Fraser of Kilmorach, he declined, adding, 'There is no one I would rather attend a farewell dinner for than Lord Fraser.' Even those who knew him could not be sure whether he meant to be insulting, but offence was taken by the remark.

In a similar vein, when he was Master of Trinity College, Cambridge, he said to a retiring Clerk of Works: 'My wife and I are glad to have got here in time to see you leave.' The clerk was deeply offended.

During the early part of Sir Anthony Eden's premiership – before the Suez fiasco – some newspapers began to speculate on Eden's future. Caught by a journalist at Heathrow Airport who invited him to comment on the press reports, RAB uttered what was to become his most famous remark. When asked whether he supported Eden, he replied: 'Well, he is the best Prime Minister we have.'

Some political commentators thought such remarks were uttered quite innocently, but those who knew him well thought differently. Indeed, some of his friends thought that this waspish irreverence contributed to his failure to become leader of the Conservative Party, a view supported by Professor Galbraith who has said that it was RAB's habit of looking on others with 'ill-concealed amusement' that stopped him from reaching the very top.

Although many Tories in the country felt he was unfairly denied the premiership, this view was by no means the unanimous view of the parliamentary party. During the war, the Conservative MP for Chichester, Major J. S. Courtauld, said of him: 'He's industrious but loopy.'

⧗

CHARLES PANNELL once observed: 'In politics, the plural of conscience is too often conspiracy.'

⧗

THE LATE Labour Cabinet minister Richard Crossman, commenting on his own party, said: 'The two most important emotions of the Labour Party are a doctrinaire faith in nationalisation, without knowing what it means, and a doctrinaire faith in passivism, without facing the consequences.'

On the left wing in the Labour Party: 'A group of people who will never be happy unless they can convince themselves that they are about to be betrayed by their leaders.'

On his own party leader, Harold Wilson: 'A tough politician who jumps from position to position, always brilliantly energetic and opportunist, always moving in zig zags, darting with no sense of direction but making the best of each position he adopts.'

On general elections: 'For the Queen, an election simply means that just when she has begun to know us, she has to meet another terrible lot of politicians.'

And, on the Civil Service: 'It is profoundly deferential –
"Yes, Minister! No, Minister! If you wish it, Minister!".'

※

HAROLD WILSON, later Lord Wilson of Rievaulx, is the second
most successful leader the Labour Party has had. He led his
party to victory in the general elections of 1964, 1966 and (just)
1974, failing only once in 1970 when he lost to Ted Heath.
Tony Blair is the only Labour leader who has beaten this record.

A significant element of Wilson's success was his ability to
manage the Labour Party effectively and, in the main, prevent
damaging splits between the left and right wings from emerging. Wilson had the knack of papering over the cracks, and has
candidly admitted how he did it: 'Leading the Labour Party is
like driving an old stage coach. If it is rattling along at a rare
old speed, most of the passengers are so exhilarated – perhaps
even seasick – they don't start arguing or quarrelling. As soon
as it stops, they start arguing about which way to go. The trick
is to keep it going at an exhilarating speed.'

Wilson's preoccupation with keeping Labour together soon
led his detractors to accuse him of pursuing expediency rather
than formulated policy. Indeed, it could be said that the views
he expressed on the Tory statesman Benjamin Disraeli could
equally apply to his own career. Of Disraeli he commented:
'He had a complete and almost proverbial lack of political
principle, often acting by instinct.'

Wilson's view on Ramsay MacDonald, Labour's first Prime
Minister: 'He still embodies a legend of betrayal to the Labour
Party, without having secured a word of tribute. He gradually
became a pathetic figure, tired, ill, rambling and taking refuge
in virtually meaningless and almost unending phrases.'

He also made less than complimentary comments on
the following:

On Stanley Baldwin: 'He was the antithesis of Lloyd
George. He would conduct the orchestra and not tire himself.

He was the finely tuned manipulator of the steering wheel: direction without engine power, the prerogative of the bosun throughout the ages.'

On Baldwin's successor, Tory PM Neville Chamberlain: 'It was not only that he was totally inadequate as Prime Minister: many are and some get by. What was tragic was that he was totally opinionated, totally certain he was right.'

On Britain's nineteenth-century Prime Minister Lord Aberdeen: 'As a leader he was weak and unfit for the premiership.'

On the Liberal Party at the end of the last century: 'Gladstone clung to the leadership and an increasingly rebellious party simply did not dare get rid of him. No one would bell the cat.'

On Herbert Morrison, who served in Attlee's Labour Cabinet: 'He was not so much disloyal as watching for a favourable opportunity to be disloyal.'

On former Tory PM Sir Anthony Eden: 'He was one of the great gentlemen of British politics – and one of the great tragedies. He had a jealous temperament.'

Wilson was more generous to his former adversary, Conservative Prime Minister Harold (later Lord) Macmillan: 'Macmillan's role as a poseur was itself a pose. He was a patrician in a non-patrician age, a dedicated professional who gave the impression of effortless government. He was one of the most articulate of Britain's premiers who regarded the premiership as a source of continuous enjoyment. He was a Disraelean, perhaps the last Disraelean Prime Minister Britain will see.'

And, more on Macmillan: 'The man's a genius. He's holding up the banner of Suez for the Party to follow, and he's leading the Party away from Suez. Now that's what I'd like to do with the Labour party over nationalisation.'

Perhaps his most effective put-down of Macmillan was the barb: 'He had an expensive education – Eton and Suez.'

With the Suez crisis in mind, Wilson later said: 'One of the laws of politics is that nothing provocative must be allowed to occur in an allied country in the year leading up to an American presidential election.'

On his own style: 'If I go on TV and look grim, they say the situation must be even worse; if I smile at all, it's complacency.'

On his own Labour government: 'I don't mind running a green Cabinet but I'm buggered if I'm going to run a yellow one.'

On former Labour Chancellor of the Exchequer Hugh Dalton: 'Apart from his loud voice, he had little to commend him. He had an infinite capacity for meeting himself coming back.'

On political power: 'Every statesman should remember his power to evoke a reaction-coefficient greater than unity.'

On the qualities required of a Prime Minister: 'No one should attempt the role of PM who cannot fall asleep the moment he is in bed with the cares and worries of the day behind him.'

Defending his own approach to the role of PM: 'A healer does not usually get a good press. Fleet Street thrives on confrontation. If a Prime Minister uses his political skills to keep the Cabinet together in pursuit of a common aim and common policies, he is condemned as devious; if he forces splits and public recriminations then, as long as he takes the right side in the division, he is a hero – but his Cabinet disintegrates.'

Deliberate leaks to the press from private and supposedly secret Cabinet meetings are not a new phenomenon. They frequently happened during Wilson's time as Premier. In a bid to stop what was happening, Wilson told his Cabinet that they should no longer take notes during his meetings. Shortly after this, transport minister Barbara Castle was observed to be making copious notes whilst Wilson was talking. The Cabinet Secretary went over to reproach her, looked at her notes and then quietly spoke to Wilson, who, to the surprise of all present, did not admonish her. Wilson later revealed that she was making out her shopping list and her notes contained nothing more than a list of vegetables. He told a colleague: 'A clear case of leeks, rather than a leak.'

Throughout most of Wilson's time at Number 10, he faced Ted Heath as Leader of the Opposition, about whom he said: 'A shiver looking for a spine to run up.'

Early in 1972 there was a political row when unemployment passed the one million mark. Wilson, at this time, was in opposition and the Prime Minister was Edward Heath. Heath had just returned from the EU negotiations (then called the EEC) in Brussels, which led Wilson to gibe: 'Heath is the first dole queue millionaire to cross the channel since Neville Chamberlain.'

Back in power after the 1974 general election, Wilson faced a difficult public expenditure round with a slender parliamentary majority. When the vote came, a number of left-wing Labour MPs abstained, which caused the Labour government to lose the motion on public expenditure. Some defended their action by saying that they could have voted with the Conservatives, but didn't. Wilson, who was furious, snapped: 'It is always an arguable question about promiscuity whether one is more open to criticism for going into the bedroom or being the lap dog outside the door.'

On his own Foreign Secretary, the unpredictable heavy-drinker George Brown: 'He is a brilliant Foreign Secretary – until four o'clock in the afternoon.'

He later referred to the comfort that the Labour left-wingers had given to the Conservatives as 'An unholy parliamentary alliance that can only be described as arsenic and red chiffon.'

To the surprise of many, he regularly outwitted his critics from within the Labour Party. When there was talk of a plot to dump him, the press inquired if he knew about it. He calmly, but memorably remarked: 'I know what's going on – I'm going on!'

On his then industry minister Tony Benn: 'Tony has some of the qualities of an Old Testament prophet without the beard. He rambles on about the new Jerusalem.'

And, later on Benn: 'He is the only person I know who immatures with age.'

Despite Wilson's considerable success in keeping Labour in power, his former Cabinet colleague Richard Crossman was not impressed: 'Harold Wilson had one overriding aim – to remain in office. He would use almost every trick or gimmick to achieve it. Whenever I go to see Harold, I look into those grey eyes – and see nothing.'

⧗

THE LATE Labour MP Bessie Braddock, often the butt of gibes herself, said of former Labour Cabinet member, Richard Crossman: 'He is a man of many opinions – most of them of short duration.'

⧗

THE COLOURFUL Sir Gerald Nabarro, late Tory backbencher, was rarely off British television screens in the 1960s, often insulting one or other of his parliamentary contemporaries – frequently one of his own party colleagues.

He was often seen driving around the streets of Westminster in one of his many vehicles with a personalised registration number (At one time he owned the cherished numbers NAB 1 all the way up to NAB 6). Short in stature but with a big booming voice and an even larger moustache, his utterances were always worth listening to, if only for the entertainment value.

Commenting on a speech by his own Chancellor of the Exchequer Harold Macmillan, he said: 'I was captivated by the Chancellor's reply and I have been poring over it ever since. I have been trying to determine exactly what he meant.'

On the attitudes of British management in the 1950s and 1960s: 'In the post-war world in Britain it has been considered in many circles to be slightly off to be eager, slightly improper to be thrusting, not done to be ambitious. Quite simply, these sentiments are drivel.'

Once, seeing a middle-aged member of the public using a telephone reserved for MPs, Nabarro grabbed the man by the scruff of the neck, beckoned a policeman and bellowed, 'These phones are reserved for use by MPs only,' demanding that the officer throw the miscreant out of the building. 'But this is Hugh McCartney,' the officer explained, McCartney at that time being a Labour Member of Parliament (and father of former Labour minister Ian McCartney). Unabashed, Nabarro walked off yelling: 'Well, he's never bloody here anyway.'

Of Labour MP Albert Murray he was dismissive: 'The man is a mere flatulent lightweight.'

Not long after his death, two Tory MPs were discussing him in the Members' Smoking Room of the House of Commons: 'The man was a complete shit.' said the first. This drew the riposte from a Tory whip: 'There is no need to be nice to him now he is dead.'

⧗

HAROLD WILSON's Deputy Prime Minister was, for a time, George Brown, the able but unpredictable and somewhat neurotic Labour MP for Belper in Derbyshire. His unpredictability increased in direct proportion to his intake of alcohol.

He served Wilson as Secretary of State for Economic Affairs and later Foreign Secretary. When he was upset with some issue he started to make a habit of threatening to resign from the government. All in all he threatened eight resignations, once on the grounds of a row with his own wife!

Wilson normally handled these threats with a great deal of tact, but not always. Once, when Brown stormed out of a meeting he was having with Wilson in a highly agitated state, Wilson waited and as expected Brown later returned to the discussions. Brown then raised a particular issue and Wilson retorted that now that the sixteenth resignation was out of the way, they could discuss matters further 'when the occasion was reached for the seventeenth'. At this Brown blew up and again stormed out of the deliberations.

When his Labour colleagues were privately debating the merits of the Sexual Offences Bill, which relaxed the law on homosexuality, Brown exploded, becoming extremely agitated and aggressive. He started insulting homosexuals and the prevailing tolerant attitude towards them. 'Society ought to have higher standards;' he bellowed, 'if this Bill gets through we will have a totally disorganised, indecent and unpleasant society. We've gone too far on sex already.' Then, to the astonishment of those present, he added: 'I don't regard sex as pleasant. It's pretty undignified and I've always thought so.' His last remarks raised quite a few eyebrows, particularly as Brown frequently went through the far more undignified process of being publicly drunk, on one occasion falling into the gutter and on another smashing his car into a wall in the precincts of the Commons!

One story, oft-repeated at Westminster but alas apocryphal, relates to Brown's attendance at a reception hosted by the President of Uruguay. Just before canapés were served, a band struck up and it is alleged that Brown, then Foreign Secretary, asked a brunette figure dressed in scarlet to dance with him. The figure replied: 'There are three reasons why I will not dance with you. First, you are drunk, horribly drunk. Secondly, this is not a dance but my country's national anthem and thirdly, I am not, as you say, "a charming young brunette" but the Cardinal Archbishop of Montevideo.'

Despite all this, he still had his fans. During this period *The Times* remarked: 'George Brown drunk is a better man than the Prime Minister [Wilson] sober.'

He resigned from the government for the final time in March 1968 over Wilson's style of leadership. Although it is reported that he later tried to see Wilson to effect a reconciliation, Wilson, who had clearly had enough, went to ground and the eighth resignation was left to take effect.

Commenting on his colleagues, Brown wryly observed: 'Many MPs drink and womanise but I have never womanised.'

Brown was sent to the Lords but he did not much care for the experience. He gradually fell out with most of his Labour colleagues and in 1976 resigned once more, this time from the Labour Party itself.

Commenting later on Labour leader Michael Foot he opined: 'The Labour Party should not be led by someone who has one eye and one leg.' One of Foot's friends, alluding to Brown's legendary drinking, dismissed Brown's outburst with the riposte: 'In the country of the legless, the one-legged man is king.'

⧗

FORMER CONSERVATIVE WHIP the late David Walder formulated the 'Walder Rules', which, even today, many say still apply without exception. Walder claimed that the first three MPs who speak from the floor at the Conservatives weekly 1922 Committee meeting are insane, and that the next three are drunk.

⧗

THE LATE Labour peer and columnist Lord Wyatt had a colourful turn of phrase. On his party's former Premier Jim Callaghan: 'He was skilful in debate, persuasive in speech – and disastrous at his job.'

On politicians: 'A good character is not merely unnecessary for becoming Prime Minister – it may be positively harmful.'

On the House of Commons: 'The House listens with great humility to humbugs and compliments them on their sincerity. It hates to hear awkward truths and abuses those who tell them. It suffers fools, particularly sentimental ones, gladly.'

⧗

POLITICIANS ARE usually accused by the press and the public of not being candid enough. Such an accusation could certainly be levelled against former Tory MP Sir John Foster, at least if his 'off the record' comments are anything to go by.

Once, he was being interviewed by Granada Television and gave a rather reactionary and patriotic response to the interviewer's questions. After the recording was over, Sir John astounded the interviewer by saying: 'By the way, you ought to know that my public pronouncements bear no relation whatever to my private views and there are three things I cannot stand – God, the Queen and the family.'

⌛

THE LATE Sir Nicholas Fairbairn was, in his heyday, a first-rate lawyer and politician. His entries in *Who's Who*, mentioned below, were always worth reading and his Commons performances, except perhaps towards the end of his life, could be nothing short of dazzling.

He was, in every sense, a colourful politician and was known, among other things, for his eccentric taste in clothes. He was often seen around the House wearing tartan trousers and unusual jackets, which he designed himself. He was exceptionally forthright in expressing his views and possessed a highly caustic tongue making it an extremely dangerous pastime to cross swords with this former Scottish law officer.

Many colleagues enjoyed his acerbic company in the Members' Smoking Room of the House of Commons, where he delighted in ridiculing and insulting anyone and everyone who passed by. More than one politician who joined him 'for a quick drink' stayed for hours until he left the building. When asked afterwards why they had stayed so long, the answer was invariably that they were frightened to leave lest their character be ripped to shreds by Fairbairn after they had departed!

In the last couple of years of his life, sadly, he became a caricature of his former self and was almost always the worse for drink. On one of his last visits to the Commons he nearly caused a riot at the Members' Entrance. Waiting for a taxi, he approached an extremely attractive young woman in an evening dress. She was an MP's wife and had just arrived to meet her husband to attend an evening function. Fairbairn, who had never seen her before, approached. 'Good evening my dear. You are very pretty. And what a beautiful dress.' So far so good. Then he decided to try his luck. 'However, can I offer some advice? I have to say you would look *far more* beautiful if you took the dress off. Can I help you in this regard?' Luckily, the policeman on duty ushered him off into a cab before the astonished woman had time to react.

He was, more often than not, a bane of his own party's Whips' Office. When his own regional whip Timothy Kirkhope MP (now an MEP) asked him not to abbreviate his name by addressing him as 'Tim', he forever thereafter loudly and insultingly referred to Kirkhope as 'Mothy'.

Although many colleagues found him exasperating, the impish grin and the boyish twinkle in his eye caused many he had offended to readily forgive him even though he usually reserved his fiercest criticisms for members of his own Party.

On the late Lord (Willie) Whitelaw he was vicious: 'He is the living person I most despise because he represents what I despise most – sanctimony, guile, slime and intrigue under a cloak of decency, all for self-advancement – it's called hypocrisy.'

Of former PM John Major he said: 'More a ventriloquist's dummy than a Prime Minister.'

And his view on Tories Kenneth Clarke and Michael Heseltine: 'I don't like Clarke and I don't trust Heseltine – Clarke's a bounder and Heseltine's a spiv.'

On Sarah, Duchess of York: 'She is a lady short on looks, absolutely deprived of any dress sense, has a figure like a Jurassic monster, is very greedy when it comes to loot, has no tact, and wants to upstage everyone else.'

When referring to another member in the House of Commons, MPs are not permitted to call each other by name, but need to refer to the constituency of the MP concerned. During a rather heated debate, Labour's Frank Dobson, the MP for Holborn and St Pancras, found himself the subject of Fairbairn's ire. Fairbairn dismissed his detractor's opinions by waving him aside, referring to Dobson as 'the MP for the two tube stations'.

On one occasion, during a speaking engagement at Edinburgh University a young female student has the temerity to mock his outfit, he retorted: 'You are a silly, rude bitch and since you are a potential breeder, God help the next generation.'

Asked about electoral law during the 1992 general election, he opined: 'Why should the bastard child of an American sailor serving in Dunoon have a vote in Scotland even though he's in America, when the legitimate son of a Gordon Highlander born in Dalmstadt who's resident in Carlisle has no vote or say in Scotland?'

During a debate in Committee Sir Nicholas crossed swords with the former Labour MP, the late Norman Buchan. Mr Buchan was becoming quite excited during the debate on an amendment to the Criminal Justice Bill, arguing that no lawyer should in future have to wear a gown 'or a uniform of any kind'. Mr Buchan went somewhat over the top claiming that the purpose of all uniform and dress was merely to identify the office of the wearer. This was too much for Sir Nicholas: 'If that's what he thinks, why does the Honourable Member wear trousers? Is it in order to have a crutch for his dignity – or to protect the dignity of his crutch?'

On former Scottish Labour MP Dennis Canavan he remarked: 'I take the view that he, who knows more about madness than anyone else, should continue his career as a merchant of discourtesy elsewhere.'

He once told a journalist: 'I was born the year that Hitler came to power, although he wasn't as good a painter as I am.'

On further European integration: 'Attempts to make Europe right and pure by being nice to those who want to divide it in their own interests won't work. All being called Schmidt and speaking Esperanto is not the way ahead.'

Whilst he was serving as Solicitor-General for Scotland he was once asked by the Scottish Labour MP John Maxton if he appreciated that the 'alarming spread of glue sniffing among fourteen- and fifteen-year-olds is due to the lack of employment caused by his government and their consequent sense of uselessness'. Fairbairn swatted him with the rebuff: 'Glue sniffing is not a habit normally indulged in by children above the age of sixteen. It is a criminal offence to employ a child below that age. But if glue sniffing induces a sense of uselessness, it amazes me that the Honourable Member has not taken up the habit himself.'

In 1988 the salmonella crisis resulted in the resignation of junior health minister Edwina Currie. Afterwards, during a routine debate Mr Fairbairn interrupted Edwina's speech with the barb: 'Does the Honourable Lady remember that she was an egg herself once; and very many members of all sides of this House regret that it was ever fertilised?' Vicious!

Upsetting in one swoop all women MPs, just before his death he said: 'They don't give me feelings of femininity. They lack fragrance. They're definitely not desert island material. They all look as though they're from the fifth Kiev Stalinist machine-gun parade. As for Edwina Currie – well the only person who smells her fragrance is herself. I can't stand the hag.'

His view of marriage shocked many of his colleagues: 'Christian monogamy, and its assumption of fidelity, is as fallacious as the Catholic concept of the chastity of priests. I am sure that polygamy and harems probably worked better. We live in a priggish and prim age.'

And when asked what were the attractions (if any) of marriage he replied: 'Apart from the depth of the relationship, you remember when you turn over in bed who you're with – and you don't have to get up at dawn and get out.'

When fellow Tory Lord (Patrick) Cormack, then an MP, attacked Sir Nicholas and referred to his 'eccentric and ridiculous utterances, bad manners and eccentric garb', Fairbairn said of Cormack: 'His manners are always appalling and his dress sense is worse. He is a squit.'

Sir Nicholas had a long running line in insults against former Prime Minister Sir Edward Heath. This being so it came as quite a surprise when the press revealed that Sir Nicholas had sent a letter to Ted congratulating him on becoming a Knight of the Garter. Of this incident Fairbairn said: 'The *Daily Telegraph* has said that while one could be rude to one's friends in private, one should be polite to them in public. Well that's the contrary to all I was brought up to believe. To write and rejoice in what was clearly for him a reason for great satisfaction for himself was the proper thing to do. But then, why can't I say he was a dreadful Prime Minister and his public behaviour is appalling? The fact that he sent my private letter to the press shows he has no manners. He has grave personality problems and torment within himself which he'll never resolve.'

And warming to this theme he said: 'To him chivalry is unknown. Since the Order of the Garter arose out of an incident in which man of little rank despised a lady of great standing, what could be more fitting?'

And on former defence minister the late Alan Clark: 'A rich goon with perverted views.'

He frequently changed the list of his own recreations in *Who's Who*. He initially listed these as 'making love, ends meet and people laugh'. This was then changed to 'draining brains and scanning bodies'. In 1990 his entry became 'growling, prowling, scowling and owling'.

Finally, just before his death, he changed his list to read: 'Drawing ships, making quips, confounding whips and scuttling drips.'

After a particularly colourful insult by Sir Nicholas a Tory backbench MP was overheard to remark: 'He is in his element again – hot water.'

THE HOUSE OF COMMONS lost an intellect of the highest calibre when veteran politician Enoch Powell was defeated in the 1987 general election. The Conservative minister fell out with Edward Heath and later went on to become an Ulster Unionist MP. On his death in 1998 generous tributes were made by politicians of all parties, although memories of his notorious 'rivers of blood' speech made in the 1960s still caused some commentators to portray him as a right-wing bigot.

Throughout his political life, any controversy he caused was usually as a direct result of his honesty. Enoch would always articulate his fears, concerns or conclusions, reached after he had logically considered the issue under discussion. However, brutal candour can create enemies and is not always a wise course for a democratic politician to take. Sometimes, a little blarney and diplomacy are necessary sweeteners when the message is unpalatable.

When a supporter told him that 'the world would be a better place with more people like you', his response was typical. Most politicians would respond with some grateful small talk, saying 'I am only doing my job,' or 'I appreciate your support', but not Enoch. Powell reflected on the proposition that had just been made and gave his conclusion. 'No, I disagree,' he began, astonishing his fan. Then he explained his reasoning to the by now incredulous disciple: 'A society for survival needs a spread of types. For example, in every battalion there's one man who deserves the VC, and one man who ought to be shot for cowardice. The battalion depends for its success upon a spectrum connecting those two.' Leaving the man speechless he finished: 'A country with everyone like me would be ungovernable.'

Curtly commenting on more EU Directives for harmonisation: 'You don't have to live under the same laws as a foreigner in order to trade with him. You don't have to take the same bath water.'

Again, on the subject of 'Europe', he was dismissive: 'Europe is nothing except a line on a map.'

Amongst his other observations, the following are worthy of note:

'History is littered with the wars which everybody knew would never happen.'

'I do not keep a diary. To write a diary every day is like returning to one's own vomit.'

'Those who lead are always out in front, alone.'

'Above any other position of eminence, that of Prime Minister is filled by fluke.'

'In politics, it is more blessed not to take than to give.'

Powell strongly felt that the way fellow human beings were treated should not depend on where they were living. He movingly argued: 'Nor can we ourselves pick and choose where and in what parts of the world we shall use this or that kind of standard. We cannot say, "We will have African standards in Africa, Asian standards in Asia and perhaps British standards here at home." We must be consistent with ourselves every-where. All Government, all influence of man upon man, rests upon opinion. What we can do in Africa, where we still govern and where we no longer govern, depends upon the opinion which is entertained of the way in which this country acts and the way in which Englishmen act. We cannot fall below our own highest standards in the acceptance of responsibility.'

Just before Powell lost his Commons seat, he was walking down a corridor in the Houses of Parliament and was greeted by the then Home Office minister, the Tory Sir Peter Lloyd, who commented how well Enoch looked. Powell scowled: 'Oh, it's come to that has it?' Lloyd was baffled. 'What do you mean?' he replied. Enoch looked him in the eye. 'There are three ages of man – youth, middle age and "Oh, you are look-ing well",' he snapped before disappearing down the corridor.

⌛

THE LATE Lord Hailsham, the former Quintin Hogg MP, had an impressive career in politics, serving as a minister under five prime ministers until his retirement in 1987. Indeed, in the early sixties he very nearly became Prime Minister himself but the Conservative hierarchy chose Sir Alec Douglas-Home instead. He would have made an interesting if unpredictable Premier and some think that had he become Conservative leader he might have prevented Harold Wilson securing a narrow Labour victory in 1964.

In his day he was an awesome orator. As a student I remember seeing an audience of eight hundred activists being spellbound by his rhetoric when he came to Leicester in 1967 to speak at a by-election in support of the Tory candidate Tom Boardman, who subsequently won what until then had been a safe Labour seat.

Hailsham was not only erudite but both colourful and emotional. One of the most effective and striking attacks (literally) ever seen in a General Election campaign took place in 1966. Quintin Hogg, as he then was, was addressing an open-air rally for the Conservative candidate Dudley Smith. During Hogg's speech, a Labour supporter, standing near to the platform, raised a huge placard on which was pasted a poster showing the head and shoulders of Harold Wilson, with the slogan 'You Know Labour Government Works' printed underneath. Hogg immediately turned the incident to his own advantage by asking the crowd to look at the poster: 'The one with the ugly face.' He then launched a violent attack on the placard with his walking stick. The young socialist was helpless. He was anchored to his place by the crowd and could not move. He was obliged to stand there, struggling to hold his poster and board upright, whilst a senior member of the shadow Cabinet smashed it to smithereens! At least part of this incident was recorded by the television cameras and even today, over thirty years later, it is still an amusing and effective piece of political theatre.

Just as years later the media came to associate the phrase 'silly billy' with Labour's Denis Healey, Hogg's 1960s warning against Labour Party policy stuck, but not in the way he intended. During one interview he said: 'If the British public falls for the programme of the Labour Party, I say it will be stark raving bonkers.'

His view of fellow Tory Cabinet minister R. A. Butler, a fellow contender for the Tory leadership in the early 1960s: 'I never numbered candour amongst his virtues… he had not the stuff within him of which Prime Ministers are made. Politics may well include the art of the possible, but weakness on matters of principle, coupled with an inability to admit that you are wrong, limits the area of what is possible.'

On socialism: 'It may be an excellent way of sharing misery, but it is not a way of creating abundance.'

On economists and their theories: 'The only thing I know about economic rules are that there are no economic rules.'

Even in the twilight of his ministerial career, his wicked sense of fun – and penchant for insults – had not deserted him. One day, during Hailsham's term as Lord Chancellor, the left-wing Bishop of Durham was making a rather polemical speech. A Labour peer who entered during this peroration was shocked to hear a loud voice bellow 'Bollocks!' at the Bishop's remarks. Astonished he looked up, expecting to see a demonstrator being escorted from the public gallery above, but all was calm. He then realised that the insulting interruption had come from the occupant of the Woolsack – Lord Hailsham.

Hailsham often delighted in repeating the following piece of self-penned doggerel:

> A Shakespearean actress played Puck,
> In the course of which she got stuck
> As she had never heard
> Of that four-letter word
> She said 'Oh what rotten bad luck.

On a partisan panelist who appeared on a TV programme posing as an independent, he snapped: 'Don't pretend to be a judge when you are an advocate.'

Active until the end, even though latterly he was only able to walk with the assistance of two canes, he died in 2001.

THE LATE Tory MP Dr John Blackburn was a likeable man who was popular in the House. He would frequently greet colleagues with open arms and a cry of 'My Son, my Son' – even when the MP was old enough to be his father!

Despite several heart attacks, he insisted on attending the Commons to vote whenever John Major's majority seemed at risk, even though the whips frequently told him to go home and rest. When I was Deputy Chief Whip I excused him from voting regularly, only to find he would reappear in votes hours later saying, 'I'm here to do my duty.' In the end, his loyalty killed him. He collapsed and died in the Commons precincts in October 1994 on the eve of the Tory Party Conference.

He rarely lost his temper and had a good sense of humour, although he was not a great orator. On one occasion, during the 1979–1983 parliament, he sat all through a long debate on the subject of crime hoping to catch the Speaker's eye to deliver his speech, which he had spent several hours preparing. He was therefore both irritated and peeved when the debate ended without him having been called. Afterwards he approached the Speaker's chair and to express his disappointment. 'Mr Speaker,' he began, 'the country, nay the world, is very disappointed in you.'

'Why is that John?' replied George Thomas, the then Speaker.

'Well, Mr Speaker, you have denied the country and the House the opportunity to hear a brilliant speech on this subject. I have in my pocket here a splendid speech and by not calling me you have denied both the House, and indeed the world, an opportunity to hear this, the best speech I have *ever* prepared.'

Such a challenge to the chair warrants, and usually gets, short shrift, but Speaker Thomas remained impassive: 'It's always the same with you John, isn't it?'

'What do you mean, Mr Speaker?' enquired Blackburn.

'Well, whenever I don't call you, you have prepared the

most brilliant speech of all time yet whenever I do call you, you always deliver a fucking awful one.'

To his credit, Blackburn not only took this justified rebuff well, he later often told the story against himself.

In 1987, the members of an overseas British parliamentary delegation to Trinidad and Tobago were being bored by a particularly long-winded host, who insisted on relating details of a serious accident he had suffered many years earlier and of how he was subsequently ill for ages. After he had been going on for almost ten minutes about the one-time severity of his condition and how he had been at death's door, Dr Blackburn, the leader of the delegation, silenced him with the query, 'And tell me, did you live?'

☒

WITH ALAN CLARK, the late Tory diarist, an insult or putdown was never far below the surface. Whilst serving a minister, he caused a furore by referring to one African state as 'Bongo Bongo land'. Of fellow Conservative and former Foreign Secretary Douglas Hurd, he shocked many when he said: 'He might as well have a corncob up his arse.'

When he was particularly rude towards fellow Conservative MP Edwina Currie, Mrs C said: 'Oh Alan, don't be so nasty.' To which he retorted: 'Ask around my dear, I am nasty.'

On life at Eton: 'Eton is an early introduction to human cruelty, treachery and extreme physical hardship.'

On the media: 'The power of television has become fearsome and it is now being abused. TV is staffed by limousine liberals.'

Widely known as a historian, when he was once asked, 'Where did you read history?' He snapped back: 'In an armchair.'

On his fellow Conservatives: 'There's nothing that so improves the mood of the Party as the imminent execution of a senior colleague.'

On his ministerial advisors: 'Give a civil servant a good

case and he'll wreck it with clichés, bad punctuation, double negatives and convoluted apology.'

On English Heritage: 'English Heritage has got too big for its boots. Its director is a prominent figure in what is sometimes referred to as café society and he is seen enjoying hospitality in many locations.'

His ability to startle remained undimmed until the end. In 1998, when politicians from all parties and also the press were united in their condemnation of English soccer hooligans in Marseille, Clark came to their defence: 'English football fans have become the targets of everyone from ordinary police to known Mafia enforcers from Argentina... Football matches are now the substitute for medieval tournaments and it's perfectly natural that some of the fans should be obstreperous.'

He didn't leave it there and went on to attack his own party's proposals to restrict the fans' freedom to travel, saying that Shadow Home Secretary Norman Fowler's plans were 'un-conservative and completely illegal wartime restrictions on people's movements'.

When called a fascist by one leading newspaper, Clark wrote a letter to the editor which objected to the slur, insisting: 'I am not a fascist. Fascists are shopkeepers. I am a Nazi.'

Commenting on the then Tory Deputy Prime Minister, Michael Heseltine, the aristocratic Clark sniffed: 'He is a man who has bought his own furniture.'

After his death from a brain tumour in 1999, at the relatively early age of seventy-one, former Chancellor of the Exchequer Norman Lamont said of him: 'He was the most politically incorrect, outspoken, iconoclastic and reckless politician of our times.'

⊠

FORMER LABOUR LEADER Michael Foot served as Leader of the Opposition between 1980 and 1983. On the left wing of his party, he was a respected author and journalist who served as a Member of Parliament between 1945 and 1992, apart from a brief hiatus between 1955 and 1960.

A passionate and renowned orator, his skills were formidable but he was not telegenic. With his long unkempt hair and his propensity for wearing a duffel coat, the public simply did not see him as a Prime Minister in waiting. This, coupled with both a bounce in the polls for the Conservatives after the 1982 Falklands War and an extremely left-wing Labour election manifesto, resulted in Foot leading Labour to its biggest electoral defeat since the First World War.

He famously called Norman (now Lord) Tebbit: 'A semi house-trained polecat.' When he was later asked to expand his views, he added: 'He is the most stupendously offensive man in the House.' This is a description that Norman would probably regard as a compliment!

On the National Anthem: 'The tune is appalling and the words are banal.'

When a minister remarked to him that he was 'too busy to read any books'. Foot remarked: 'Men of power have no time to read; yet the men who do not read are unfit for power.'

He described his own Party's plan to abolish the voting rights of hereditary peers and create a House of Lords comprising only life peers, as 'a seraglio of eunuchs'.

On John Major's government: 'Napoleon in his first 100 days recaptured Paris without a battle. John Major in his first 100 days buried Thatcherism without a tear. Thereafter, they were both destroyed for their previous misdeeds.'

Foot passed away in 2010 at the grand old age of ninety-six.

⚖

FORMER PRIME MINISTER Sir Edward Heath, who died in 2005, served as an MP between 1950 and 2001. In his later years he was never afraid to speak his mind – an attribute which did not endear him to some of his parliamentary colleagues, particularly as he repeatedly attacked Margaret Thatcher, his successor as party leader. Acknowledging this fact, when speaking at the Conservative Party Conference in 1981, he amusingly said: 'Please don't applaud – it may irritate your neighbour.'

He was once offered a job by Lord Reith of the BBC. He turned it down with the barb: 'I couldn't work for God Almighty.'

He struck a chord with many when he commented on the high fees of directors of Lonhro Plc: 'The unpleasant and unacceptable face of capitalism.'

During a tour of the North-East just before he became Prime Minister he was taken through the slums of Newcastle. He surprised an aide when he remarked: 'If I lived here, I wouldn't vote for Harold Wilson.' He paused and added, 'I wouldn't vote for myself either – I'd vote for Robespierre.'

On the British press: 'A greater part of our press is run by foreigners; the Murdoch Empire and the Black Empire, and they have little interest in this country and its people. All they're interested in is their own products and making their own money.'

On Harold Wilson: 'A brilliant, if cynical party manager, who successfully got through his first period in office. But in the end, I ask, what did he really achieve? Or what did he really believe in?'

On his own party: 'The natural position of the Conservative Party is middle of the road. Always. Tony Blair realises that, and that is why he was so eager to seize this ground before the 1997 election. It remains to be seen how much of it he'll be able to keep.'

On Britain: 'We may be a small island but we are not a small people.'

Just before he died, he gave his view of Tony Blair: 'Like Harold Wilson, who faced me in the Commons, Blair has a habit of adjusting himself to events as they come along. The look is more important to Blair than the substance and it is this that is getting him into increasing trouble. Wilson, for all that one might say about him, did at least have a proper respect for Parliament. I am appalled by Tony Blair's disdain for Parliament.'

When one supporter criticised him for the fact that he was unmarried, he snapped back: 'What I do know is that a man who got married in order to be a better prime minister wouldn't be either a good prime minister or a good husband.'

Whilst some ministers seem to thoroughly enjoy political office, Heath nearly always gave the impression that life as a minister was a burden. Near the end of his life he seemed to confirm that this was indeed his view when he said: 'You must not expect prime ministers to enjoy themselves. If they do, they must not show it.'

THE LATE CONSERVATIVE MP Sir David Lightbown was extremely taciturn most of the time and this was just one of the reasons why he was an excellent government whip, under premiers Margaret Thatcher and John Major.

However, he never refrained from speaking his mind if he felt that a parliamentary colleague was being disloyal and he was quite prepared to be disagreeable if he felt that the miscreant deserved to feel the lash of his tongue.

This could be a terrifying experience. Lightbown, a former footballer, was physically a huge man and his very presence could be intimidating to young backbench MPs – and he knew it.

He always smiled wryly when the press referred to his weight because they invariably described him as 'the Commons' most-feared whip, who weighs eighteen stone'. As this was a considerable *understatement* of his size, he was flattered rather than insulted.

Once, in the Commons Tea Room, a new MP was bragging about his former occupation. 'I used to be a Plant Manager,' he boasted. Lightbown was unimpressed. 'I bet it was his job to water them,' he muttered as he left.

Never one to mince his words, despite all whips being instructed to keep quiet in public, he went on television during the 1992 Conservative Party Conference to call the Maastricht rebel Tory MPs 'nutters'.

On one occasion, seeing John Prescott enter the House of Commons Tea Room, Lightbown shouted: 'Make yourself at home John – hit somebody.'

He once petrified a young provincial journalist who had dared to criticise the Whips' Office, of which Lightbown was a member, by giving him a menacing stare and threatening him with retribution: 'Listen, sonny, one of my ancestors helped kill King Edward II by ramming a red-hot poker up his arse. If you don't watch out the process will be repeated.'

He was given a knighthood on leaving the Whips' Office in 1995 and died later that year after suffering a heart attack while watching a rugby match. He was sixty-three.

⌛

FORMER LIBERAL MP, the heavyweight Sir Cyril Smith, won the Rochdale seat in a 1972 by-election. He once said of the British Parliament: 'The place is the longest running farce in the West End.'

On the post-prandial activities of his political colleagues: 'The consumption of alcohol does tend to encourage those MPs of all parties who can neither speak with effect nor be silent with dignity.'

In 1975 Smith was appointed the Liberal Chief Whip and soon came under intense pressure from the press in light of a sexual scandal involving then Party leader Jeremy Thorpe. Smith soon resigned from the Whips' Office, allegedly on health grounds but his colleague David (now Lord) Steel gives a different assessment, saying: 'Cyril was not an ideal Chief Whip because he did not handle a crisis well and had a tendency to say anything to a news camera.'

A common joke on the size of the Parliamentary Liberal Party in the 1970s was that only one taxi would be needed to transport the entire party. However, after Smith's election, it was said that the party could now fill two taxis.

❧

FORMER PREMIER the late Jim (later Lord) Callaghan was not regarded as a great success as Prime Minister. Summing up his own philosophy he said: 'You never reach the promised land. You can only march towards it.'

❧

FAILED PARLIAMENTARY CANDIDATE and successful businessman the late James Goldsmith once remarked: 'The trouble with marrying your mistress is that you create a vacancy.'

❧

WILLIE WHITELAW (later Lord Whitelaw) was a popular figure in the Conservative Party in the 1970s and 1980s, except with the late Sir Nicholas Fairbairn MP.

He had a slightly bumbling style that endeared him to many. On one occasion he famously accused his political opponents of 'trying to stir up apathy'.

On another he was scheduled to speak at a by-election in favour of the Conservative candidate Stan Sorrell. Whitelaw caused laughter all around when he could not quite remember the candidate's name and after hesitating, urged the electors 'to vote for Stan Laurel'.

❧

FORMER LABOUR MINISTER the late Robin Cook carved out for himself a formidable reputation as a parliamentary debater.

He became Labour's first Foreign Secretary in eighteen years when Labour returned to office in May 1997, although after the 2001 election Tony Blair demoted him to the lower-ranking position of Leader of the House of Commons. In this role his intellect and sense of humour won him many friends across the political spectrum and MPs of all parties were genuinely shocked and upset by his death in August 2005, when he collapsed whilst mountaineering.

I came into regular contact with him whilst he was Leader of the House as I was then serving as Shadow Deputy Leader. I soon came both to respect and to like him. He had an incisive mind and a quick wit, certainly, but he was also a compassionate man who was willing to consider the views of others, including those of his political foes. He is still widely missed.

Commenting on the poor opinion poll showing of the Tory opposition in the late 1990s, he said: 'Conservatives cannot get off the back foot because that foot is so mired in the mud of the last Tory government.'

In 1990, before her downfall as Prime Minister, he said of Margaret Thatcher: 'Papua New Guinea is the only other country with the poll tax. The time has come for the Conservative Party to conclude that Mrs Thatcher could serve Great Britain best as our Ambassador there.'

In 1994, of his own aspirations, he joked: 'My looks and personality are very much of the school swot. I'm not good-looking enough to be Party leader.'

Cook, however, had a rather endearing thesis about holidays, saying in 2004, during the last winter before his tragic death: 'You should never trust a man who leaves the country at Christmas.'

Always a loner, one of his colleagues said shortly before his death: 'What is a conspiracy in the Labour Party?' Answer: 'Robin Cook on his own.'

THE LATE CONSERVATIVE Eric Forth MP was a House of Commons creature. If Labour MPs were expecting an early night, he would deliberately get up and speak in the House at length just for the hell of it. Forth was extremely adept at the parliamentary filibuster, causing Labour MPs to refer to him as 'Bloody Eric', a description he welcomed.

Commenting on the difference between British Prime Minister Tony Blair and former US President Bill Clinton he quipped: 'Blair is just Clinton with his zipper up.'

Explaining his own position in politics he once said: 'All this sucking up to minorities is ridiculous. There are millions of people in this country who are white, Anglo Saxon and bigoted – and they need to be represented.'

He opposed the BBC's spending money on a Nelson Mandela concert in 1988: 'Those who want the arts and who support them should pay for them themselves.'

A master at getting around the rules of procedure and keeping his utterances perfectly in order, he managed to imply that PM Tony Blair was a liar without being brought to heel. During Blair's tenure as PM, Forth nicknamed Prime Minister's Questions 'PMPs'. This led to the inevitable question 'PMPs? Don't you mean PMQs?'. To which Forth responded: 'No. PMPs – Prime Minister's Porkies, of course.'*

MENTION THE NAME of Lord Stratford at Westminster and few will know who you are referring to. On the other hand, if mention is made of his lordship's better known Commons moniker of Tony Banks, then politicians of all parties will agree that here was one of the most colourful of Labour's parliamentarians, who died tragically young.

His quick wit and withering tongue ensured that he did not last long as a minister!

---

* 'Porkies' is short for 'Pork Pies' which is rhyming slang for lies.

Before the 1997 election he gleefully described the Conservative Chancellor of the Exchequer, Ken Clarke, as someone who 'in his usual arrogant and high-handed fashion, dons his Thatcherite jackboots and stamps all over local opinion. He is like Hitler with a beer belly.' He later added: 'He is a pot-bellied old soak.'

He was an avid fan of the theatre, unlike former Conservative backbencher Terry Dicks, who was opposed to public subsidy of the arts. Referring to Mr Dicks, Banks said: 'He is an unreconstructed Member of Parliament. When he leaves the chamber, he probably goes to vandalise a few paintings somewhere. He is to the arts what Vlad the Impaler was to origami. He gives us a laugh.'

And warming to his criticism of Mr Dicks, his favourite *bête noire* during the term of the John Major Conservative government, he said: 'In arts debates, he plays the court jester. He has a muscular approach. He claims that the ballet is something for poofters in leotards. That is the level of his contribution. He is to the arts what *The Sun* is to English literature, or what the *A Team* is to embroidery. He is living proof that a pig's bladder on the end of a stick can be elected to Parliament.'

On Margaret Thatcher when she was PM: 'She is a half-mad old bag lady. The Finchley whinger. She said the poll tax was the government's flagship. Like a captain she went down with her flagship. Unfortunately for the Conservative Party, she keeps bobbing up again – her head keeps appearing above the waves.'

Surprisingly, Banks escaped rebuke from the Speaker for once accusing Margaret Thatcher of acting 'with the sensitivity of a sex-starved boa constrictor'.

Expanding his views of Lady T: 'She is about as environmentally friendly as the bubonic plague. She is a natural autocrat surrounded by a bunch of sycophants, many of whom have betrayed everything in which they once claimed to believe. She is far more influenced by the example of Attila the Hun than Sir Francis of Assisi. She is a petty-minded xenophobe who struts around the world interfering and lecturing in an arrogant and high-handed manner.'

Former Labour MP Doug Hoyle was one day bemoaning the closure of British shipyards, arguing it would have been better if we had put the shipyards in mothballs. He then corrected himself and said that he would have preferred to have kept the shipyards open and instead put the then Trade and Industry Secretary, Peter Lilley, in mothballs. This led Tony Banks to gibe: 'They are the only balls he has.' Mr Hoyle agreed to bow to what he described as Mr Bank's 'superior knowledge of the minister's anatomy'.

On another occasion, during a debate on conservation in the Antarctic, the late Labour MP Peter Hardy pointed out that modern-day prospectors could do an enormous amount of damage in a small amount of time due to new technology. He illustrated his point by telling the House: 'Some people may imagine that a prospector is a hoary old man riding on a mule with a backpack of beans and dried bacon, hoping to extract a few bits of rocks with a hammer and a shovel and so discover gold.' At which Tony Banks interrupted: 'This sounds like Nicholas Ridley.'

Banks added later: 'Britain still has the reputation of being the dirtiest nation in Europe. That must have something to do with the raw sewage contained in Nicholas Ridley's speeches.'

Commenting on John Major's performance on *Desert Island Discs* whilst Prime Minister: 'He should have chosen something from *The Beggar's Opera* because there is a whole chorus on the London streets which could join in.'

Again, on former PM John Major: 'He revealed himself as a Thatcherite with a grin.'

On (Lord) Michael Heseltine: 'His contributions to debates are as if the House was not made up of Members of Parliament, but of delegates, all with their blue rinses and red necks applauding to the rafters, rather similar to when he makes one of his speeches to the Conservative Party Conference.'

On Conservative heavyweight Nicholas Soames: 'The

amiable food mountain clearly likes his grub. At the Dispatch Box he could probably persuade MPs that arsenic is quite palatable if suitably chilled.'

On the Conservative government of John Major: 'There is very little which was decent in that government of second-hand car salesmen, Arthur Daleys and low lifes generally – on second thoughts, I have probably been unfair to second-hand car salesmen.'

During a defence debate he snapped: 'When Conservatives describe weapons of death and destruction they become positively orgasmic. Looking at them, those are probably the only orgasms that they are ever likely to have. Margaret Thatcher used to tremble with excitement at the thought of being able to press the nuclear button.'

On former Prime Minister John Major: 'Where did Major go so badly wrong and become a Tory? I think that it was when he got turned down for the job of bus conductor. He had his heart set on punching tickets and helping little old ladies on and off the bus, but he was spurned. At that point he vowed hideous revenge on us all, but to be able to get it he first had to push a little old lady from Finchley off the bus. Having achieved that, he has now turned his attention to the rest of us. Our fate is to be even more horrible. We are to be buried alive under charters. I thought that the Citizen's Charter was just one document, but there are more and more charters in store.'

When interrupted by Conservative gibes he airily brushed them aside: 'It appears that we are in the midst of a convention of small order waiters.'

On the Young Conservatives: 'It is the Tory Party equivalent of the Hitler youth.'

On the state of Britain after eighteen years of Conservative government: 'Britain is heading pell-mell towards the status of a banana monarchy but without the benefit of bananas. What Victorian values mean to Conservatives is that many of them would be quite happy to see little boys once again earning pennies by going up chimneys. There are times when I find it difficult to work out whether the Conservative government is vicious or ignorant. I have come to the conclusion that it is both.'

When former Foreign Office minister Tim Sainsbury was answering questions, Tony Banks bawled at him: 'Yankee lick-spittle.' One MP, who was hard of hearing, thought Banks was ordering a type of cream cake sold in Sainsbury's. However, the barb was un-parliamentary and the Speaker promptly ordered Mr Banks to withdraw.

Comparing the difference in speeches between Labour's Tony Benn and former Tory MP Neil Hamilton, Banks commented: 'Comparing the two speeches is like comparing Demosthenes with Alf Garnett.' This led a Tory government whip to shout: 'Which is which?'

After a kiss-and-tell story appeared detailing how Chelsea fan and then MP David Mellor wore a football kit during sex, he said: 'Since the great days of Jimmy Greaves, it's the only time anyone's managed to score five times in a Chelsea shirt.'

However, not all of his colleagues were fans of Mr Banks. The late Labour MP Andrew Faulds described some of his contributions as 'puerile comments from an inevitably loqua-cious colleague'.

Mr Faulds was not the only socialist who had mixed feel-ings. During a rather lengthy speech Mr Banks expressed his disagreement with Tony Benn, who at the time was not in the chamber. Saying that he regarded Mr Benn's arguments as 'somewhat bankrupt', Mr Banks informed the House that he would ensure that his remarks were pointed out to Mr Benn 'as he probably does not spend a great deal of time reading my speeches – but then who does?', which led Labour front-bencher Peter Snape to snipe: 'You do.' Displaying his knack of dispelling criticism from whatever quarter it emanates, Tony Banks responded: 'I most certainly do not bother to read my speeches because I know what a load of rubbish they are before anybody hears them.' No one in the House felt that they could argue with that!

However, it was not long after Labour's 1997 election victory that he got himself into trouble again during that year's Labour Party Conference, putting his own future in doubt. On the same day that Tony Blair made his main address to the nation, Labour's *other* Tony caused a sensation when he lambasted Tories William Hague and Michael Portillo as well as his Labour colleague Peter Mandelson in a diatribe in highly dubious taste.

In September that year, Mr Banks was one of half a dozen Labour ministers to address the left-wing Tribune Rally at the Corn Exchange in Brighton. Referring to the Conservative leadership election Mr Banks said: 'And now to make matter worse, they have elected a foetus as party leader. I bet there's a lot of Tory MPs who wish they hadn't voted against abortion now.'

This attack was widely held to be unacceptable.

However, this was just for starters. Banks went on to claim that former defence minister Michael Portillo's plan for 'world domination' had come to grief on election night and he then likened him to Pol Pot, the former Khymer Rouge dictator, who was responsible for the deaths of more than a million people. Banks continued: 'At one moment Portillo was polishing his jackboots and planning the advance. And the next thing he shows up as a TV presenter. It is rather like Pol Pot joining the *Teletubbies*.'

Turning on his colleague Peter Mandelson, he compared him to a figure out of *Dracula*. Mandelson had just failed to secure a seat on Labour's ruling National Executive Committee, having lost out to veteran left-wing MP Ken Livingstone. Banks quipped: 'Those Labour Party members who voted for Mr Livingstone should either not go out on their own at night – or take some garlic with them.'

He seemed to be thoroughly enjoying himself as he then went on to suggest that Labour's Milbank headquarters – where the general election campaign was controlled – was 'making cloned Mandelsons and storing them in the Millennium Dome at Greenwich', the project then being overseen by Mandelson. He added: 'And when the clock strikes midnight on 31 December 1999, millions of Mandelsons will march from the Dome and civilisation as we know it will be at an end.' These insults backfired and Banks was forced by Labour Party bosses to issue an apology.

However, he showed little remorse. Only a month later he told the *New Statesman* that he thought his own party's spin doctors had drawn attention to his remarks to deflect press criticism of remarks made about the minimum wage at the same time by Peter Mandelson.

Of the Liberal Democrats, he said: 'They are woolly-hatted, muesli-eating, Tory lick-spittles.'

On footballer Paul Gascoigne: 'When God gave Gascoigne his enormous footballing talent, he took his brain out at the same time to even things up.'

On retiring from the lower house in 2005, Lord Stratford, as he became, said he was stepping down from the House of Commons because dealing with constituents' problems was 'intellectually numbing, and tedious in the extreme'.

On his own attitude to loyalty to his party: 'Bringing the leadership to its knees occasionally is a good way of keeping it on its toes.'

He suffered a serious stroke in early January 2006 whilst on holiday in the USA and died a few days later at the tragically early age of sixty-two.

☒

CONSERVATIVE CABINET MINISTER, John, later Lord, Biffen, who died in 2007 aged seventy-six, was respected across the political spectrum for his honesty and independence of mind. He was the one politician with whom Tony Blair said he would willingly share a desert island.

In an age when spin and political conformity were gaining ground, he held on to his principles – even if it meant the premature end of his Cabinet career.

He entered Parliament in 1961, but he was never content meekly to toe the party line, voting against incomes policy, Rhodesia sanctions and entry to the EEC.

As a result, he remained on the backbenches under the leadership of Edward Heath, with whom he had an uneasy relationship, but he flourished under Heath's successor Margaret Thatcher, who appreciated his monetarist economic views – he had been a disciple of Enoch Powell in the 1950s and 1960s, sharing his free market beliefs.

Mrs Thatcher made him Chief Secretary to the Treasury in her first Cabinet – one of an inner circle of 'dries' who would drive through the Thatcherite revolution in the teeth of opposition from the 'wets' on the front bench.

He gained a reputation as a deep thinker, who avoided scoring easy points against his political opponents.

He was made trade minister and then Leader of the House of Commons, a role in which he was said by political commentators – and even opponents – to have excelled.

When, in 1986, he called with characteristic frankness for a 'balanced ticket' to fight the next general election, it was seized on by Thatcher's opponents as a sign he saw her as a vote loser.

'No one seriously supposes that the Prime Minister would be Prime Minister throughout the entire period of the next parliament,' he told Brian Walden in a 1986 *Weekend World* interview. 'The Prime Minister will make her most effective contribution to the Conservative Party by being what she is and not by trying to be something different. Others then have to provide the balance in that situation.'

He was famously branded a 'semi-detached member of the Cabinet' by Mrs Thatcher's press secretary Bernard Ingham, following the *Weekend World* interview and was sacked from Cabinet after the 1987 election.

Biffen retaliated by saying Ingham was the 'sewer and not the sewage' and describing the Thatcher government, after he had left it, as a 'sort of Stalinist regime'.

Years later, he became more philosophical about his sacking, saying: 'I shall go through life as "semi-detached"... that halter has been put round my neck by Mr Ingham. Nothing I can do about it.'

Amongst his other comments, the following are worthy of note:

'Second to being a football manager, being a Cabinet minister is a short-lived experience.

And, in a similar vein: 'You can't complain about being scratched if you work in a menagerie.'

On the House of Commons: 'It is theatre. It always has been theatre and as long as it has the vitality of trying to represent the wide range of opinions that are argued outside of a saloon bar and are put in a rather different form in this place – it will retain its vitality.'

On being called 'semi-detached': 'I think that Bernard Ingham put a patent on that phrase. I have no complaints. I lived a very contented life in semi-detachment for some time after I was demolished.'

He became a life peer in 1997 and continued to campaign against the growth of EU power until his death of kidney failure.

⧗

THE SEVENTH EARL of Onslow, who died in 2011, was a self-confessed 'parliamentary hooligan' who often said he was proud to be a 'disloyal Conservative', adding that his duty was 'to the constitution rather than his political party'.

He had a penchant for outrageous bow ties and colourful language. Commenting on his own place in politics he said: 'any House which has me in it needs its head examined.'

When someone attacked the fact that hereditary peers had an automatic right to sit in the House of Lords (which they did before Tony Blair's reforms) he astonished his detractor by agreeing with him, saying: 'I am a hereditary peer who sees the illogicality of having any power over his fellow citizens just because his forebear got tight with the Prince Regent.'

And, further commenting on himself: 'I was actually too stupid to go to university, but I was very privileged to go to Eton.'

HERE TODAY

Political invective has changed over the years but so too has the venue. The packed public meeting where a candidate addresses his electors, fields questions from the floor and has the opportunity both to insult his opponents and parry with hecklers, is no more. Today most political insults are either well rehearsed for release in a TV or radio studio, dictated to journalists, or hurled across the floor of the House during debate.

It is a fact that media coverage of politics in the run up to an election has resulted in the public reaching saturation point well before a general election campaign is over. Consequently, few bother to attend public meetings and these days few candidates hold them.

The major parties have reacted to this by staging the glittering political rally, which has replaced the public meeting. This 'supporters only' convention is an occasion where one's own party members are encouraged – even sometimes mandated – to attend, wave flags and cheer on one's own party leaders.

Although the advent of multiple television channels has had the effect of toning down the invective, thankfully it has not been entirely removed from the political dictionary. This section contains a selection of the most memorable contemporary barbs uttered in recent years.

⌛

NORMAN TEBBIT (now a Lord) is a former Conservative Party Chairman and he remains a formidable performer. Whatever the forum for debate, when Norman is on form you cross swords with him at your peril. He is, undoubtedly, one of the most acid-tongued politicians of recent times.

When asked who had the most influence on him, his mother or his father, he replied: 'I don't think either of them had. I think I had more influence on them.'

On Labour's former leader, Neil (now Lord) Kinnock: 'I have never rated Neil Kinnock as anything but a windbag whose incoherent speeches spring from an incoherent mind.'

And commenting further on Kinnock: 'More gimmicks than guts. I sometimes wonder whether he exists at all.'

When an MP sarcastically suggested to Norman that he was someone who no doubt held the view that 'God was a paid-up member of the Conservative Party,' Tebbit replied: 'Yes, of course he is. God could not be a socialist because of the process of evolution.' When asked to explain what he meant, he said: 'Evolution means getting rid of the dinosaurs and replacing them with some more efficient and up-to-date animals. Any socialist would have been dedicated to protecting the dinosaurs in the name of compassion or conservation or something. Thus dinosaurs would never have been allowed to go. So God can't be a socialist.'

On the Labour Party: 'It is a party full of envy, people with failures and richly tainted with smug hypocrisy. It shows malice towards personal success.'

On his own philosophy: 'A centrally controlled state leads to unpleasant consequences. Socialism is bound to become authoritarian.'

Norman once astonished a group of MPs, of which I was one, when he suddenly broke off from talking about the economy in the Commons Members' Lobby to watch veteran Labour MP David Winnick walk by. After watching in silence, he turned back and remarked: 'That man walks rather strangely. He has either got a bad tailor, suffers from piles or he's shit himself.'

This was mild compared to some of Norman's other utterances. When, in the 1970s, he was upset by something said by Labour MP Tom Litterick, Tebbit snapped: 'Go and have another heart attack.' At the time Litterick was seriously ill and he died shortly afterwards.

When he was told that Labour Cabinet ministers in office were at least well-meaning, he exploded: 'Well-intentioned and well-meaning people are the most dangerous. You cannot have socialism unless you control incomes and prices. So you go the way of Hitler and Mussolini.'

To those who attack the special relationship with America: 'Anti-American talk is a sign of cheap and dirty parties seeking cheap and dirty votes.'

On the Liberal Democrats: 'They are Enid Blyton socialists – a dustbin for undecided votes.'

When Labour was at its nadir under Michael Foot in the early 1980s, one Tory MP crowed with glee that 'the Labour Party is dead'. Tebbit quickly corrected him: 'Not dead – just brain-dead.'

When he was told that he spent too much time trying to appease the party faithful, he shot back: 'The faithful won't vote for you unless you're faithful to them. I stand up for what I believe is right.'

On Tony Blair: 'He likes to style himself as the people's Prime Minister but the way the truth is concealed and distorted would do credit to the former People's Republics of Eastern Europe. He appears to have no clear political views except that the world should be a nicer place and that he should be loved and trusted by everyone and questioned by no one.'

On New Labour MPs: 'Like glazed-eyed parrots, they all recite precisely the same words, transmitted by email, fax or pager from Labour headquarters at Millbank.'

And, warming to this theme, his view on the House of Commons during the Labour government of Tony Blair: '"Blair's Babes" are shepherded through the division lobbies baa-ing like the well-fed sheep they are, without even sight of their great Leader. He is too busy hosting parties for Labour luvvies and showbiz junkies at Number 10, or patronising the nation with his views in a variety of silly voices on the selection of England's World Cup team. There is a whiff of arrogance and it is more than nannying.'

Unlike most of his predecessors, who have gone quietly into retirement, Lord Tebbit has continued to give the Conservative Party the benefit of his opinions. In 2002, he warned the then Tory leader that he was being undermined by 'spotty youths, researchers, assistants and party apparatchiks'. 'Iain Duncan Smith needs to clear the squabbling children out of Central Office,' he opined, urging Mr Duncan Smith to sack Party strategy director Dominic Cummings and Conservative chief executive Mark MacGregor, and the party to rid itself of 'squabbling children'.

Mr MacGregor, ex-leader of the Federation of Conservative students, which was shut down by Lord Tebbit during his time as Party Chairman, was singled out for criticism. Norman also attacked the calibre of staff employed in Tory Central Office, saying they were too willing to 'gossip to reporters with their critical analysis based on two years of experience'. He went on: 'Mr Duncan Smith should get a higher calibre of more experienced people in Central Office and make it very plain that their job is to obey orders and not go off out criticising people who have appointed them.'

Shortly afterwards, he took a swipe at Francis Maude MP and other modernising factions of his own Party, including Michael Portillo and Kenneth Clarke. Tebbit said that (the then) Tory Leader Iain Duncan Smith should remember he was voted in 'to follow a traditional path', adding: 'I think somebody needs to give a slap in the face to the people who have dedicated themselves to heading in the wrong direction. Iain Duncan Smith should follow his instincts and he should recall that he was elected by the Conservative Party on the basis that he was not of the Mr Maude School, not in the Portillo school, not in the Clarke school, but in the traditional school of the Conservative Party – they wanted to get back to it.'

Warming to his theme, he said: 'Mr Maude thinks that's the way to lose elections – well he perhaps knows more about losing elections than I do – but certainly I think that what the party needs to do is to rally around its leader.'

On Labour's former Defence Secretary Geoff Hoon he was withering: 'I've met Boy Scouts with more military bearing.'

Once, whilst campaigning for future Tory Chairman Jeremy Hanley in the 1980s, Norman was interrupted at a public meeting by an excitable young heckler. Tebbit tried to soothe the situation by saying, 'Calm down my lad.' It didn't seem to work and the young man retorted: 'My lad? You're not my father.' Tebbit silenced the barracking with the gibe: 'I would quit whilst you're ahead lad – I'm the only father you'll ever know.'

Before Tony Blair's resignation in 2007, during a radio interview, the reporter ventured to suggest that Norman was calling Tony Blair a liar. Norman shocked the reporter with his denial: 'I never accused Tony Blair of being a liar. He certainly isn't one.'

Then, he explained himself: 'To be a liar, you need to know what is the truth and what are lies and then deliberately decide to tell a lie. Tony Blair is a fantasist and he doesn't know the difference.'

And, on former Premier Gordon Brown: 'Dull, uninspiring, brown. A man with no charisma and a record of imprudent borrowing and spending to put Northern Rock's mild profligacy in the shade.'

On the defection to Labour of Tory MP Quentin Davies in June 2007: 'This defection will raise the average standard of members on the Conservative side and lower it on the Labour side.'

On supporters of New Labour: 'Some of them are so sick that they see a paedophile behind every tree, global warming in every sunny day and a potential rapist in every man.'

Showing that his talent for abuse is not restricted to criticising only non-Conservatives, in 2011 he said of his own party leader: 'I still do not know where, apart from a Big Society gay wedding in Westminster Abbey, David Cameron really wants to go.'

And on the Conservative-led coalition government: 'After all, what are coalition politics? Ghastly, messy and incoherent.'

Tebbit has also frequently been at the receiving end of acerbic abuse. However, unlike most politicians, the more offensive the nickname the more he seems to take pleasure in them. Failed Labour leader Michael Foot once famously called Norman 'a semi-house-trained polecat'. His reaction to this was to enshrine a polecat in his coat of arms when he was elevated to the House of Lords, although he did suggest to Foot that he (Foot) should 'put a bridle on his foul-mouthed tongue'.

Other less than flattering soubriquets thrown at Norman include 'The Chingford Strangler' and 'Dracula'.

During the 1987 General Election, Tebbit informed PM Margaret Thatcher that he wished to leave the government after the election in order to care for his wife, who was badly injured in the 1984 Brighton bombing. He stood down from the Commons in 1992 and was given a life peerage. Shortly after he left the government Margaret Thatcher said that she 'bitterly regretted' losing a like-minded person from the Cabinet.

⌛

COLOURFUL TORY MP Dr Sir Rhodes Boyson MP was a popular after-dinner speaker at Conservative Party fundraising events during the 1970s and 1980s. His populist right-wing views and Victorian schoolmaster image were appreciated by the Tory grassroots if not always by the party leadership.

With his 'mutton chop' sideburns and traditional dress, it was no surprise that he once said: 'A man is not properly dressed without a waistcoat.'

Commenting on Winston Churchill, he said: 'When the

Second World War was won, my Father, like the rest of the nation, thanked him for his efforts and voted for his removal for office.'

On the Lib Dems he said: 'They are a colour supplement with nothing inside.'

On what he thought should be the maxim for every minister: 'Every man has two masters – his philosophy and his daily responsibilities. If you take decisions without bearing in mind what you are moving towards you destroy your philosophy. If you get bogged down in administration and don't keep asking yourself questions, you destroy yourself.'

On education: 'Children who fail their exams at eleven and fourteen should have to spend their summer holidays in the classroom.'

He surprised many with his view on single parents: 'An intentional one-parent family is probably the most evil product of our times.'

Reactionary he certainly was, but he was also good after-dinner entertainment and Conservative audiences knew it. He would regularly attract a bigger crowd when he was the guest speaker than many leading ministers of his day.

A workaholic, he once stayed at my house after making a speech nearby. 'I like a full English breakfast and I rise at 6 a.m.,' he told me as we retired to bed at about one o'clock in the morning. I could not help giving the reply: 'I like one too – but I rise at eight, so call me when it's ready.'

⧗

LABOUR VETERAN Tony Benn, now retired from the Commons, on the House of Lords: 'A Chamber elected by nobody and accountable to nobody.'

And further expressing a view of the House of Lords when it was still largely a hereditary chamber: 'Its members get there, not by first-past-the-post but by a first-past-the-bedpost system.'

And on the New Labour government of Tony Blair: 'The Blair government has no industrial policy and seems to have made protection of the rich one of its main objectives.'

Commenting on the photo-finish US presidential election in 2000, he said: 'George W. Bush won the presidential election by having a very big majority – not in the country but in the Supreme Court.'

Asked his view of Labour leader Gordon Brown, he was vitriolic: 'Gordon Brown? He's vacuous, ridiculous and utterly pathetic.'

On getting to the top in politics: 'When you get to Number 10, you've climbed there on a little ladder called 'the status quo'. And when you're there, the status quo looks very good.'

On Lady Thatcher: 'Mrs Thatcher will be remembered not as a great Executive leader, because every Prime Minister is powerful, but because she is a teacher. The weakness of the Labour Party over a long period is that it hasn't done any teaching.'

Again on Lady T: 'She believes in some things. It is an old fashioned idea.'

On Tony Blair: 'I did not enter the Labour Party forty-eight years ago to have our manifesto written by Dr Mori, Dr Gallup and Mr Harris.'

Returning to his attack on New Labour, he took a swipe at the large number of current Labour MPs who are prepared to ask Tony Blair helpful questions at Prime Minister's Question Time: 'There are so many planted questions now that it ought to be renamed *Gardeners' Question Time*.'

And, on his differences with Tony Blair: 'I am not *New* Labour, I am a member of the Labour Party. New Labour is actually the smallest political party in the world. All its members are in the Cabinet.'

Asked what he saw as the answer to Britain's problems under Mr Blair, he retorted: 'What Britain needs is a Labour government.'

⌛

FORMER LABOUR Cabinet minister and Labour veteran, Denis, now Lord, Healey was a knockabout Commons performer who was a bruiser in debate. In the 1980s he memorably insulted Margaret Thatcher saying: 'I often compare Mrs Thatcher with Florence Nightingale. She stalks through the wards of our hospitals as a lady with a lamp – unfortunately, in her case it is a blowlamp.'

Later he added: 'Margaret Thatcher says that she has given the French President a piece of her mind – this is not a gift I would receive with alacrity.'

And on his own Party's former leader, Harold Wilson: 'He did not have political principle. He had no sense of direction and rarely looked more than a few months ahead. He had short-term opportunism allied with a capacity for self-delusion, which made Walter Mitty appear unimaginative.'

His view of former American President Lyndon Johnson: 'He exuded a brutal lust for power which I found most disagreeable. He boasted acting on the principle "Give me a man's balls and his heart and mind will follow." He was a monster.'

On a speech by the Conservative Sir Geoffrey (now Lord) Howe: 'I think we have all enjoyed another lugubrious concatenation of meaningless clichés.'

But Healey's most famous putdown was his assertion that being criticised by Howe was 'like being savaged by a dead sheep'.

Telling a story about his former colleague David Owen, who left the Labour Party to found the short-lived SDP: 'Four fairies attended the birth of David Owen. Number one said, "You'll be good looking." Number two said, "You'll be clever." Number three said, "You'll be very ambitious." Number four said, "You'll be all these things and you'll also be a shit."'

Winston Churchill once remarked that Clement Attlee was 'a modest man with much to be modest about'. A Tory whip with a grudging respect for Healey sniped: 'Healey's a vain man – with a lot to be vain about.'

🕱

FORMER CONSERVATIVE PARTY Chairman Lord (Cecil) Parkinson, taking a swipe at the Blair Labour government, quipped: 'The trouble with New Labour MPs is that most of them don't trust each other – and they're right.'

On life in politics: 'I have my own Parkinson's Law: in politics the whips give you what they think you deserve and deny you what they think you want.'

On himself: "It is better to be a has-been than a never-was.'

And, early in 1998, poking fun at his own political comeback as Party Chairman he said: 'I have at least proved one thing – you can boil a cabbage twice.'

At the time of Margaret Thatcher's defeat as Conservative Party Leader he mused: 'The Labour Party is led by a pigmy and we are led by a giant. We have decided that the answer to our problems is to find a pigmy of our own.'

On leaving the House of Commons in 1992: 'I'm a great believer in leaving politics when you've reached your ceiling... though I did lower the ceiling somewhat.'

🕱

MARGARET HILDA THATCHER became Prime Minister in May 1979 and remained in office until 1990, making her not only Britain's first woman Prime Minister but one of our longest-serving premiers.

Upon first arriving at 10 Downing Street, she said, paraphrasing the Prayer of St Francis: 'Where there is discord, may we bring harmony. Where there is error, may we bring truth. Where there is doubt, may we bring faith. And where there is despair, may we bring hope.'

She was first elected Conservative Party Leader in 1975 and led her party to victory in 1979, 1983 and 1987 before being deposed by her own MPs, following a challenge by Michael Heseltine.

She later said of her challenger: 'He is all glamour and no substance.'

It seems surprising now but she was regarded by many political observers as an unknown quantity when she challenged Edward Heath for the Tory leadership after his second general election defeat in 1974, having held only the relatively junior Cabinet position of Secretary of State for Education. There were also the patrician voices of the Conservative party elders who thought that *no* woman could ever be up to the job of being PM. It was not long, however, before it was clear that she was not going to be a 'soft touch' for anyone.

It was the late French President François Mitterrand who said of her: 'She has the mouth of Marilyn Monroe and the eyes of Caligula.'

More invective aimed at her came from overseas, when the Russians called her 'the Iron Lady'. But what was intended as an insult backfired badly as it was immediately used by her supporters as an indication of her steadfastness. The taunt stuck – but not in the way it was intended.

Slapping down a colleague and summing up much of her own approach to politics, she said: 'Do you think you would ever have heard of Christianity if the Apostles had gone out and said, "I believe in consensus"?'

On the Labour government of Jim Callaghan: 'He presided over debt, drift and decay.'

On the sensitivities of most politicians: 'If you are working with politicians, you should remember that they have very large fingers and very large toes and you can tread on them remarkably easily. I, however, have stubs.'

In opposition, she silenced a Labour minister with: 'The honourable gentleman suffers from the fact that I understand him perfectly.'

One apocryphal story going around the Tea Room at Westminster in the mid-1980s was that when Lady T's receptionist answered the phone she used to say, 'I am afraid that Mrs Thatcher is not available at present. Who should I say was going to listen?'

Amongst her other sayings, the following are the most memorable:

'If your only opportunity is to be equal, then it is not opportunity.'

'Nobody would remember the Good Samaritan if he had only good intentions; he had money as well.'

'You can strike your way down, but you have to work your way up.'

'I sometimes think that the Labour Party is like a pub where the mild is running out. If someone does not do something soon, all that is left will be bitter and all that is bitter will be left.'

'A typical Labour Budget – giving away money that they haven't even borrowed yet.'

'President Clinton is a great communicator. The trouble is, he has absolutely nothing to communicate.'

'Being powerful is like being a lady. If you have to tell people you are, you aren't.'

'Being Prime Minister is a lonely job. In a sense, it ought to be: you cannot lead from the crowd.'

When asked by Geoffrey Clifton Brown MP, several years after she had retired, what she would do differently if she had a second chance at being Prime Minister, she replied without hesitation, silencing him with the answer: 'I think I did rather well the first time round, don't you?'

Former Home Secretary Kenneth (Lord) Baker, commenting on Mrs Thatcher's style, said: 'She categorised her ministers into those she could put down, those she could break down and those she could wear down.'

And, the view of late USA President, Ronald Reagan: 'She is the best man in England.'

DAVID STEEL (now Lord Steel) led the Liberal Party from 1976 until 1988. He stood down from the House of Commons in 1997 and is now a member of the House of Lords.

He once silenced a heckler with the riposte: 'Of course I don't disagree with everything you say. Even a broken clock is right twice a day.'

On himself: 'I like good food and decent wine as much as Roy Jenkins does, but I keep quiet about it.'

On the achievements of Margaret Thatcher: 'She turned the British bulldog into a Reagan poodle.'

⌛

FORMER CONSERVATIVE defence minister Tom (now Lord) King on filibustering: 'Those not inclined to speak can sometimes be provoked to do so by those who are not inclined to shut up.'

⌛

LORD (NIGEL) LAWSON is a serious intellectual heavyweight whose contributions to debate are always of substance.

He served as Secretary of State for Energy before becoming Chancellor of the Exchequer during Margaret Thatcher's premiership. He remained Chancellor of the Exchequer for longer than any of his predecessors since Lloyd George, but following a disagreement with Thatcher he resigned in October 1989. His length of service as Chancellor has subsequently been beaten by Gordon Brown.

When in office, Lawson had little time for political small-talk. As a Cabinet minister, he eschewed the boring but necessary job of 'chatting-up' his own Party's backbenchers before a difficult debate.

Indeed, sometimes he actually appeared to *enjoy* upsetting his colleagues. One of these occasions was a PPS meeting held in the Lower Ministerial Conference Room, underneath the

Commons Chamber. This was a yearly occasion, ahead of the Budget, to give PPSs the opportunity to let the Chancellor of the Exchequer know their views before he finalised his fiscal proposals. It was really little more than a public relations exercise. The job of being a PPS is generally a thankless one. These 'ministerial bag-carriers' work unpaid for ministers in the hope of one day attaining office themselves. This meeting was to give them the impression of being consulted before the Chancellor finalised his Budget plans, to make them perhaps think that their views *did* matter after all. Most knew it was something of a charade but they also knew their attendance would be expected and that the sessions would be chaired by the Chief Whip – the man who advises the Prime Minister of suitable candidates for promotion. This therefore presented an opportunity to show the Chief who of those present was indeed promotion material. Most attending therefore asked questions and in past years the then Chancellor responded politely and encouragingly. When Lawson was faced with this meeting, he did not hide his contempt. At the time, I was a PPS and consequently one of those in attendance. It was a memorable occasion.

'Nigel, you have started well,' a PPS pompously began, 'by abolishing a different tax in each Budget. But please Nigel, whilst continuing to maintain a sound economy, also continue with tax abolition and this year make it Stamp Duty.'

Lawson's features were impassive. 'You are right that I have abolished a tax in each Budget. If fiscal circumstances allow, this is something that I will continue to do. So far as Stamp Duty is concerned, when I first cut the level of this, the tax take went up because of increased taxable activity. Then, when circumstances allowed, I cut the stamp duty level again and much to the surprise of my officials the tax take did not go down but it went up, again because of increased dutiable activity. But, you know, if I abolish Stamp Duty completely, I think the tax take will go down. Next....!'

There was laughter all round and one PPS with a very red

face. It was very amusing but after that episode, the questions dried up, the meeting finished early and this annual event was thereafter abandoned.

Although invariably on top of his brief, Lawson did not always bother to acquaint himself with the mundane background facts necessary for any minister undertaking a regional tour. In 1987, when touring seats in the East Midlands, Lawson came to speak for Tory candidate Andrew Mitchell, who was standing for Parliament for the first time in the Gedling constituency. The General Election was already underway and Lawson attended a public meeting on Mitchell's behalf. He astounded the audience – and Mitchell himself – by telling the crowd during his speech that they should 're-elect Andrew Mitchell' because he was 'doing such a good job in the House of Commons'. Mitchell, who went on to win, said afterwards that his constituents subsequently never believed another word uttered by a Cabinet minister.

On former ministerial colleague James Prior: 'An affable but short-fused Heathite squire.'

Amongst his other quips the following are worthy of note:

'You don't make the poor rich by making the rich poor.'

On economists: 'I would not take too much notice of teenage scribblers in the City who jump up and down in an effort to get press attention.'

'The Conservative Party has never believed that the business of government is the government of business.'

Long after he had left office, Lawson appeared on the Clive Anderson chat show on BBC TV to promote his book on dieting. Anderson, rather smugly, made a few jokes at Lawson's expense. Not realising perhaps that he was treading on thin ice, Anderson went on and on about Lawson's weight loss. Showing a flash of his old self, Lawson suddenly hit back saying, 'Well, it's better than having no neck!' Anderson appeared shocked at this swipe at his own physique, which was brutally effective. So effective in fact, that ever since I witnessed the episode, I have been unable to watch Anderson on television again as each time he appears I find my eyes involuntarily drawn to where his neck should be!

In 2006 he seriously upset some scientists and all of the green eco-lobby when he questioned their assumptions about global warming. The Kyoto Agreement, under which many of the world's industrialised countries agreed to reduce carbon emissions, was an 'absurd response' to supposed global warming, he said, adding, 'It will do virtually nothing to slow change as the US has not signed up and developing economies like Brazil, China and India will increase their building of coal-fired power stations.'

For good measure he continued: 'In primitive societies it was customary for extreme weather events to be explained as punishment from the gods for the sins of the people; and there is no shortage of examples of this theme in the Bible, either – particularly but not exclusively in the Old Testament. The main change is that the new priests are scientists well rewarded with research grants for their pains, rather than clerics of the established religions, and the new religion is eco-fundamentalism.'

And, commenting further on climate-change fanatics: 'The new religion of global warming is *The Da Vinci Code* of environmentalism. It is a great story and a bestseller. It contains a grain of truth and a mountain of nonsense.'

On the dithering of the Labour government: 'To govern is to choose. To appear to be unable to choose is to appear to be unable to govern.'

On British politics: 'We already have a sabbatical system. It's called opposition, and I've had enough of it.'

And, with his tongue near his cheek, he once told an interviewer: 'The only thing I won't tolerate is intolerance.'

Unlike many politicians Lawson has always been comfortable with his own views. On one occasion when he was a Cabinet minister, he was briefing his own Party's backbench MPs on his latest policy when the then junior backbencher Peter Lilley started to argue with him, questioning what he had to say. So strident was Lilley that some ministers might have taken offence and complained to the whips. Lawson did indeed approach the whips but not to complain: he asked for Lilley to be appointed as his PPS!

⧖

FORMER LABOUR LEADER, later Euro-Commissioner and now a Labour Peer Lord (Neil) Kinnock brought his party back towards the centre ground and for this he deserves some credit. However, he failed to deliver victory at the 1992 General Election, something that many had predicted. Although he deserves recognition for modernising Labour, he also deserves some blame for Labour's 1992 loss. He was, simply, unelectable as Prime Minister and the sight of him ranting 'We're all right' at Labour's Sheffield rally brought Tory voters out in their droves.

Although generally verbose, an insult is usually not far from the surface. He once famously described former Conservative Party Chairman Norman (now Lord) Tebbit as 'a boil on a verruca'.

On Tories Norman Fowler and Nigel Lawson, before Lawson undertook his spectacular diet: 'Norman Fowler looks as if he is suffering from a famine and Lawson looks as though he caused it.'

On former Labour minister David Owen: 'He possesses an ego fat on arrogance and drunk on ambition.'

On Prince Phillip: 'I *am* prepared to take advice on leisure from Prince Phillip. He is a world expert on leisure. He's been practicing it for most of his adult life.'

Lord Kinnock has criticised his former ally Peter Mandelson, claiming the ex-business secretary has become a 'caricature' of himself. Kinnock's criticism came in the wake of Mandelson's book which described feuding between Gordon Brown and Tony Blair, alleging Mr Blair called his successor 'mad, bad and dangerous'.

Lord Kinnock said it focused too much on a 'pathetic personality clash' between the Brown and Blair camps.

Kinnock said: 'We have an account barely two months after the general election, and we have a book that either has been written at breakneck, indeed a rate of genius, velocity, or was being written many, many, many months before the general election.'

Kinnock, who employed Peter Mandelson as Labour's campaign co-ordinator for the 1987 general election, said: 'I take some responsibility for Mr Mandelson because I gave him his first significant job.' He added: 'My view of Peter was that he wasn't as good as he thought he was, and he was certainly not as bad as many people said he was. The problem is with Peter, so much was said about him as, for instance, the Prince of Spin, and the Prince of Darkness, that he inhaled and he's actually come to believe that caricature of himself.'

⧗

FORMER FOREIGN SECRETARY and Conservative leadership challenger Douglas (now Lord) Hurd, bemoaning the current trend in British politics, said: 'We are becoming a nation of strong journalists and weak politicians.'

In 1988, he helped to set up the charity Crime Concern but once, whilst Home Secretary, he tried to explain away the rise in crime by responding: 'There's so much more to nick these days.'

On his former leader: 'Margaret Thatcher, growing up in a bombed and battered Britain, derived a distrust which has grown with the years not just of Germany but of all continental Europe.'

Other comments worthy of note are:

'People are very interested in politics, they just don't like it labelled politics.'

'We should be wary of politicians who profess to follow history while only noticing those signposts of history that point in the direction which they themselves already favour.'

✕

ROY HATTERSLEY was a challenger for the Labour leadership in 1983 but lost out to Neil Kinnock. He became Deputy Leader of the Labour Party that same year, a post he held until 1992.

On former Labour leader Tony Blair: 'He built a government which was untainted by dogma. Tony Blair took the politics out of politics.'

On Blair's style of government: 'The Cabinet met for just thirty minutes on a Thursday morning. Tony was very near to giving Cabinet government a lethal injection.'

On Margaret Thatcher's performance during PM's Questions: 'You could fire a bazooka at her and inflict three large holes, but she still kept coming.'

Amongst his other comments, the following are worthy of note:

'In British politics, being ridiculous is more damaging than being extreme.'

'Familiarity with evil breeds not contempt but acceptance.'

'In my opinion, any man who can afford to buy a newspaper empire should not be allowed to own one.'

'Morality and expediency coincide more than the cynics allow.'

'The proposition that Muslims are welcome in Britain if, and only if, they stop behaving like Muslims is a doctrine which is incompatible with the principles that guide a free society.'

On former Labour Home Secretary Roy Jenkins, who defected to the SDP: 'In politics, arrogance and integrity go hand in hand.'

On the hereditary peer the Earl of Onslow: 'He is a walking advertisement for parliamentary reform.'

He stood down from the House of Commons in 1997 and shortly thereafter entered the House of Lords as Baron Hattersley.

✕

LABOUR'S FORMER Deputy Prime Minister John (now Lord) Prescott is a lively parliamentary performer, although one always feels that a sudden loss of temper is bubbling just below the surface. It is probably for this reason that he acquired the nickname 'Thumper'.

On William Waldegrave when he was made the Secretary of State responsible for the Citizen's Charter: 'He has been described by the John Major as the minister for little people – he seems more like the minister for paperclips to me.'

On the policy of privatisation when pursued by the Conservatives: 'It is to do with kickbacks, greed and sleaze in the Tory Party.'

Dismissing an attack from the Liberal Democrats, Prescott described them as 'always holier than holy'.

On the Conservatives' plans on rail privatisation: 'This is not a Passengers' Charter. It is more a cherry-picker's charter – ripe for exploitation by property speculators, by route operators and by the Tories' City friends growing fat on commissions and fees resulting from the disposal of public assets.'

His view on former Tory Chairman Lord Parkinson was terse: 'He's a nutter.'

On the Conservative Party: 'The Tories are so green, they keep recycling their leaders.'

In 2006 he took a swipe at Conservative leader David Cameron, saying: 'He claims he is a liberal. He claims he is "New Labour Cameron. Environmental Cameron. Fox hunting Cameron." Fox hunting Cameron? That's the only Tory policy he's happy to stick with!'

And again on Cameron: 'He's like a rainbow when you think about it. The Yellow Cameron. The Red Cameron. The Green Cameron. The Blue Cameron. What we've got is Cameron the chameleon. He can change the colour of his skin at will but the political animal underneath is Conservative to the core. Let me give Dave a little bit of advice, as he is a PR man. Politics is not, despite what he thinks, only about image. I suspect that if it was I would not be the Deputy Prime Minister.'

During the same speech, he spluttered with righteous indignation that a Tory would dare to talk about traditional Labour issues: 'Compassionate Conservatives? Compassion? Social Justice? Don't make me laugh. They might call themselves compassionate and caring. But we know different. They change the label any time they like – but it's still the same old poison in the bottle.'

But it was in the ad libs and asides that Prescott got the biggest laughs, playing the class warrior card for all it was worth, once quipping: '"Dave" Cameron, or "David" to you and me, is just an ordinary lad from Eton.'

He also referred again to Cameron the 'PR man', saying that Cameron is an untrustworthy toff. It was the sort of attack that New Labour was meant to have banished and that Tony Blair himself could never get away with, being an ex-public schoolboy himself.

Further commenting on the PM: 'He is trying to be a Tony Blair Mark II.'

On Lib Dem MP Vincent Cable, who was once a member of the Labour Party: 'He's had more parties than Paris Hilton.'

On being a politician: 'I don't think there's any other job which suits my temperament.' (He could have added 'boxer' surely?)

And on that punch in 2001 – when he walloped a protester who lunged at him: 'I told the Prime Minister [Tony Blair] that I was following his orders and connecting with the electorate.' The punch was no surprise to those who know him. His wife has admitted that his temper is 'unbelievable' adding, 'upstairs in one mood, downstairs in another'. Before 9 February 1998, not many Tory MPs had heard of the anarchist rock band Chumbawamba, but now many admire group member Nigel Hunter (who uses the ridiculous stage name of Danbert Nobacon) for throwing a bucket of water over the Prescott at the 1998 Brit Awards.

In 2006 it emerged that Prescott had been having an affair with his diary secretary Tracey Temple, an attractive woman many years his junior. This led to speculation at Westminster as to how New Labour would 'spin' the story in the press. One Tory wag suggested that Tony Blair was about to blame Margaret Thatcher for the secretary being willing to sleep with Prescott, on the grounds that it was Thatcher who, many years earlier, had abolished free eye tests!

On the Deputy Prime Minister: 'Nick Clegg talks about Alarm Clock Britain but why does his government keep hitting the bloody snooze button?'

And a Tory backbencher's view of the former Deputy PM: 'He's a cross between Norman Tebbit, Andy Capp and Les Dawson.'

⌛

FORMER CONSERVATIVE Deputy Prime Minister Michael, now Lord, Heseltine was a tremendous Commons performer. Whether in Parliament, out on the hustings or in a TV studio, when he was on form he could wipe the floor with anyone. I recall sitting next to him in a meeting when he was Deputy PM and watching him write five bullet points down on a card, draw a line and then write down two more. I asked what he was doing. 'I am appearing on the *Today* programme tomorrow', he replied, 'And these are my five answers – and if I can, I will mention the two final points.'

'But surely they haven't given you the questions in advance?' I enquired.

Heseltine smiled: 'No. But whatever the questions are – these are my answers!'

The following day I listened to the programme and, true to his word, he gave his pre-selected answers with aplomb, managing a score of six out of seven. It was a dazzling performance.

On Neil Kinnock, he snapped: 'The self-appointed King of the Gutter' adding: 'He is a latter-day Duke of York leading a one-legged army: left, left, left...'

On Kinnock's successor John Smith: 'He is a fence-sitter. His policies are wall-to-wall whitewash.'

On former Lib Dem leader Paddy Ashdown: 'A one-man band who has transformed a party without a leader into a leader without a party. And he was a leader with more answers than there were questions, and more news conferences than there were newspapers.'

He effectively pointed out the difference between *old* Labour under Michael Foot and *New* Labour under Tony Blair: 'They used to be the barmy army. Now, they're the smarmy army.'

In the 1990s he was speaking at a by-election meeting when a man in the audience wearing a large Labour rosette started protesting that the stewards were trying to force him to remove his hat. He noisily resisted their attempts to make him sit down and remove his titfer. Heseltine silenced him: 'I know why you don't want to take off your hat. It's because there's absolutely nothing underneath it.'

Amongst his other comments, the following are the most memorable:

'The essence of being a Prime Minister is to have large ears.'

'You cannot restore our cities while running down our countryside.'

Rightly drawing attention to the fact that at the top of the Labour party there are more Scots than Englishmen, he referred to Gordon Brown, Donald Dewar, Robin Cook, Brian Wilson, Dr John Reid and the others as 'Scotland's Revenge'.

When Gordon Brown was in opposition, not having yet served as a minister, he sought to set out his credentials as a future Chancellor of the Exchequer by referring in a speech to 'neo-classical endogenous growth theory and the symbolic relationships between government and investments in people and infrastructures'. This part of his speech, it was later revealed, was written by his then aide, Ed Balls (now an MP and shadow minister). A few weeks later, at the Conservative Party Conference, Heseltine referred to Brown's unintelligible vision and repeated the words above, reminding his audience that they were actually written by Labour aide Ed Balls. For maximum effect, Heseltine then paused, before continuing: 'So there you have it. Labour's economic vision for the future... it's not Brown's... its Balls!' Some would say it was a cheap jibe but it brought the house down.

Attacking new Labour leader John Smith in the 1990s: 'I always knew that Neil Kinnock belonged in the economic nursery. Now, God help us we've got twins.'

Of his own career, he has made a number of comments, the following being the most memorable:

'I don't believe in the concept of retirement.'

'There comes a point when having more money makes no difference.'

'I am humble enough to recognise that I have made mistakes, but politically astute enough to know that I have forgotten what they are.'

⧗

SIR JOHN MAJOR was hailed as a refreshing change when he took over the reins of the Conservative Party from Margaret Thatcher in 1990. Towards the end of her term as Prime Minister, she was accused of being domineering, bossy, arrogant, out of touch and unwilling to consider the opinions of others. John Major was different. He listened. He consulted. He reflected on the concerns of others and was often cautious in his approach. This, plus a Labour leader whose temper always appeared to be hanging on a hair trigger, contributed to his surprise general election win in 1992.

But public confidence in him did not last long. Disillusionment soon set in – even amongst some members of his own party – and his willingness to consult was soon portrayed by the press as indecision. He could be brilliant in a one-to-one interview in a TV studio. However, whenever he made a speech and raised the volume of his voice he also raised its pitch and the rather thin timbre of his vocal chords, not noticeable when he was in conversation, did not carry well on a public platform.

But most of all it was Major's rapidly shrinking parliamentary majority which severely limited his room for manoeuvre. Major often took the blame for vacillation, when the real culprit was parliamentary arithmetic.

The then Leader of the Opposition, Tony Blair, was extremely astute. Realising Major's small parliamentary majority was limiting his options over a whole range of policy issues, he attacked the man himself, describing him as 'weak, weak, weak'. This theme was taken up by some sections of the press and this was electorally very damaging.

Occasionally, Major's own ministerial team were critical of him too. Then Tory minister Nicholas Soames called his aims for a 'classless society' a 'load of ullage'.

And soon after his election as party leader, one Tory MP said of Major: 'I cannot stand his lowlier than thou attitude.'

But Major often scored in a speech. Of New Labour he said: 'Unlike Labour, Conservatives aren't ashamed of our past. Unlike Labour, we haven't abandoned our principles and we haven't had to reinvent ourselves.'

Taking an effective swipe at Tony Blair's rhetoric, he said: 'Have you noticed how the less a politician has to say, the more overheated the language is? When every aim becomes a "crusade", every hope a "dream", every priority "a passion", then it's time to duck for cover. When I hear Blair lace a speech with words like "tragedy", "triumph" and "destiny" – then I think of Ralph Waldo Emerson: "The louder he talked of his honour, the faster we counted our spoons."'

And again on Blair: 'He is sanctimonious and cloaks himself in righteousness.'

On proportional representation, he has forcefully argued of the dangers of hung parliaments: 'To offer the electorate a proportional Parliament that mirrors its opinions, but is unable to take decisions that mirror those opinions, offers a false prospectus to the elector.'

Amongst his other *bon mots* the following are worthy of note:

'Privately educated Tony Blair and privately educated Harriet Harman. You know what they say. New Labour, Old School Tie.'

On one occasion, Prime Minister Major was ordered by the Speaker to withdraw his summing up of Tony Blair, then opposition leader, as 'a dimwit'.

On Labour's record in office: 'Labour often say they want to soak the rich. But they're the only party in history who regularly manage to soak the poor.'

Once during his premiership Major, like Gordon Brown several years later, was caught off guard by an open TV microphone. Not realising he was still broadcasting, he labelled his rebellious Cabinet members as 'bastards' and promised to 'crucify' them live on air.

Once, when giving an interview as Prime Minister, a reporter expressed surprise at Major's reply to one of his questions and said, 'Isn't that rather off-message?' Major retorted: 'What do you mean? I *am* the message.'

After he had stepped down as Conservative leader and the country had experienced over a year of Labour government, Major gave his views on Blair's style: 'He has "dumbed down" political debate to avoid scrutiny of Labour in office. It is all very well appearing on the *Des O'Connor Show* but it should not replace serious debate in Parliament. I cannot imagine Gladstone or Disraeli dumbing down politics like this.'

Commenting on Labour minister Jack Straw, he also revealed some of his own political tactics: 'Jack Straw has just made a speech in a very reasonable tone of voice. That makes me suspicious. When I was a minister and I was excessively reasonable, it usually meant that I had something to hide, or that I sided with the opposition, but did not wish my own party to realise this.'

On one occasion, Major asked the Russian leader Boris Yeltsin to describe the state of Russia in one word. 'Good', Yeltsin replied. Not entirely satisfied with this, Major then asked him if he could describe the state of Russia in *two* words. 'Not good', Yeltsin snapped back.

BBC interviewer John Humphrys claims he is still baffled by Major's response during the Tory leadership election when Major resigned to seek his own re-election. According to Humphrys, when he asked Major why he had taken this extraordinary step, he received the reply: 'When your back's against the wall, the only thing to do is turn around and fight.'

Major also caused a few others to scratch their heads when he said: 'The world has gone through tremendous change recently – both nationally and internationally.'

He did however hit the mark when he said of Labour leader Neil Kinnock: 'When it comes to the crunch, the trade unions will put their arms around Mr Kinnock and say, "Neil!" And he will, he will.'

To some observers, especially those who worked with him, Major ultimately failed the Harold Wilson test of the qualities required of a Prime Minister. Wilson's theory was that 'no one should attempt the role of PM who cannot fall asleep the moment he is in bed with the cares and worries of the day behind him.'

⌛

FOREIGN SECRETARY and former Tory leader William Hague is an excellent Commons performer. However, brilliance in debate does not always translate into votes as Hague and the Conservative Party discovered in 2001 when, despite a spirited election campaign, he led the Tories to their second landslide defeat.

Surprisingly, one of the main criticisms levelled at Hague by electors across Britain during his four years as Tory leader was his Yorkshire accent and his rather nasal delivery! I even had electors in East Yorkshire criticising his South Yorkshire accent, so goodness knows what they were saying down south!

This subject was, at the time, taken up by the late British

ventriloquist Arthur Worsley, who said to me: 'Hague sounds like someone trying to impersonate Mike Yarwood impersonating Harold Wilson.'

Despite his poor poll showing as Tory Party Leader, Hague remains a respected figure in the Commons and is now widely regarded as an effective minister. His utterances are always worth listening to.

As might be expected, Hague has been extremely critical of both Brown's and Blair's style of government. Taking a swipe at New Labour he said: 'This is the government of the nanny state. This is the government who tell people how to live. They tell people, "Don't drink, don't smoke, don't hunt, don't have a pension, don't eat beef on the bone, don't save, don't drive a car; if you drive a car don't park it." Tony Blair preaches to us – and Labour's budgets represent the collection plate being passed round after the service.'

After news of Cherie Blair's £2,000 hairdressing costs for a short USA trip was made public, Hague alluded to his own disappearing hairline and amusingly quipped: 'The most expensive haircut I ever had cost a tenner – and £9 went on the search fee.'

On the former Prime Minister's attitude to the Mother of Parliaments: 'Blair wants a rubber-stamp Parliament where the MPs only turn up to fawn over him.'

On the difference between Blair and his one-time 'Cabinet enforcer' Jack Cunningham: 'Tony Blair gave up the Bar for politics. Jack Cunningham appears to sometimes give up politics for the bar!'

On Deputy Prime Minister John Prescott's transport plans: 'After all the promises and all the hype, it is now clear that it is a complete dog's breakfast!'

On the embattled Paymaster General Geoffrey Robinson, who had been widely criticised for his offshore tax trusts, before Robinson's resignation: 'Blair appointed as the minister responsible for offshore tax avoidance a man with offshore tax trusts. This is breathtaking hypocrisy. I suspect that the

Swiss-bank family Robinson will stay in business and out of tax.'

Following his absence during a short illness, Hague bounced back with a vicious swipe at the New Labour government in the wake of lobbying revelations, where one lobbyist appeared to suggest ministers were available upon payment of a fee. Hague commented: 'Even with my sinuses, I could smell the stench coming out of these [lobbying] revelations. This is a government for sale.' Continuing, he challenged Blair: 'When are you going to stop protecting the money-grabbing cronies you've surrounded yourself with?' He later added: 'They are feather-bedding, pocket-lining, money-grabbing cronies.'

Returning to the charge, Hague later said that the Blair government had 'too many cronies and not enough principles'.

In opposition, Hague was usually devastating at Question Time and he has often said that the ideal question to ask is one where no answer is particularly satisfactory. Explaining this, he says he often mused when he was Leader of the Opposition of asking Tony Blair if he believed in Santa Claus, on the grounds that if he said 'yes' he would look ridiculous and if he said 'no' then to every child in the land he would look heartless.

On Labour: 'The British Labour Party is an organisation where your best friend will plunge a knife in your back and then call the police to tell them that you are carrying a concealed weapon.'

On Blair's first year as PM: 'In just one year, a man with confident early pledges has become full of meaningless waffle.'

On New Labour: 'They are for everything but nothing: tough, tender; hot, cold; soft, hard; fast, slow; for you, for me; to give, to take; to stop, to start.'

On former Foreign Secretary Robin Cook: 'The Foreign Office is being run like a *Dad's Army* outfit by a Foreign Secretary who combines the pompousness of Captain Mainwaring, the incompetence of Private Pike and the calm of Corporal Jones.'

On the EU single currency: 'It was inevitable that the *Titanic* would set sail, but that does not mean it was a good idea to be on it.'

When Gordon Brown presented a Budget, but not all of the tax changes were announced, Hague quipped: 'His Red book in this case is the unread book.'

On the law and order plans of the last Labour government: 'Wouldn't it be better to have a watertight law designed to catch the guilty, rather than a press release law designed to catch the headlines?'

Almost immediately after he stood down as Conservative leader, Hague's popularity started to climb, causing some to talk of a possible comeback as Leader. This did not impress Labour's Tony Banks, who said at the time that the British public will never elect as Prime Minister 'someone who looks like a foetus'.

Hague was untroubled by such talk. After he quit as party leader he was in great demand as a public speaker, he wrote two critically acclaimed books (on William Pitt the Younger and William Wilberforce) and regularly penned a newspaper column. Observers estimated that he was earning well over £1 million a year from these activities, which is far more than he would ever hope to earn during a whole Parliament as Prime Minister.

However, the lure of high office proved irresistible and it was not long before he returned to frontline politics as shadow Foreign Secretary under Tory leader David Cameron. Following the formation of the Coalition government after the 2010 general election, he duly became Foreign Secretary.

Although not named as a 'deputy leader' Hague has also been given the task of standing in for Cameron during Prime Minister's Questions. He soon showed that he had lost none of his old sparkle. When Gordon Brown's premiership hit trouble in 2009, Hague said: 'I think Gordon Brown has now achieved the impossible. He has made the Labour Cabinet even more dysfunctional and divided than it was before.'

And, on his time as Conservative Party Leader: 'I have discovered that being leader of the Conservative Party and wearing a hat are incompatible.'

⧗

HISTORY WILL credit Tony Blair for bringing to an end eighteen years of Conservative government – the longest period of one-party rule since the Crimean War. And he did it by a far bigger margin than anyone expected, winning the largest parliamentary majority for any party since 1832.

Many have now forgotten that when he was first elected as Labour leader, Blair was given the nickname of 'Bambi', so unsure was his initial touch. However, as he found his feet – which did not take him long – this soubriquet soon disappeared.

Indeed, MPs rapidly noticed that his confidence grew by leaps and bounds in a very short space of time. He soon developed what appeared to be an absolute faith in himself, which to some Tories appeared to be close to hubris.

However, there is no doubting the charm that this public school barrister exuded, particularly on television, although critics would say his apparent artless sincerity was rehearsed and calculated.

Blair's modus operandi was markedly different from John Major. He imposed a rigid and centralised control of the government machine from Downing Street.

On his predecessor John Major: 'He presided over the most wasteful, inefficient and incompetent government in living memory. His hope before the 1997 election was that the public forget VAT on fuel, Black Wednesday, BSE, the doubling of crime, the doubling of debt, the poll tax, arms for Iraq, cash for questions, Scott, Nolan, business failures and negative equity. Major pretends he has no responsibility for the state of the nation he has governed. It's as if he had just landed from Mars.'

Blair also took a swipe at current Speaker John Bercow

when he was a backbench Conservative MP: 'His hallmark is to be both nasty and ineffectual in equal quantities.'

On the official opposition: 'The policy of the Conservative party was a mess before the election and has been a catastrophe since. If there is any brain left in the opposition it is time that they manifested it.'

On being attacked by the Tories on Europe: 'The one issue that I would have thought it very unwise to raise is the subject of Europe, where the Conservative party is split from head to toe.'

On former Tory leader William Hague: 'He requires lessons in how to be Leader of the Opposition. If he is really good to me, I might tell him. Instead, he gets up and asks what might impress a sixth-form debating society but does not impress me.'

And again on Hague: 'Quite the most bizarre experience is to be preceded by the Leader of the Opposition running around the country, holding press conferences and saying what a disaster everything is. The fact is that no one pays the slightest attention to him but that is more a reflection on him than anything else.'

On the Conservatives' economic philosophy: 'These are people who believe that a strong economy can be built on sweatshop wages. They believe that the answer to the problems of the economy is low wages.'

Continuing his attack on the Tories under William Hague: 'Hague and his party have still not worked out why they lost the last election – he ought to try to work out where the Conservatives stand on some of the policy issues that face us.'

Dismissing an attack on Labour's foreign policy towards Sierra Leone, Blair described a Commons row as 'an overblown hoo-hah'.

But former Euro Commissioner Leon Brittan pinpointed what many agreed was a symptom of Tony Blair's style of government: 'It's government by spinning.' And, a Tory whip on Tony Blair: 'Tony is a real politician. He can say absolutely nothing and mean it.'

The left wing of the Labour Party never liked Blair, viewing him as a closet Tory. One prominent socialist summed up the view of many on the left by describing Blair as 'Phoney Tony', and a number of Labour left-wingers soon came to use the soubriquet 'Phoney Blur' in view of his large-scale dumping of his party's socialist policies and principles.

In 1997, expressing his own frustration at leading a party which had been in opposition for so long (eighteen years), Blair said that he had 'a PhD in Opposition'.

In 2006, following the election of David Cameron as Conservative Party leader the previous autumn, opinion polls showed that for the first time in over a decade, Labour and the Tories were neck and neck. Asked to comment on this, Blair's reply was shrewd: 'My maxim is never under-estimate the Conservative Party and never overestimate the Lib Dems.'

Blair did once raise more than a few eyebrows when he solemnly stated: 'I don't make predictions – I never have and I never will.'

After becoming Labour leader, Blair said of himself: 'Last year I was Bambi, this year Stalin. I have gone from Disneyland to dictatorship in twelve short months.'

Although they have been regularly accused of being voting fodder, not all of Tony Blair's backbenchers have kept their heads down, especially after Blair's 2005 election victory. Veteran and idiosyncratic Labour MP Austin Mitchell, who in 2002 temporarily changed his name to Austin Haddock, described New Labour as a 'children's crusade which regards older MPs as useless and yet the young make the biggest messes'. He went on to blame Gordon Brown for 'locking the government into deflation' and Peter Mandelson for 'the Dome disaster', whilst calling former minister Harriet Harman 'the Minister for Social Insecurity'. He added: 'Boy wonders run Labour and to be old is a bit of an inconvenience.'

When a furore erupted in 2002 over the fact that Cherie Blair's advisor, Carole Caplin, was going out with Australian conman Peter Foster, one wag quipped: 'What is the differ-ence between Peter Foster and Tony Blair? Peter Foster has convictions.'

According to Labour colleagues, Tony Blair once described Gordon Brown, then his Chancellor, as 'mad, bad, dangerous and beyond redemption'.

Mr Blair has been quoted as saying that even the then Deputy Prime Minister John Prescott was 'scared' by Mr Brown. 'He knows there's something wrong with him,' Blair reportedly said.

Lord Mandelson has admitted Tony Blair described Gordon Brown as 'flawed, lacking perspective and having a paranoia about him'.

He is also quoted as saying: 'He's like something out of the mafiosi. He's aggressive, brutal... there is no one to match Gordon for someone who articulates high principles while practising the lowest skulduggery.'

Charismatic and telegenic Blair certainly was, but accord-ing to some, including Norman Tebbit, he suffered as a leader by always wanting to be liked. This desire was not always fulfilled. After one meeting José Bono, the Spanish politician, branded Blair 'un gilipollas integral'.

Whatever his long-term legacy, Tony Blair now belongs to a select group of former politicians: although he did not beat Margaret Thatcher's record for length of service, at least he left office on a date of his own choosing, which is more than most manage to achieve.

⌛

FORMER CONSERVATIVE Leader Iain Duncan Smith is the self-professed 'quiet man' of politics. His brief span as party leader (2001–03) led many to conclude that he lacks both colour and charisma but he showed that in politics there can be life after death when he bounced back as Work and Pensions Secretary under PM David Cameron.

Even though most of his party colleagues think he was not a success as leader, he could still sometimes hit the mark in debate.

When 'Blair Babe' former Labour MP Oona King revealed that when she was young she had wanted to be 'either Prime Minister or an air hostess', Duncan Smith, glancing at Blair, said that he saw no conflict in these ambitions: 'Both an air hostess and the Prime Minister spend their days repeating the same pre-prepared and utterly predictable announcements before jetting off around the world.'

On the Lib Dems: 'At the next election, printed after their party symbol each ballot paper should also contain a warning about them ... "contains nuts".'

On Blair's immigration policy failure: 'Whilst Tony Blair has been travelling around the rest of the world, the rest of the world has been travelling here.'

On one of Blair's soundbite replies: 'The Prime Minister is not juggling with balls, he is talking them.'

Showing that he possessed little by way of powers of clairvoyance, in 2003, just before his ousting as Tory leader, Duncan Smith said: 'I will give up politics and do more writing, but only after I've been Prime Minister for a good few years.'

Just before his downfall in October 2003, a long-time critic, Conservative backbencher Anthony Steen, said of him: 'I have come to the conclusion he is murally dyslexic. This means he doesn't see the writing on the wall.'

Duncan Smith himself once commented: 'I would rather have played rugby for Scotland than be Prime Minister.' It now looks certain that neither ambition will be fulfilled.

⧗

THE MOST ASTONISHING political comeback of recent times, if only for a short while, was performed by Tory Leader Michael Howard in 2003.

Written off as an unwelcome old face of the last
Conservative government in 1997, some six years later he
was chosen by acclamation by his parliamentary party to
take over from Iain Duncan Smith, ruthlessly pushed aside
for an older man.

Howard soon showed himself to be a heavyweight more
than up to the task of taking on Tony Blair, with Prime
Minister's Questions becoming a gladiatorial contest worth
watching once again.

Although he later failed in his ambition to win the 2005
election and become Prime Minister, Howard's legacy to the
Conservative Party is far greater than many appreciate.

After he had lost the General Election of 2005 and decided
to stand down as leader, rather than stand back and watch the
election for his successor from the sidelines, he stayed on for
six months and during this period calculatingly promoted his
favourites, the then little-known David Cameron and George
Osborne. He also made the arch-moderniser Francis Maude
the new Conservative Party Chairman, thus dramatically
changing both the direction of his party and the prospects
for the leadership contenders, and all after he had decided to
throw the towel in.

There is little doubt that both Cameron and Osborne
would, in the light of their abilities, have made it to the top of
the Conservative Party in time, but Howard's actions substan-
tially expedited the process

On Gordon Brown, reworking the wording of an old advert
for Gordon's gin, Howard observed: 'He is a happiness Hoover.
The gloom-monger in chief. When the story is grim, and the
policies are dim, one knows that "it's got to be Gordon".'

Attacking Chancellor Brown's revised economic forecasts,
he jibed: 'These are the downgraded forecasts of a downgraded
Chancellor.'

On former Labour leader Neil Kinnock: 'As a pretender to
the nation's driving seat, he has some notable qualifications.
He loves reverse gear. His three-point turns are masterly. And,

as for his principles, he never sets out without a complete set of spares.'

When, in 2003, after his coronation as Conservative leader, Labour MPs started referring to Mr Howard as 'Dracula', he quickly turned the jibe back on his detractors, saying: 'For too many Labour MPs, words like "choice" and "competition" are as welcome as a clove of garlic to Dracula.'

When Tony Blair tried to defend his plans for university top-up fees (then opposed by the Conservatives) as a means of broadening access to education, Howard shot back: 'This grammar school boy is not going to take any lessons from that public school boy on the importance of children from less privileged backgrounds gaining access to university.'

On PM Tony Blair: 'Mr Blair may regard sticking to election promises as opportunism; we do not.'

On the Blair government: 'Heads don't roll in this government. They simply take time out.'

Responding to the Prime Minister Blair's taunts that he, Howard, was an opportunist, he snapped: 'This is the man who joined Michael Foot's bandwagon to get into the Labour Party; joined the Campaign for Nuclear Disarmament bandwagon to get on in the Labour Party; and turned over his Chancellor's bandwagon to take over the leadership of the Labour Party. Tony Blair is Mr Bandwagon.'

He stood down from the House of Commons in 2010 and shortly afterwards entered the House of Lords as Baron Howard of Lympne. There is talk at Westminster of a possible ministerial comeback under David Cameron.

⌛

FRENCH POLITICIAN Jacques Chirac began his career as a civil servant before entering politics and going on to become Mayor of Paris, French Prime Minister and then President of France, an office he held between 1995 and 2007.

Despite all of his civil service training, he has been extremely undiplomatic about British cuisine: 'The only thing Britain has ever done for European agriculture is mad cow disease... After Finland, it is the country with the worst food.'

⧗

FORMER LIB DEM Leader Sir Menzies Campbell is well-liked in Westminster, but he was forced to resign the leadership of his party in 2007 following a series of jibes and comments about his age. Following his resignation, Nick Clegg said that Campbell had been treated 'appallingly' and subjected to 'barely disguised ageism', a view shared by the charity Age Concern.

Sir Menzies has admitted that he had been irritated by the 'cliché ridden' media coverage of him whilst Lib Dem leader, adding: 'If I had a fiver for every time someone gave me a zimmer frame in a newspaper cartoon then I'd be a very rich man indeed.'

Campbell has said of leading the Lib Dems: 'One of the things I learned very early on, is that the leader of the party – the opposite of the harlot – has the responsibility but not the power.'

⧗

FORMER BUSINESS SECRETARY Peter (Lord) Mandelson is known as either the 'Prince of Darkness' or the 'King of Spin', depending on what your politics are. Rather immodestly, when in office he frequently referred to himself as 'The Quality Controller'.

Within hours of Labour's election victory in 1997, when he was neither a Cabinet minister nor a departmental one, he issued instructions to government departments to clear future policy announcements through Prime Minister Tony Blair's Office. He explained his action by saying: 'It is important to have a strong centre of government. Civil servants can sometimes be rather tunnel-visioned.'

He certainly wielded huge influence and power within the New Labour government of Tony Blair. This was clearly due to Tony Blair's patronage but he surprised many by making a comeback to mainstream UK politics in 2008, showing that he had won Brown's patronage as well! He is an expert at what some regard as the main evil of British politics today – 'spin doctoring'.

Of the Tories under William Hague, he said: 'By addressing only the diary column end of politics, the Conservatives are reinforcing the public's opinion of them as out of touch and irrelevant to the issues of today. By concentrating their firepower on dishwashers and diary secretaries the Tories devalue their attacks and emphasise why they were so distrusted by the electorate.'

He then went on to describe the official opposition under Hague as 'pathetic and frivolous'.

In the late 1990s, taking a swipe at Michael Howard (before he became Tory leader and after he had ceased being Home Secretary) for his criticism of Foreign Secretary Robin Cook for sacking his diary secretary Anne Bullen, he said: 'Michael Howard has traded the responsibilities of high office for breathless interviews about a diary secretary. The man who sacked the Director General of the Prison Service to cover his own back and was successfully sued for damages, has taken to his high horse on personnel matters.'

Such was Mandelson's perceived power over New Labour MPs during his time as a DTI minister that Conservatives used to tell a story of a newly elected New Labour MP who went for a haircut wearing earphones connected to a Walkman tape recorder. The MP refused to remove his headset and insisted that the barber work around them. Whilst sitting in the chair the MP fell asleep, so to make his job easier, the hairdresser removed the earphones. After a couple of minutes, the MP slumped forward – dead. Shocked, the barber picked up the headset to hear what it was the MP was listening to, and he heard the voice of Peter Mandelson saying: 'Breathe in... Breathe out... Breathe in... Breathe out...'

Arch media manipulator Mandelson was forced to resign in 2001 as Northern Ireland Secretary following accusations that he had helped one of the Hinduja brothers gain a British passport in return for a £1million donation to the Labour Party. This was Mandy's second resignation following a career gaffe. His first, in 1998, followed the disclosure that he had accepted a £373,000 home loan from the then Paymaster General Geoffrey Robinson MP.

Proving that there can be political life even after a second death, he became Britain's Euro Commissioner in 2004 before bouncing back to UK domestic politics as Business Secretary in 2008.

In 2009, when Gordon Brown's premiership hit trouble, Mandelson nearly came a cropper when the press gleefully reported upon a leaked email written eighteen months earlier by Mandelson (now Brown's Business Secretary), in which he described Brown as 'self-conscious' and 'angry'.

Amazingly and brazenly, Mandelson claimed the message, written before he joined the Brown government was 'not intended to be hostile'. He said the email, written in January 2008 – months before he returned to Cabinet – had been 'misrepresented' by the press. 'It was not hostile to or about the Prime Minister,' he claimed, adding: 'What it said is that Gordon Brown needs to be what he is, be what he stands for and believes in and the values he has – and not listen to people who are trying to glue some artificial persona onto him.'

The *Mail on Sunday* published extracts from the email, sent to former Labour spin doctor Derek Draper, and they were part of a wider email debate about a book called *The Political Brain* by US psychology professor Drew Western, which looked at which qualities made politicians successful. The paper reported that Lord Mandelson had written that Mr Brown was 'not as comfortable in his own skin' as his predecessor, Tony Blair. Mandelson added that Brown was 'a self-conscious person, physically and emotionally'.

This leak came in June 2009 at the end of a bitter week

for Brown, in which Labour was heavily defeated in local elections; six ministers left the government and his leadership was the main issue, with James Purnell's resignation as Work and Pensions Secretary coming with a call for Brown to 'stand aside' and Caroline Flint MP quitting as Europe minister, complaining she had been used as 'window dressing'.

But Mandelson has had some harsh words for his political opponents too. Commenting on Conservative leader David Cameron, he said: 'He likes people to think he is cuddly and compassionate but he's a fraud. He is different when he thinks people are not listening or looking. And the sentiments he expresses are not shared by his party, so there is a double fraud going on.'

On the Blair–Brown relationship: 'The unbridled contempt that some people around Gordon Brown had for Tony Blair and those who worked for him was very destructive.'

Amongst his other comments, the following are worthy of note:

'I believe that if you treat China as an enemy, then it is likely to become one.'

'Having viewed Europe as an extension and projection of itself, France now finds Europe developing a mind and identity of its own which embraces France but is not controlled by France.'

'I do not share the half-in, half-out attitude to the EU of some in Britain. Britain's place is in Europe.'

A Labour MP in the Commons Tea Room once said of Mandelson: 'Peter reminds me of a character from a horror film. He's Dr Mandelstein.'

⌛

JUSTICE SECRETARY Kenneth Clarke is a political bruiser who could easily have become the leader of the Conservative Party if he had been prepared to modify his views on Europe. He now says that Europe is a 'settled issue' so far as the Conservative

Party is concerned. If only he was prepared to say the same thing when contesting the leadership he might have won. But at the time he was not prepared to trim his sails and the parliamentary party voted instead for other less-obviously qualified candidates: William Hague in 1997, Iain Duncan Smith in 2001 and David Cameron in 2005. Characteristically, at the time he said to those who questioned his actions: 'What is the point of being in politics at all if you cannot pursue your own beliefs?'

Showing no signs of modifying his views, in 2000 he described William Hague's policy on Europe as: 'Way out.'

Attacking his successor as Chancellor shortly after Labour's 1997 victory, his remarks showed some remarkable prescience. Clarke said: 'Gordon Brown has transformed from the Iron Chancellor to the Big-handed Chancellor, with uncontrolled spending in just about every Department in Whitehall. He will end this parliament short of taxation and short of economic growth. His cheering supporters may ring the bells today but they will wring their hands shortly hereafter.'

On Gordon Brown: 'He has based his policies on 'the Dolly Parton School of economics – an unbelievable figure, blown out of all proportion, with no visible means of support.'

On Brown and his Treasury team, when Labour was still in opposition, Clarke quipped: 'They are eighteen-year-olds in the saloon bar trying every bottle on the shelf.'

On New Labour policies: 'The idea of Labour backing business, keeping taxes low and reducing the deficit is completely absurd. It isn't just a matter pigs flying, it's a whole farmyard on a mission to deep space.'

On government generally: 'If I had to say which was telling the truth about society, a speech by a minister of housing, or the actual buildings put up in his time, I should believe the buildings.'

On Tony Blair: 'He took on the powers of a sort of medieval monarch, where he decided most things on his sofa for his ten years in office.'

Offering unsolicited and no doubt unwelcome advice to his own party leader David Cameron, early in Cameron's leadership, Clarke said: 'David Cameron had to persuade the public to see him as a future prime minister by being "statesmanlike" in everything he does. He has the opportunity to be prime minister and the public are looking to him as a possible prime minister – that's a huge advance – but they're not certain yet, and because he's new, he's inexperienced, they're getting to know him. I think he's capable of doing it. What he needs to approach everything with is a statesmanlike attitude of thinking, "What am I going to do in government?"'

Then, with a hint of criticism, he added: 'You need the odd soundbite, but not too many. He faces a long slog until the next general election and has to show he is a responsible person capable of governing the country – without being boring. That should make him resist people who want him to make crazy promises, react to events, get a quick headline in one of the right-wing newspapers. He's got to calm his party down on the sillier things. He's got to lead his party responsibly into new areas, look as though he can govern a modern country.'

Conservative MP Philip Davies said of Clarke: 'He does have a tendency towards political pigheadedness. His law and order beliefs are like his pro-Euro beliefs. He is equally wrong and equally adamant about both.'

And, another Tory MP's view of our Ken was: 'He's the sort of person who crosses the road to *join* a fight!'

Showing that statement is indeed still true, Clarke surprised many by making a return to the front line of the political fray at the age of sixty-eight by joining David Cameron's shadow Cabinet in 2009 and going on to become Justice Secretary after the 2010 election. So long as Clarke remains in the House of Commons, it would be unwise to write him off for any post.

And, finally, Ken on himself: 'Of course I'd have loved to be Prime Minister. But I'm not nursing a grievance.'

꙳

FORMER PRIME MINISTER Gordon Brown is an intellectual heavyweight who must take a large part of the credit for helping,
initially at least, to get rid of Labour's pre-1997 reputation
for financial incompetence in office, if not their penchant
for increasing taxes. That is until he became Prime Minister
himself, when his reputation began to deflate faster than the
British economy!

Widely regarded as a dour and somewhat humourless Scot,
this is a reputation he has encouraged by telling us, just before
Tony Blair's retirement, that we should 'look forward to a new
thirst for seriousness'.

Unfortunately for him, Brown's honeymoon with the
public was very short-lived indeed, evaporating in October
2007 when he appeared unable to decide whether to call a
general election or not. This led Tory MP Michael Gove to
jibe: 'Gordon Brown is the man who came to dither.'

In a similar vein, another Tory MP quipped: 'He is
Incapability Brown.'

Damaged goods he certainly became, but he was still able
to land effective blows on his opponents. Commenting on
the then new Tory leader David Cameron, he said: 'The only
change he represents is that he changes his mind all the time.'

He accused the Conservatives of 'retreating to the old
agenda on Europe, the old agenda on grammar schools, the
old agenda on spending and the old agenda on tax cuts',
adding, for good measure: 'The wheels are falling off the Tory
bicycle, and it is just as well that David Cameron has got a car
following him when he goes out on his rounds.'

On what Cameron stands for: 'He has nothing to offer
but slogans.'

On Lib Dem leader Nick Clegg: 'He is a flip-flopper.'

On the Conservative Party in 2008: 'Since 1997 the Tories
have had: four leaders – now four systems for electing their
leader; seven shadow chancellors, I remember them well,

well most of them, and I look forward to welcoming the eighth. With the current one they made a virtue of skipping a generation. On the evidence so far they should probably skip another one.'

Despite all the years of building up a reputation as an iron Chancellor, Brown's standing with the electorate evaporated quickly once he entered Number 10. The dour but strong and effective Chancellor somehow morphed into a stubborn and hopeless PM, who was seen as pathologically incapable of telling the truth. Brown added to this perception when he came under attack for proposing spending cuts. Unable to bring himself to admit curbing government spending, in 2009 he was widely derided when he tried to rebuff an assault from David Cameron with the confident declaration: 'Total spending will continue to rise. It will be a 0 per cent rise in 2013/14.'

When in a magazine interview Brown compared himself to Heathcliff, the Tory Shadow Chancellor George Osborne jibed: 'If he is a Heathcliff, then it is only because he cannot decide whether to come down from his Dithering Heights.'

And a Labour backbencher, commenting on Gordon Brown's performance as PM, joked: 'He does not have the Midas touch… it is more of the Andrex touch.'

The presenter of *Top Gear*, Jeremy Clarkson, caused a furore in 2009 by calling the Prime Minister a 'one-eyed Scottish idiot'. In typical Clarkson fashion, he later professed to apologise, saying: 'I apologise for calling him one-eyed and Scottish.'

Brown's 2009 woes did not end there. Later in the year, he was branded a 'disgruntled dour Scot who most voters see as uncaring'. Surprisingly, these damning comments came in a book by former Labour First Minister of Scotland and ex-Labour MP Henry McLeish!

The book also contained comments from psychologist Anne Ellis, who claimed that the Prime Minister's personality 'just does not cut the mustard in popularity stakes' and warned he may lose the next election to a 'much more pleasant personality'. She made the remarks in a profile of Mr Brown contained in the book *Scotland – A Suitable Case for Treatment* by Mr McLeish, which looks at Scotland and the Scots.

In the book Ellis suggests Mr Brown could learn a lesson from the current Scottish First Minister Alex Salmond, who she describes as 'a consummate politician if ever there was one'. Ms Ellis says Mr Brown is 'a very typical example of a dour Scot' and adds: 'He has no time nor interest in courting popularity as he wants to get on with solving the problems of the world. What he has failed to see is that in today's terms the role of politician, due to media attention, is more a public relations job than any other.' With friends like these...

Brown himself greatly compounded his woes during the 2010 General Election by making a huge gaffe when he insulted a Labour voter, not realising his Sky News microphone was still on. Whilst out campaigning he had met pensioner Gillian Duffy, a life-long Labour supporter. His TV microphone recorded him privately attacking Mrs Duffy as a 'bigot' for daring to raise immigration with him – seconds after telling her she was a 'good woman'.

Dubbed 'the bigotgate scandal', the press showed him holding his head in his hands as his comments were replayed. He was quickly forced into making no less than two apologies, first by phone, then by going to Gillian Duffy's home to express 'profound regret'.

He also sent a grovelling email to Labour supporters apologising for hurting the party's campaign, saying: 'You know I have strengths as well as weaknesses. You also know that sometimes we say and do things we regret. I profoundly regret what I said this morning.'

His gaffe prompted anger amongst many colleagues, who feared he had given voters a devastating insight into his own character and undermined the party's stance on a key issue.

Lord Mandelson tried to lead a damage limitation exercise,

pleading that the Prime Minister was 'slightly tired' and 'letting off steam' but admitting there could be 'no justification' for his remarks; but Brown never really recovered from this incident.

Commenting on Cameron and Clegg in 2010, Brown remarked: 'These two guys remind me of my two children at bath time.'

After losing the 2010 General Election, he said: 'I am not someone who wants to go around being a public relations officer to myself.'

⌛

COALITION PRIME MINISTER David Cameron was not even on the radar screen of most political pundits in May 2005, but just six months later he was elected Conservative leader by a land-slide and pretty much without having to announce any policy details whatever.

The then 39-year-old Old Etonian had dazzled that year's party conference with his youthful dynamism and charisma, reportedly telling journalists he was the 'heir to Blair'. He was helped by a rather lacklustre speech by his leadership oppo-nent David Davis MP.

Before becoming leader, he was the Conservatives' campaign co-ordinator at the 2005 general election and briefly shadow Education Secretary. Before that he was special advisor to Home Secretary Michael Howard and Chancellor Norman Lamont during the 1990s, before spending seven years as a public rela-tions executive with commercial broadcaster Carlton.

Since his election as leader, Cameron has sought to place Conservatives firmly in the centre ground of British politics, but his assault on traditional Tory subjects, such as grammar schools, has brought him into conflict with some of the party's traditional grassroots supporters.

On his own past: 'I didn't spend the early years of my life thinking "I'd better not do anything because one day I might be a politician", because I didn't know I was going to be a politician. I did lots of things before I came into politics which I shouldn't have done.'

On citizenship: 'If you don't speak English, you can't participate fully in national life. Government needs to make this clear.'

On Tony Blair: 'The most inaccurate characterisation of Blair that we have seen was his early depiction as "Bambi". Bambi? Blair will cross the road to pick a fight but mostly he likes to fight his own party.'

To demonstrate he is above what some describe as 'Punch and Judy' politics, David Cameron began his first Prime Minister's Questions by attacking Labour's then Chief Whip Hilary Armstrong for 'screaming like a child', and indicated that he wished to see less kettle-calling in the House. However, this restraint did not last long and David Cameron later went on the attack, saying: 'Tony Blair came into politics wanting to soak the rich and ban the bomb but has spent his time as Premier sucking up to the rich and dropping bombs.'

In September 2007, when Prime Minister Gordon Brown praised Conservative former Prime Minister Margaret Thatcher and said she was 'a conviction politician' like him, who (again like him) 'saw the need for change', David Cameron exploded: 'What a cheek! If we had listened to Gordon Brown no one would have been able to buy their council house. Unions would run the country and we'd probably be speaking Russian.' He then appeared to relent, adding mockingly: 'Gordon is a conviction politician all right – convicted of robbing people's pensions, introducing stealth taxes and failing to reform the health service.'

Later, commenting on Brown's problems, he said: 'Brown compounded calling off the election by then saying it was nothing to do with the polls, which was a massive mistake. It was a lie and it was treating people like fools.'

Back in 2006, Cameron sparked a furore by calling the United Kingdom Independence Party 'fruitcakes, loonies and closet racists, mainly'. This led Roger Knapman, then leader of UKIP to retort: 'We don't have to kill the Tory party – David

Cameron is doing a good job of killing it himself.' Knapman later added: 'The real fruitcakes are the people who elected a socialist to lead the Conservative Party.'

But Cameron bounced back with a vengeance in the autumn of 2007 after a series of Labour blunders, including the general election that never was. When a charge of incompetence was levelled against Brown, Cameron, alluding to Brown's reported control-freakery, sniped: 'He tries to control everything – but he can't run anything.'

On the financial crisis of 2008: 'Gordon Brown is perpetrating a "con" on the public over Northern Rock, and going from Prudence to Del Boy without touching the ground.'

Cameron then posed a question about his predecessor in Number 10: 'Who was it who said that he, and he alone, had rewritten the laws of economics to end boom and bust? The answer is Gordon Brown. And my message to Gordon Brown is this: you have had your boom, and your reputation is now bust.'

Cameron, in a further attack on Brown, said: 'He is an analogue politician in a digital age.'

On himself: 'I think I'm canine rather than feline. I like company, I like people, and that is much more dog-like than cat-like. And I'm more of a dog lover.'

On religion: 'I'm a pretty classic Church of England "racked with doubt and scepticism" believer.'

On his own political philosophy: 'My favourite political quote is by Disraeli: he said the Conservative Party should be the party of change but change that goes along with the customs and manners and traditions and sentiments of the people rather than change according to some grand plan. I'm going to be as radical a social reformer as Mrs Thatcher was an economic reformer, and radical social reform is what this country needs right now.'

On leadership: 'You appoint good people, and trust their decisions, but you have to know when to step in. William Hague has really helped me, because he made all the mistakes the first time round.'

Asked for his favourite political joke, before the formation of the coalition government, Cameron replied: '[Lib Dem
leader] Nick Clegg, at the moment.'

On former Prime Minister Tony Blair: 'He wasn't tough
enough with his team. They kept saying, I am sorry, I'm not
going to accept this, I don't want to go. Well, I'm sorry but in
my position when I want someone to go I simply tell them,
and then that's that. You have to be tough about it.'

On one of his own MEPs, Daniel Hannan: 'He does have
some quite eccentric views about some things – and political
parties always include some people who don't toe the party line.'

Sensing that the new Labour leader has not yet made a
big impact on the public, the Prime Minister often claims that
Ed Miliband has 'absolutely no idea' what he would do if in
power, adding: 'You are just demonstrating complete political opportunism, total opportunism. You are behaving like a
student politician and frankly that's all you'll ever be.'

Ed Miliband shot back with a reference to Cameron's days
in the Bullingdon Club at Oxford: 'I was a student politician.
But I was not hanging around with people who were throwing
bread rolls and wrecking restaurants.'

On Labour's Ed Balls: 'I wish he would occasionally shut
up. I may be alone in thinking him the most annoying person
in modern politics but I've got a feeling the Leader of the
Opposition will one day agree with me.'

On Labour's Ed Balls and Ed Miliband: 'A shadow
Chancellor who can't count and a Labour leader who doesn't
count... Ed Miliband was the nothing man when he was at
the Treasury, he's the nothing man now he's trying to run the
Labour Party.'

Controversially, on why he does not use the social-
networking site Twitter he said: 'The trouble is the imme-
diacy of it... too many twits might make a twat.'

When the Labour leader sneeringly referred to claims in the
WikiLeaks cables that Foreign Secretary William Hague had
said that he (Hague), David Cameron and Chancellor George

Osborne were all 'children of Thatcher', the Prime Minister snapped back, to laughter from MPs, 'I'd rather be a child of Thatcher than a son of Brown.'

But not all Conservatives are Cameron fans. When the Tory leader made a point of announcing that he would end the 'generous pension scheme' for British MPs, even though this was not an issue being pursued by any other political party at the time, one Tory MP, referring to the wealth of Cameron's family snapped: 'It's all right for him. He's already got a generous non-parliamentary pension scheme – he married it.'

One senior Tory backbencher has said of Cameron's style: 'He unfortunately mistakes being stubborn with strong leadership.' And former Labour Minister Tony McNulty commented: 'He is vacuous and his policies are "wash and go".'

After the announcement of the Lib–Con coalition, in which the Lib Dems got more than their fair share of ministerial jobs, one disappointed Tory MP was heard to say of the PM: 'He clearly is a man who can drive a soft bargain.'

⧗

THE NEW LEADER of the Labour Party Ed Miliband was a surprise winner in 2010, beating his brother David, who was the favourite, convincingly – but only after support from the trade unions was counted.

Ed Miliband was a television journalist and then became a Labour Party researcher, before rising to become one of Gordon Brown's confidants when he was Chancellor of the Exchequer. He has been the Member of Parliament for the constituency of Doncaster North since 2005.

In 2007 then Prime Minister Gordon Brown appointed Ed Miliband first as minister for the Cabinet Office and then as Secretary of State for Energy and Climate Change, a position he held from 2008 up to Labour's defeat in the 2010 General Election. On 25 September 2010 he was elected Labour Party leader.

Giving PM David Cameron some unsolicited advice during a Commons row he said: 'He should not get so angry. It will cloud his judgement.'

More recently, the Labour leader has compared David Cameron to 'Flashman', one of literature's most famous bullies.[*]

Mr Cameron, hitting back, likened his opponent to ski-jumper Eddie 'the Eagle' Edwards.[†]

On Communities Secretary Eric Pickles: 'A megaphone diplomat. He displays all the hallmarks of someone who is arrogant and high-handed. We are all fed up of him throwing up smokescreens and insulting people's intelligence.'

Miliband accused the Cameron government of being the 'same old Tories' after George Osborne delivered his second Budget speech to the House of Commons.

Dismissing Mr Osborne's economic plans, he said growth figures showed the Chancellor's strategy was failing and called on him to change course. Ridiculing the Chancellor's stated aspiration of wanting to be a blend of 1980s Conservative heavyweights Nigel Lawson and Michael Heseltine, Ed Miliband quipped: 'Instead we have the same hubris and arrogance of the early 1990s, the same broken promises, the same view that unemployment is a price worth paying.'

He then described George Osborne as 'Norman Lamont with an iPod', adding: 'And no doubt on his playlist, we have 'Je Ne Regrette Rien'.'

On his upbringing: 'I come from a generation that suffered school lessons in portacabins and crumbling hospitals. I tell you one thing, for the eighteen years they were in power the Tories did nothing to fix the roof when the sun was shining.'

---

[*]   Flashman is the villain of the nineteenth-century novel *Tom Brown's Schooldays*.

[†]   Eddie Edwards, was a British skier who was the first competitor to represent Great Britain in Olympic ski jumping. Edwards finished last in both the 70m and 90m events.

On his beliefs: 'I don't believe in God personally but I have great respect for those people who do.'

'There is a defining difference between me and David Cameron... and that is optimism.'

'The most important thing I have learned is that gossip and tittle-tattle of Westminster is actually irrelevant to most people's lives.'

And on politicians: 'Politicians should never feel safe or insulated from those they represent.'

Although many Conservatives have taken to referring to the Labour leader as 'Red Ed', Mr Miliband has decided he now wants to be officially known by his full name. Perhaps for reasons of gravitas, he has instructed the Official Report of proceedings in Parliament to stop referring to him as 'Ed' and henceforth to record his name as 'Edward'.

⧗

LIB DEM LEADER and Deputy Prime Minister Nick Clegg narrowly won his party's 2007 leadership contest. Some say his victory was more to do with his looks than his intellect or ability. However, he made a workmanlike start, even if he has largely remained rather too polite for the likes of this book. During his first few days as leader, he said that jokes and insults will not be part of his leadership style.

However, shortly after he made this statement he pleasingly showed signs of not intending to adhere to his own mantra. Asked about the last Labour government, he said: 'When Gordon Brown said he wanted a government of all the talents, no one realised that incompetence was going to be one of them.'

The difficulty Mr Clegg initially had was in addressing the perennial question facing the third party in UK politics – what do they stand for? A question that many felt he had conspicuously failed to answer until his sparkling performance in the first ever televised Leaders' election debates. From then on he could do no wrong and surprised everyone, perhaps even himself, by becoming Deputy Prime Minister in the coalition government of 2010.

Commenting on his party's political opponents in 2008, he retorted: 'Labour – old, tired and incompetent. The Conservatives – reactionary, remote and regressive.'

He later branded Labour a 'Zombie government' adding: 'They're the living dead: no heart, no mind, no soul, just stumbling around with no idea what to do. A cross between *Shaun of the Dead* and *I'm Sorry I Haven't a Clue*. They're so desperate to protect their own jobs, they can't be bothered to protect other people's.'

For most of 2008 and 2009 Nick Clegg spent his time denouncing the Labour government, but in September 2009 he decided to turn his fire on the Conservatives – describing David Cameron as a 'conman' and his policies variously as 'phoney' or 'fake'.

Later, before the coalition government was formed, he commented further on Conservative leader David Cameron, saying: 'He is the conman of British politics. He will say anything to win the 2010 election.'

When the phone hacking scandal arose in 2010, it appeared that amongst the politicians whose phones might have been tapped by a *News of the World* journalist was Labour MP Chris Bryant. This led Clegg to remark: 'Every time Chris Bryant asks a question I find it more and more baffling why anyone should want to hack his phone and listen to his messages!' All of the House enjoyed this putdown – except Chris Bryant.

JOHN BERCOW was a pugnacious, witty, robust, intelligent and fluent right-wing Conservative MP, before he became the Speaker of the House of Commons.

Since his election as Commons Speaker, Bercow has been

willing to embrace parliamentary change and has acted to
ensure better scrutiny of the executive, frequently allowing
backbenchers to ask urgent questions on pressing issues of
the day.

However, he has not endeared himself to everyone and once
said, not entirely in jest, that he had always had 'a relationship
of trust and respect with his party whips – they didn't trust
him and he didn't respect them'.

He has made some irreconcilable enemies amongst a few of
his former party colleagues.

When he was still sitting on the Tory benches, his whip
for a time was Simon Burns MP. Shortly after his election to
the chair, Mr Bercow rebuked Burns for his heckling during
Prime Minister's questions, calling him 'boring and boorish'.

After the 2010 election, Bercow was re-elected as Speaker
and Burns became a health minister. When Bercow again
reprimanded Burns, this time for the rather trivial 'offence'
of turning away from the microphone whilst addressing the
House, Burns exploded, calling him a 'stupid, sanctimonious
dwarf' during health questions. The offending remarks were
made from a sedentary position and not picked up by the
Commons Hansard reporters, but those in the Press Gallery
heard and it was reported everywhere.

The following day, Labour's Chris Bryant inquired on a point
of order whether Mr Speaker was worried about being 'short
with ministers'. Bercow replied that he'd 'always been short'.

However, Prime Minister David Cameron kept the story
going by telling a Press Gallery lunch that Simon Burns had
bumped the Speaker's car whilst leaving the Commons, to
which the Speaker retorted: 'I am not happy.'

'Which one are you then?' Burns was alleged to have replied.

Although he has his critics, Speaker Bercow has never
been one to mince his words. He recently described the *Daily
Mail* as a 'sexist, racist, bigoted, comic cartoon strip'. He then
paused before apologising for breaking the trade descriptions
act by describing the *Mail* as a 'newspaper'.

One Conservative MP, commenting on Mr Bercow, remarked: 'He is a vain man who would read the weather forecast as if he was Henry V at Agincourt.'

But the Speaker is more than up to the task of dealing with such abuse. He said recently: 'I have two categories of opponent – snobs and bigots,' adding, 'I think that bigotry can be cured, because I once held those views myself, but, as far as I am aware, there is no cure for snobbery.'

⧗

CHANCELLOR OF THE EXCHEQUER George Osborne is an excellent debater.

When, as Chancellor, Osborne announced he was working closely with the Lib Dem MP Vince Cable to 'do everything to make Britain one of the most competitive places in the world to do business', he added: 'I know that might surprise some of you. Many people said we wouldn't get on, that we'd trade cruel nicknames, that we would knife each other in the back, that we'd try to end each other's careers. Who do they think we are? The Miliband brothers?'

Before the 2010 general election, commenting on his opposite number, he said: 'Alistair Darling will never recover his reputation for competence. He is now, politically, a dead man walking... If Gordon Brown could make a decision he would move him.'

On Gordon Brown: 'This man had in front of him confidential Treasury advice that he's got to cut spending by 10 per cent. What a disgrace that he spent his Conference speech unveiling a list of new unfunded spending commitments when he can't pay for the last lot. When he should have been giving this country a lead, he went shopping on Brighton Pier with the nation's credit card. The Iron Chancellor has turned into the plastic Prime Minister.'

However, some of Osborne's jibes have been described as 'below the belt' and beyond what is acceptable. In 2009 a charity criticised Osborne after he appeared to suggest Gordon Brown could be 'faintly autistic'. He denied the charge after being criticised by the National Autistic Society following a light-hearted exchange at a Tory fringe meeting. Mr Osborne, then the shadow Chancellor, had been recalling his ability to retain odd facts, when the journalist hosting the event joked he might have been 'faintly autistic'. In reply, Mr Osborne said: 'We're not getting on to Gordon Brown yet.'

Later, in 2010, Labour MPs were upset when Osborne, now Chancellor, likened a gay shadow minister to a 'pantomime dame'. The comment came after Chris Bryant MP accused the Chancellor of delighting in playing 'Baron Hardup' and suggested he 'play Prince Charming instead'. Mr Bryant said the response was either 'homophobic or just nasty'.

The Chancellor has insisted it was just a 'Christmas joke' in the pantomime theme begun by Mr Bryant and was not homophobic.

⌛

FORMER WORK AND PENSIONS Secretary David Blunkett has a sharp tongue; however, he seems to have reserved most of his vitriol for members of his own party.

Commenting on his own position at the Home Office after four years of Labour government, he claimed he inherited 'a giant mess' from his Labour predecessor (Jack Straw), adding: 'God alone knows what Jack did for four years.' He went on to call his party's Culture Secretary Tessa Jowell 'weak'; say that Patricia Hewitt, the then Trade Secretary, 'doesn't think strategically'; claim that Labour's Education Secretary Charles Clarke 'hadn't developed as expected'; accuse Gordon Brown of being 'a bully'; and declare that the Prime Minister 'doesn't like being told the truth'.

He lasted only a week as Home Secretary after these comments were published, but after the 2005 election he was

brought back to frontline politics by Tony Blair by being made
Work and Pensions Secretary.

In 2010, he again returned to the subject of his party
colleagues, saying of Lord (Peter) Mandelson: 'Peter fell in
love with himself at an early age. His tragedy is that he rarely
heeds the wise advice he gives others.'

Of himself he has said: 'I have built my reputation on
honesty and I have sometimes been too honest.'

⧗

FORMER LIB DEM Leader Charles Kennedy has a nice line about
the trials and tribulations of politics – but which could equally
apply to life in general. In 2004, after a particularly gruel-
ling week, he commented: 'Things equal out pretty well. Our
dreams seldom come true, but neither do our nightmares.'

However, just two years later, he had cause to disagree
with his own creed. After months of rumours about his
drinking, Mr Kennedy finally owned up to having a drink
problem early in 2006. From his perspective, this may have
been a mistake because instead of clearing the air, Kennedy
immediately faced a battle to retain control of his party.
The row intensified rather than subsided after he publicly
admitted that he had sought professional help. When the row
showed no signs of abating, within days he was gone, returning to the backbenches after losing the support of half of the
Lib Dem Party.

Although Charles Kennedy has now joined a long list of
British politicians known for hitting the bottle, not all saw
it as a problem. Wartime leader Winston Churchill had quite
an appetite for brandy and champagne. On one occasion,
wobbling through the Commons, Churchill encountered MP
Nancy Astor who accused him of being 'drunk – horribly
drunk', to which he famously retorted: 'Yes, madam, I am
horribly drunk. But you are ugly – horribly ugly... but in the
morning I will be sober.'

Commenting on bravery, Kennedy has said: 'Courage is a peculiar kind of fear.'

〰

JOHN REDWOOD has a sharp intellect. Brought back to the front-line by Conservative leader Michael Howard in 2004 and demoted by David Cameron in 2005, he is regarded as being an inflexible right-winger by some Conservatives. This elicited the following retort from Redwood: 'I think in politics it is better to make up your mind and stick with it.'

Of Tony Blair, he has said dismissively: 'He is a man who has no single political principle within him, who will change his views as often as opinion polls and spin doctors tell him to.'

When he found himself having to listen to a long speech delivered in French during a dinner at Claridges recently, he was heard to mutter: 'Thank God for the English Channel.'

Following a number of policy U-turns by the coalition government after the 2010 election, his advice to Conservative backbenchers wanting to be loyal was: 'Don't worry. If you rebel today you are agreeing with tomorrow's coalition poli-cies. A rebel today is tomorrow's coalition loyalist.'

〰

FORMER FOREIGN SECRETARY David Miliband, commenting on the possibility of a Conservative election win under David Cameron before the 2010 election, said: 'I don't want people laughing at my country because a bunch of schoolboys have taken over the government. The Tories are not a government in waiting. They are a national embarrassment.'

And on David Cameron: 'Cameron has shown not leader-ship but pandering, not judgement but dogma.'

〰

SCOTTISH NATIONALIST Leader Alex Salmond is the current First Minister of Scotland. He also served as a British MP between 1987 and 2010.

Of the delights of Scotland, he has said: 'Sun, sand, but too cold for sex.'

When Gordon Brown decided not to call a general election in the autumn of 2007, after allowing speculation to mount for several weeks that he would, Salmond said the Prime Minister had lost 'an enormous amount' of credibility, adding: 'Gordon Brown is not so much the Grand Old Duke of York – more the big Feartie from Fife!' He continued: 'Gordon Brown obviously looked at the polls north and south of the Border and ran away at the first whiff of grapeshot. Those whom the gods seeks to destroy they first render ridiculous and this shambles leaves Gordon Brown looking totally ridiculous.'

Salmond later quipped: 'Labour are a shambles north of the border and shaky south of the border.'

On Scotland: 'Nations are nations if they feel themselves to be a nation and Scotland had 1,000 years as an independent nation before the union.'

⌛

LIB DEM heavyweight Vince Cable hit the mark and caused widespread laughter across the Commons chamber when, in winter 2007, during the then Prime Minister Gordon Brown's woes over missing data files, defence cuts and Labour sleaze, he pointed out 'the Prime Minister's remarkable transformation in the past few weeks from Stalin to Mr Bean, creating chaos out of order, rather than order out of chaos'.

This barb was not only funny but also hit home, causing a lot of stony silent faces on the Labour side.

On Conservative Shadow Chancellor George Osborne, before the creation of the 2010 coalition government: 'His business experience is limited to serving at the Bullingdon Club bar.'

And, after becoming a minister, he gave his view on ministerial economic predictions: 'When my job was attempting to predict future economic developments for the Shell oil company, I was frequently reminded of an Arabic saying: "Those who claim to foresee the future are lying, even if by chance they are later proved right."'

☒

FORMER LABOUR MP and former Secretary of State for Health Patricia Hewitt risked the ire of her own electorate with the following: 'Fifty per cent of the public doesn't actually know what the term fifty per cent means.'

☒

LIB DEM MINISTER Lynne Featherstone giving the benefit of her views: 'Thinking is really undervalued. People don't seem to do it anymore.'

☒

CONSERVATIVE BACKBENCHER David Davis MP is a former Tory leadership challenger, but his hopes of leading his party were swept away by a brilliant conference performance from David Cameron.

Not regarded as a great orator, Davis can still be hard-hitting in debate. Once, when asked his view on a colleague, replied: 'He is about as much use as the Pope's testicles.'

On one occasion, when he found himself not only standing next to Labour veteran Tony Benn, but also agreeing with him, he declared: 'This is the libertarian wing of the maverick tendency.'

During Foreign Office questions, when Robin Cook was still in opposition, Davis was at the Despatch Box, facing Cook. Labour's Barry Sheerman MP shouted out: 'Two-faced Tories.'

Davis immediately turned the insult back on Labour. Looking at Cook, he replied: 'Well, no one would accuse Robin Cook of being two-faced. If he was, he wouldn't wear that one!'

Although the press savaged his party conference speech during his bid for the Conservative leadership, Davis later won their plaudits for the shortest, sharpest answer given by a guest at the monthly parliamentary lunch for political journalists. In July 2007, at the lunch, Davis was asked, first, what advice he thinks former Blair spin doctor Alastair Campbell would have given him had he been running his campaign to be leader of the Tory party and, second, what he believed David Cameron's biggest mistake had been so far. After no more than a millisecond's pause, Mr Davis replied: 'He would have advised me not to answer the second question.' It is the only time a guest has won a loud round of applause halfway through his appearance at this event.

When faced with someone who was praising the doctrine of collectivism, he retorted: 'Socialism only works in two places: in heaven where they don't need it, and in hell where they have already got it.'

Most politicians, both friend and foe alike, feel that Davis has irreparably damaged his chances of any political comeback by his shock decision to resign his seat to fight a by-election in protest at one of the policies of the last Labour government. He did it without widely consulting his party colleagues and it was a strategy with considerable risk and electoral cost.

This apparent reluctance to be a team player and his unwillingness to accept compromise was summed up by a parliamentary neighbour who said of him: 'Davis's attitude is generally: "Do it my way – or you take the highway."'

⌛

INTERNATIONAL DEVELOPMENT MINISTER Alan Duncan MP was covertly recorded by campaigner Heydon Prowse in 2009. Asked why people would no longer want to become MPs,

Duncan replied: 'Basically, it's being nationalised, you have to live on rations and are treated like shit.'

These were brave words because when, as was inevitable, Duncan's outburst reached the public domain they caused uproar. Although initially telling his MPs that Duncan had his support, Leader David Cameron then changed his mind and demoted the Rutland and Melton MP, and removed him from the shadow Cabinet.

Before his demotion, Duncan had a sharp rebuke for PM Gordon Brown, quipping: 'In a very short period of time he's gone from being a control freak to an out-of-control freak.'

⧗

NOT MANY outside the world of politics understand the purpose of parliamentary whips, although they do realise that whipping is something of a black art. Most perceive that whipping involves the arm-twisting of our MPs or councillors.

Party whips, or 'whippers in' as they were once known – the name comes from fox hunting parlance and not some sadistic ritual – originated in the early eighteenth century. At Westminster, all parties have whips: they are MPs whose job it is to secure the maximum possible attendance of their own party colleagues, in the right voting lobby, during a vote.

Understandably, the press usually focus on this: the whips' ability – or sometimes inability – to secure votes for their own party on difficult issues. But, although this is the prime duty of any whips' office, there is more to whipping than just that. In one way, a good whips' office is like a sewer. The work is mainly underground, is largely unseen and may not be very pleasant but it is essential to the workings of both Houses!

Although the whips' main duty is one of management and persuasion, they also act as a conduit for the passage of information. They will note the emerging views of party colleagues. For example, any dissent from Conservative MPs about the way the coalition government is handling an issue will be conveyed by government whips to the Chief Whip, who in turn will notify the Prime Minister. This could lead to greater efforts to sell the policy to the government's own supporters, or a change of policy or, where there is a government with a small majority which fails to take heed, defeat on the floor of the House.

Party whips have various methods of persuading colleagues not only to wait for a late vote but also to support their own side when the vote comes. Many years ago it used to be the practice of the Conservative Party to station a whip at each exit of the Palace of Westminster during the early part of the evening. This custom was known as 'all doors'. The whips would then stop all of their own party's MPs as they were leaving, telling them to remain until all votes had been concluded.

This system had one serious flaw. The whips had to be able to recognise immediately all members of their own party – no mean feat just after a general election. On one occasion, during 'all doors', Walter Bromley-Davenport MP, a new junior government whip was trying to prevent Conservative MPs from leaving before the business had finished. He approached a familiar-looking young man whom he took to be a new Tory MP. 'Where are you going?' he snapped.

'I'm going home,' came the reply.

'No you're not, you're staying for the next vote,' Bromley-Davenport retorted.

'Why should I stay for the next vote?' the obstinate young man replied. At this Bromley-Davenport lost his temper. 'You are staying here!' he shouted and kicked the young man in the seat of his pants. He was mortified to discover shortly afterwards that he had been addressing the Belgian Ambassador! His career in the whips' office ended the next day.

Later, during the early 1970s, new Tory whip John Stradling-Thomas could have suffered the same fate. He had had a bad day and noticed senior Conservative MP, Sir Gerald Nabarro, leaving the building. 'Where are you going? There will be votes later this evening,' Stradling-Thomas said.

'I am not staying late. I am going home,' replied Nabarro.

'All right then, FUCK OFF,' Stradling-Thomas shouted, 'and leave the hard work to the rest of us.'

Nabarro looked shocked but never said anything as Stradling-Thomas stormed off. Minutes later Stradling-Thomas began to panic that Nabarro might well complain to the Chief Whip about his behaviour towards a senior member of the party. Would he be summoned to explain himself, he wondered. Stradling-Thomas heard nothing more about the incident and when he checked Hansard the next morning, he has surprised to see that Nabarro had stayed and voted in all the divisions that had taken place!

Today, new technology has come to the rescue. Whips of all parties now notify their colleagues about voting via Blackberry.

⧗

THE FAUX PAS of Mr Bromley-Davenport could never have happened to former MP Sir Sydney Chapman whilst he was a whip, because he was far too courteous and polite.

During the 1987–92 parliament, when Sir Sydney was serving as a senior whip, he once had to telephone a number of backbenchers to ask them to return for an unexpected late vote. Upon telephoning the Tory backbench MP Andrew Mitchell he was informed by a French-sounding female voice at the other end of the phone that the MP was not at home but was expected shortly. Sir Sydney explained who he was and said that he wanted to speak to the MP urgently and could be contacted in the whips' office. Mr Mitchell never telephoned back, nor did he appear at the vote, despite Sir Sydney's very clear instruction.

On seeing Mr Mitchell in the House the next day, Sir Sydney inquired why he had not returned the call and why he had not voted. 'Oh was it you?' the MP said. 'When I got home the au pair said that she had a phone call from a very strange man and that when he started to talk about whipping, she just put down the phone.'

The government whips' office is the only department in government where the incumbents choose who is to be newly promoted to their number. In all other departments the choice is that of the Prime Minister, although the PM does have a veto over the whips' choice if he feels the person is unsuitable. The whips make their choice by a 'blackball' system, whereby any one whip can object to a person being admitted to the office.

Sir Sydney Chapman is a former Vice-Chamberlain of Her Majesty's Household, and as mentioned, was a senior member of the Tory government whips' office in the 1990s. He frequently used to tell the story of a particular MP who was rather over-ambitious and pushy. A rumour circulated that the said MP was about to be invited to join the whips' office. To his colleagues' amazement the MP breezed in to the Commons Smoking Room and started to order champagne all round. As each whip entered, the MP would bellow out: 'Ah, here comes my *friend*.' He was therefore extremely disappointed when the official announcement the next day revealed that someone else had got the position. Taking the unprecedented step of trying to find out what had gone wrong, he approached one of the whips and said: 'I had heard that I was to be the new whip. Presumably I was blackballed because one of the whips didn't like me. Tell me, who was it?' He was silenced with the reply: 'Well, I can't actually say how many blackballed you – but have you ever seen sheep shit?'

At a meeting before the 1997 election, when the Conservatives were over twenty points behind in the opinion polls, Mr Chapman was asked at a meeting to describe his position in British politics. He replied: 'A politician is someone who thinks only of the next election but a statesman is some-one who thinks beyond that to the next generation. Ladies and gentlemen, standing before you, you see a statesman. In view of my party's standing in the polls at the present time, I just *dare not think* of the next election.'

Before the 1992 general election, Ken Hind MP, a Northern Ireland Office PPS (the lowest form of government life), was giving his views on the tactics of the IRA to a number of Tory MPs in the Members' Tea Room. He gave an extremely long and tedious explanation of why IRA bombers behaved in a particular way and was totally oblivious to the fact that his colleagues had long since tired of his tedious and pompous exegesis. Rambling on, he referred to a recent terrorist attack and claimed that his theory showed that the bombers had actually hit the wrong target, adding: 'The IRA actually meant to bomb M&S but instead they hit B&Q.' Mr Chapman, who as I have said is normally the epitome of civility, could stand it no longer. Interjecting, he ended the discussion with the barb: 'Perhaps the bombers were dyslexic.'

At the beginning of his parliamentary career, Sir Sydney postulated his own 'Chapman's Law of Politics'. The shorter the title, he asserted, the more important the post. Clearly then at the other end of the scale, he explained to an audience that he himself was 'Parliamentary Private Secretary to the Joint Parliamentary Under-Secretaries of State at the Department of Health and Social Security'.

Chapman certainly had a point. I am always suspicious of any politician who is not a household name and who has an entry in *Dod's Parliamentary Companion* which is longer than that of the Prime Minister of the day. I kid ye not. There are a few of them and if you look them up, you will see what Sydney was getting at.

A fellow Tory MP said of Sir Sydney: 'He must be an optimist. Even his suit has its shiny side.'

🏵

FORMER GOVERNMENT Chief Whip and Foreign Office minister Lord Goodlad likes to tell the story of a Russian dissident who is questioned on suspicion of subversion by the KGB. They raid his house and confiscate all of his property which is taken away for examination, including his pet parrot. He is arrested and asked if he wants to say anything which could be used in evidence at his trial. 'Yes,' the dissident replies, 'I just want you to know that I don't agree with the political views of my parrot.'

𝕏

A FEW YEARS AGO, a new Conservative MP, upon hearing that a colleague had been accused of corruption, approached his then Chief Whip to ask how he could be sure, when accepting a gift, that he was not breaking the House of Commons' rules. He was stunned by the chief's reply. 'The guidelines are simple,' he was told. 'If you can eat it, drink it or fuck it, it's not bribery.'

𝕏

FORMER RESPECT PARTY MP George Galloway is a colourful but controversial character, starting his political career as a Labour MP before returning as the only representative of 'Respect', the party he formed before the 2005 general election. He is an impressive speaker with a vivid turn of phrase. When he called journalist Christopher Hitchens a 'drink-sodden former Trotskyist popinjay', some MPs had to reach for their dictionaries. (Popinjay is an old-fashioned and obsolete word for one who is vain.)

However, in return, Mr Galloway is, so far as I am aware, unique in that he is the only MP to have ever been insulted by officials of a country using another obsolete word. He was recently banned from visiting Canada, being described by the Canadian authorities as an 'infandous' person. This caused many to scratch their heads in puzzlement, as the word does not appear in many popular dictionaries today. It means, however, 'too odious to express or mention'.

𝕏

LIKEABLE AND COLOURFUL London Mayor Boris Johnson is a former Conservative MP and one-time opposition culture spokesman. When asked why he left journalism for politics he quipped: 'Because they never put up statues to critics.'

When in the Commons, he took a swipe at the Blair government with the jibe: 'Only three governments in history have tried seriously to enact a ban on hunting with hounds and they are Saddam Hussain's Iraq, Adolf Hitler's Germany and Tony Blair's New Labour.'

However, former defence minister and former Liverpool Labour MP Peter Kilfoyle was one parliamentary colleague who was not enamoured with Boris and (successfully) called for his sacking over a 2004 article in *The Spectator* about Liverpudlians 'wallowing' in grief over the execution of Iraq hostage Kenneth Bigley. Mr Kilfoyle snapped: 'Boris Johnson's article is not only grossly offensive to hard-working and decent Liverpudlians, it is also inaccurate, representing shoddy and lazy journalism.' Kilfoyle went on to describe Mr Johnson as 'a buffoon', a 'joke of an MP', and concluded: 'Boris Johnson may be a clown, but no one is laughing. He should be sacked. Is it any wonder that Liverpool is a Tory-free zone?'

One would have thought that the Liverpool row would have tempered Boris's tendency for making outspoken comments about UK cities, but no. A few months later, he gleefully labelled Portsmouth as 'a city full of drugs and obesity'. Predictably, Portsmouth councillors demanded the then MP apologise for his remarks. Surprisingly, rather than slapping Boris down, the first reaction of the Conservative Party was to issue a statement saying that 'figures backed Mr Johnson's comments and politicians should not criticise him for speaking the truth'.

What Boris actually said was: 'Here we are, in one of the most depressed towns in Southern England, a place that is arguably too full of drugs, obesity, underachievement and Labour MPs.' This led the city's MPs to call on the Conservative Party to sack Mr Johnson from his front-bench position as the shadow minister for higher education. Sarah McCarthy-Fry, former Labour MP for Portsmouth North, said: 'Boris Johnson is not fit to be a front-bench spokesperson. His insensitive remarks will do nothing to encourage young people in Portsmouth to go on to higher education and David Cameron should sack him.'

Diplomacy is not one of Boris's strong suits. In 2006 he apologised to Papua New Guinea's High Commissioner in London after he had linked the nation to 'cannibalism and chief-killing'.

Since quitting the Commons in 2008 and becoming London Mayor, he has confounded his critics and has become a serious and popular leader of Britain's capital city.

However, despite his change of job, his colourful turn of phrase has not deserted him. On the Lib Dem Leader Nick Clegg shortly before David Cameron started wooing him, Boris declared: 'He is like some cut-price edition of David Cameron hastily knocked off by a Shanghai sweatshop to satisfy unexpected market demand.'

On the plethora of regulations introduced by the last Labour government: 'Under Labour, councils are not obliged to have libraries, but they are obliged to have officers to count the number of bats and stag beetles.'

And on own image: 'Someone, I can't think why, once called me a disfigured albino gorilla.'

⧗

FIERY VETERAN Labour MP Dennis Skinner, widely known as the 'Beast of Bolsover', is adept at the art of throwing speakers off their stride by a well-placed interruption or comment.

Indeed, Skinner has often been called to order by the chair following his out of order interventions. He has actually been asked to leave the chamber no fewer than nine times since 1979, including a five-day ban in 1981.

On one occasion, when Margaret Thatcher rose for Prime Minister's Questions, he bawled out: 'Here's the Westminster Ripper.'

Towards the end of John Major's time as Prime Minister, he

started calling him a 'Ken Barlow replica', adding (and mixing his soaps): 'We ought to get John Major a walk-on part in a rerun of *Crossroads*.'

In July 1992, he was rather basic in his abuse when insulting the then Agriculture Minister John Gummer, calling him 'this little squirt of a minister'. This criticism upset the then Speaker, Betty Boothroyd, who ordered Mr Skinner to withdraw his remarks. He refused and was ordered to leave the chamber for the rest of that day's sitting.

Later, commenting further on John Gummer, he showed no repentance, saying: 'He used to be the wart on Thatcher's nose.'

And he was banned for yet another day in 1995 when he accused Conservative ministers of a 'crooked deal' to sell off the coal industry.

On the 1990 Conservative leadership election, when Margaret Thatcher was defeated, he opined: 'They turned out Margaret Thatcher like a dog in the night.'

A few weeks earlier, however, before the result of the challenge to Margaret Thatcher was announced, a journalist eager to obtain a quote from an MP bumped into Skinner in a Commons corridor. 'What difference will it make if Michael Heseltine wins the Tory leadership race?' he enquired. 'None at all,' replied Skinner. Rather puzzled by this response, the journalist asked why. Dennis replied: 'Because they are both millionaires and both peroxide blondes.'

During the 1992 general election, when it was revealed that Lib Dem leader Paddy Ashdown had had an affair, Skinner started referring to the leader of the Liberal Democrats as 'Paddy Pantsdown'.

On the press: 'In Britain, there is no such thing as a free press. Most of it is owned by a clique of millionaires.'

When, in 2003, the press reported that Prince Charles might leave the country if fox hunting was banned, Skinner's response was characteristic: 'I think it's wonderful. I was already keen to vote to get rid of fox hunting. I'm twice as enthusiastic now. What a bonus!'

During 2003, when it was apparent that Conservatives were rather unhappy with their then leader Iain Duncan Smith, tales of plots and a proposed coup abounded at Westminster. This lead Denis Skinner to ask of Tony Blair: 'In view of the renewed interest in crime figures, especially on the Tory benches, will my Right Hon. friend consider whether back-stabbing should become a criminal offence?'

In December 2005 Skinner was once again banned from the Commons for a day, this time for comments about shadow Chancellor George Osborne and cocaine. During Treasury questions, Skinner commented that coalfield areas would have 'thanked their lucky stars' for the 1.75 per cent growth now being forecast for the year by Chancellor Gordon Brown. Then, referring back to the 1980s, Mr Skinner said: 'The only thing that was growing then were the lines of coke in front of Boy George and the rest of the Tories.'

Speaker Michael Martin demanded that Skinner withdraw his claim but the veteran MP referred to Sunday newspaper claims – denied by Tatton MP Mr Osborne – that he had taken cocaine. Skinner retorted: 'That was in the *News of the World* and you know it.' And he continued to refuse to withdraw his remarks when the Speaker repeated his demand, defiantly saying: 'No, I'm not withdrawing it… it's true'. Speaker Martin had no alternative but to order Skinner to leave the chamber for the rest of the day.

Later, George Osborne said that this incident was 'pretty desperate and personal stuff' adding: 'When the Labour Party gets personal you know they are rattled. It is exactly this kind of behaviour that puts people off politics and which David Cameron is trying to end.'

Mr Osborne, later the same day appearing on BBC1's *Question Time*, said: 'We were having a debate this morning on the economy, a huge issue of importance to everyone.' He ruefully added: 'Dennis Skinner threw this abusive rant at me and he is on the front page of the newspapers.'

⧗

FORMER CABINET minister John Gummer (now in the House of Lords as Baron Deben of Winston) joined the Conservative Cabinet in 1989 as minister for agriculture, becoming Secretary of State for the Environment in 1993.

On rural deprivation, he hit the mark when he said: 'Poverty is considered quaint in rural areas because it comes thatched.'

In 1993, he was called a 'drittsekk' (Norwegian for 'shit-bag') by the then Norwegian Minister of Environmental Affairs, Thorbjorn Berntsen, who ranted: 'John Gummer is the biggest shitbag I have ever met.' This came after Gummer had refused to discuss the issue of acid rain during a policy dispute with Norway over the slaughter of whales.

It cannot have been wit that caused a few raised eyebrows, however, when Gummer said: 'It is not the future I am talking about. I am talking about tomorrow.'

⧗

VETERAN LABOUR MP Sir Gerald Kaufman has an acid tongue and is generally extremely effective in debate. Once, after a speech by former MP Tim Smith, in which he loyally praised his own party's policies, Mr Kaufman snapped: 'I knew he had learnt to speak but I did not know he had learnt to crawl.'

On the Conservative Party: 'When the Tories think they are facing electoral defeat they dive head-first into the political sewer. The 1945 Gestapo scare has its equivalent in the 1992 scare that Saddam Hussein might take a risk or two. The Tory bogeymen may change, but the Tory's lack of principle remains the same.'

On Nigel (Lord) Lawson: 'His style is a mixture of bluster, smugness and arrogance.'

On his former boss Harold Wilson: 'He is the only man I know who deliberately acquired a sense of humour.'

On the Conservative government of John Major: 'They are particularly puny and petty. They brandish their nuclear weapons like some macho symbol.'

And on John Major and his predecessor: 'The thing about Mrs Thatcher was there was a character to assassinate. The problem with Mr Major is that you look and look – and where is it?'

However, Mr Kaufman has also found himself to be on the receiving end. Tory backbenchers have unkindly taken to calling him 'Kermit'.[*]

⌛

CONSERVATIVE PEER Baroness Warsi of Dewsbury is Britain's first Muslim Cabinet minister. She disarmed many of her critics when in 2008 she said of herself: 'I am the youngest member of the Upper House, and so I have every right to make mistakes.'

On political life: 'Why go into politics if you are not going to be brave? If you stand on the sidelines, politics is the wrong game.'

On life in general: 'As long as I can say that whilst I had the opportunity I did all I could, then that is a great achievement.'

⌛

FORMER LABOUR MP Peter Kilfoyle dismissed Conservative peer, Lord (formerly Sir Patrick) Cormack summarily with the following: 'By his own admission he is the patron saint of lost causes.'

And the Liberal Democrats received similar treatment: 'They have changed their name from the Liberals but I could suggest an even better name: the Party of Janus, because Liberal Democrats have the unique ability to face both ways at once.'

⌛

---

[*]   After the frog character in the TV show *The Muppets*.

IN 2008, veteran Labour MP Paul Flynn was stripped of a parliamentary allowance for making fun of other MPs on his online blog.

Flynn was told to remove some of his posts and when he refused he had part of his communications allowance removed.

But Mr Flynn – whose blog had been praised for its outspoken take on Westminster life and was once described as 'magnificently rude' by *Daily Mail* sketch writer Quentin Letts – said the authorities were not concerned about bias on his site. They were instead trying to impose the same rules of etiquette that apply in the Commons chamber on the internet, which he said amounted to censorship.

'They didn't have any complaints about the party political content, it was the courtesies of the House,' he complained. 'But I have never seen the rules written down. They just rang me up after reading my blog and said, "You can't say that".'

In one post, Mr Flynn compared his Labour colleague Peter Hain to a *Star Trek* character 'who liquefies at the end of each day and sleeps in a bucket to emerge in another chosen shape the following morning'.

He also turned his satirical fire on the publicity-hungry Lib Dem MP Lembit Opik, who had recently failed in his bid to be elected Lib Dem president. Flynn called him a 'clown' and a 'turkey', whose speciality is 'mindless political populism over intelligence'.

Other MPs branded a 'turkey' included Tory Nigel Evans, who Mr Flynn described as 'a tabloid newspaper made flesh'.

He was also critical of other Labour colleagues such as Richard Caborn and Ian McCartney who are consultants to the nuclear industry, dubbing their payments 'cash for comrades'.

Long before he started blogging, Flynn still could be insulting. Back in 1997 he took a rather basic swipe at former National Heritage Secretary David Mellor, saying: 'When he loses his seat, he can get an alternative job delivering gorillagrams without the aid of a monkey suit.'

Mr Flynn seems to have something of a penchant for primate-related belligerence. Of John Major's Welsh ministerial team he said: 'The three Tory Welsh office ministers have become the three unwise monkeys of Wales who neither see, hear, nor talk of unemployment, but hide from it.' And, getting round the Commons rules, which forbid accusations of cheating or dishonesty, he added: 'Are they three monkeys or three cheetahs?'

⧗

JUST AFTER he was elected to the House, former Tory Chairman Sir Jeremy Hanley MP was surprised to find himself sitting next to the Reverend Ian Paisley MP. Hanley remarked: 'I didn't know you were on our side.' To which he received the retort from Paisley: 'Never confuse sitting on your side with *being* on your side.'

⧗

FORMER TORY MP, and now TV personality, Ann Widdecombe, commented on the track record of Tony Blair's New Labour government: 'The first Labour promise was "We will stick to the previous government's spending plans". Their second promise was "We will reduce hospital waiting lists". The Labour party made twin promises at the same time and yet they now have the nerve to blame keeping one promise for breaking the other.'

On writing: 'It always amazes me that reviewers expect characters in novels to converse in prose worthy of Austen or Tolstoy. Nobody in real life does. Not even Oliver Letwin.'

Widdecombe has herself often been the butt of parliamentary insults, once being famously dubbed 'Doris Karloff' and on another occasion being described as 'someone who looks like an Albanian librarian'. However, she has endearingly taken this in her stride and of herself she has said: 'I've been a role model for the odd-looking and it's a part I've been happy to play.'

On Conservative leader Michael Howard, she famously said: 'He has something of the night about him.'

Sometimes insults can be effective even when they are unintentional. During the 2005 General Election campaign, whilst Widdecombe was waiting to catch a train north to attend a political meeting, she began drinking from a plastic cup of coffee, courtesy of one of the quick food bars on the platform. To avoid the dripping liquid, she held out the lid of the plastic mug in front of her and some wag who passed by dropped a coin in it!

⌛

LABOUR PEER Lord (Paul) Boateng was once stopped in his tracks for using the term 'Sweet FA' during a speech because the Chair wrongly thought it was a way of using the 'F-word'.

Had Mr Boateng been quicker on his feet, he could have pointed out to the House that the term is, in fact, nineteenth-century naval slang for packed mutton. It refers to Fanny Adams, who was murdered in 1867, cut into pieces and thrown into the river at Alton, Hampshire.

⌛

Attacking the pomp and ceremony of the State Opening of the UK Parliament, Labour firebrand Jeremy Corbyn snapped: 'We should start behaving like a modern parliamentary democracy, not a Ruritanian nation stuck in the eighteenth century.'

⌛

THE INVARIABLY sun-tanned Robert Kilroy-Silk first entered politics as a Labour MP. He then left British politics to become a television presenter before standing – successfully – for the UK Independence Party in the 2004 European Parliament elections. He then left them in 2005 to found a new party called 'Veritas', from which he in turn resigned as leader later the same year.

After he was elected as a UKIP MEP for the East Midlands, he let it be known that he wished to lead his party, in place of former Conservative MP Roger Knapman. His ambitions were not universally welcomed by his party and its supporters and this was not surprising. After describing his party's PR advisor Max Clifford as a 'self-confessed lying PR man', Kilroy himself came under attack from Clifford, who described the would-be leader as 'a showman', 'permanently orange' and 'a legend in his own mind', adding for good measure: 'If his leadership bid fails, with his colouring and total obsession with his own voice, he would be the perfect front man for Orange mobile phones.'

⧗

COLOURFUL LABOUR MP Stephen Pound for Ealing North is always worth listening to in debate and his insults are not always thrown at his political opponents. Commenting on then Labour Deputy PM, he said of John (now Lord) Prescott: 'It's very difficult to say why somebody should get 130 grand a year for playing croquet.'

He has been accused of calling Arsenal's former England defender Sol Campbell a 'fairy' during a Premier League football match. Pound was allegedly heard making a string of offensive remarks whilst ranting from an executive box. An Arsenal fan who was present at a match told a newspaper 'Usually, if you are an away supporter in a box, you keep very quiet. We were in front of this executive box and I heard a stream of abuse. I turned round and recognised Stephen Pound. He called out to Sol Campbell – saying, "You are a big effing fairy."'

Once, when the subject under discussion turned to UKIP, and its high-profile former MEP Robert Kilroy-Silk, he became vicious, describing Kilroy-Silk as: 'An orange-skinned, Spanish resident escapee from the dregs of daytime television whose one word manifesto is "No".'

❍

FORMER DEPUTY LEADER of the Conservative Party Peter Lilley explaining the difference between a New Labour backbench MP and a supermarket trolley: 'A supermarket trolley has a mind of its own!'

On New Labour's tax policies: 'An interesting illusion. They have raised taxes massively with their left hand and given back a small amount with their right hand.'

And on Labour's Paymaster General Geoffrey Robinson: 'He is well-known for dodging answering questions about either his own taxes or the taxes that he is imposing on others.'

❍

FORMER JUSTICE MINISTER Jack Straw on former Conservative minister Lord (Norman) Fowler: 'He speaks in tongues of double-talk, saying one thing one day and another the next.'

And on the qualities needed in politics: 'If you can't ride two horses at once you shouldn't be in the circus.'

At the beginning of 2008, Straw gave some New Year's advice to PM Gordon Brown on how to achieve eternal electoral success: 'He should abolish January. It's cold, damp, dark, depressing. Even the root of the word is deeply uninspiring – based on Janus, the Roman god of the doorway. Only the Romans would have had a god for doors!'

❍

CONSERVATIVE CHAIRMAN of the House of Commons Procedure Committee, Greg Knight, on Labour's Douglas Alexander MP: 'Forgotten but not gone.'

In 1987, and at a time when he sported a beard, Knight was interrupted at a public meeting in Derby by a man who shouted out: 'Aren't all politicians liars?' Stroking his beard, he retorted: 'Well, at least you can't call me a barefaced one.'

When John Prescott was Labour's transport spokesman, Mr Knight was, for the most part, a government whip. During one particular debate, Prescott was outlining what changes he would like to see in the transport field and suggested that British law should be changed to allow random breath-testing of motorists. Knight, sitting on the government front bench, muttered 'what rubbish' at this suggestion and Prescott exploded. He abandoned his speech and accused Conservatives of not taking the issue of random breath tests seriously. 'The only thing they really take seriously is bringing back the death penalty,' Prescott bellowed. Then, pointing at Knight, he added: 'I bet he supports hanging.'

Knight shot back: 'Yes, but not random hanging.'

One evening when Knight was dining in the Members' Dining Room with a couple of MPs, fellow Tory, the affable and ebullient Nicholas Soames, joined his table. Soames had hardly sat down, when he jabbed a fork into one of his colleagues' meals and bellowed: 'Is this tripe?'

Knight answered: 'To which end of the fork are you referring?'

On former Shadow Home Secretary David Davis MP, his political neighbour: 'David doesn't do 'touchy-feely'. If someone ever asked him to give them a few kind words, he would probably toss them a Mills and Boon novel.'

Again on David Davis: 'He's the kind of person who would throw a drowning man both ends of the rope.'

These are some of his other comments:

On the Rev. Ian Paisley MP: 'Just occasionally I wish he would use words of one decibel.'

On David Blunkett MP: 'A man who has made a meteoric disappearance.'

On the late Eric Forth: 'I won't say his sideburns were long, but when I first met him I thought he was on the phone.'

On the French: 'They are a well-balanced people. They have a chip on each shoulder.'

On former Labour Deputy Prime Minister John Prescott MP: 'I don't know why people keep picking on John Prescott – all he ever wanted was a place to lay his hat – and a few people.'

On the art of political whipping: 'Whipping, like stripping, is best done in private.'

On one particular Conservative whip: 'There are only two things I dislike about him… his face.'

On the Alternative Vote: 'A system where everybody gets what nobody wants.'

⧖

FORMER MINISTER and actress Glenda Jackson once surprised her audience when she remarked: 'Homelessness is homelessness, no matter where you live.'

⧖

MARTIN SALTER used to represent one of the Reading seats, but no one ever dared to refer to him as a New Labour MP. When someone once did during the 2005 election, he snapped: 'New Labour hasn't got this far down the M4.'

⧖

TORY BACKBENCHER David Amess MP has refreshingly said of himself: 'I am interested in everything and expert in nothing.'

⧖

SENIOR LABOUR MP Alun Michael, after being attacked in debate by John Bercow when he was still a Conservative MP, said: 'He is a case of a backbench member being tough on the English language and soft on his thinking.'

⧖

TORY MP and government whip Robert Goodwill on life in Britain under Labour: 'Under an EU-obsessed Labour government, if a youth is cought selling an ounce of cannabis he will, of course, be arrested – not for possessing the drug but for selling it in ounces.'

MUSIC-LOVING former Labour Home Secretary Alan Johnson MP on David Cameron and Nick Clegg, during the 2009 MPs' expenses crisis: 'They are acting like the *Self*-Righteous Brothers.'

And on Conservatives: 'The party of inherited wealth, private education and conspicuous affluence.'

TORY LORD (Tim) Renton was rather a good arts minister under John Major and he proved to be one of the few politicians to better Labour's Dennis Skinner. When, asking an arts question, the Bolsover MP inquired of him: 'How many civil servants are (a) men or (b) women?' the Renton reply was terse: 'All of them.'

LABOUR MP Diane Abbott commenting on Blair's New Labour government: 'It was a *Boys' Own* project – a highly centralised government, and all men.'

SCOTTISH NATIONALIST MP Andrew MacNeil, commenting on the purpose of Prime Minister's Question time: 'The primary reason for PMQs is twofold. It is for MPs to make sure their vocal chords are working and also to give the Speaker an opportunity to make a speech.'

☒

LEAVING NO DOUBT about his Royalist views, Tory MP Sir Peter Bottomley commented: 'I would much prefer a bad monarchy to a good president.'

☒

LABOUR MP and former minister Jim Murphy on the House of Lords: 'It is the single largest regular gathering of pensioners in Britain.'

☒

BUT PENSIONERS can still be witty, as Tory peer Baroness Trumpington, a former smoker, recently proved: 'At the age of eighty there a very few pleasures left to me – but one of them is passive smoking.'

And when asked on the radio programme *Desert Island Discs* what one luxury item would she choose if marooned, she replied: 'The Crown Jewels – in order to maximise my chances of being rescued.'

☒

DISGRACED FORMER MP Phil Woolas, who was barred from becoming an MP for three years as a result of some hard-hitting but inaccurate election leaflets, took a swipe at Nick Clegg, saying the Liberal Democrats have chosen 'a manager not a leader' and adding: 'The Liberal Democrats are in deep trouble and they know, in their hearts, that they are stuck; not just with the blandest leader since their foundation, but with his approach that they neither understand nor share. They have thrown away their brand.'

LORD COGGAN shocked a quite a few when he criticised both the frenzy surrounding the death of Diana, Princess of Wales and the Princess herself.

He said: 'Britain has become godless. Man is made with a hollow which only God can fill. Then along came this false goddess and filled the gap for a time. But, like all false gods, she could not last.'

He then added, for good measure: 'The British people identified with someone who had pretty loose morals and certainly loose sexual morals. A period of disillusionment is bound to set in.'

LORD (KENNETH) BAKER served as a Cabinet minister under Margaret Thatcher for some seven years, most notably as Home Secretary. Later commenting on how Mrs T operated as Prime Minister, he remarked: 'Mrs Thatcher categorised her ministers into those she could put down, those she could break down and those she could wear down.'

He has never indicated, however, into which category he fell.

LIKE ANY other employer, a Member of Parliament occasionally needs to dismiss staff. Some employees, who see it coming, leave of their own volition, just ahead of dismissal. One particular MP, who was delighted when an incompetent researcher finally moved on, provided the following reference: 'She has worked for me for over a year and when she left, I was completely satisfied.'

In a similar vein, another wrote: 'She has worked for me now for over six months, completely to her own satisfaction.'

LABOUR'S ATTORNEY-GENERAL Baroness Scotland caused uproar and the resignation of a Commons parliamentary aide in protest when it was discovered that she had been employing an illegal immigrant as a housekeeper in 2009. In trying to play down the incident, for which she was fined £5,000, she actually made matters worse by saying of her actions: 'It's like driving into the City and not paying the Congestion Charge. It's not a criminal offence.'

⧗

WITTY OLD LABOUR MP Austin Mitchell is well worth listening to in debate. In 2002 to draw attention to the plight of fishermen in his Grimsby constituency, he changed his name by Deed Poll to Austin Haddock before later returning to his former moniker.

He once revealed that he had two ambitions: 'My New Year resolution is to find where the Labour Party has been buried, and the tomb of the Unknown Socialist.'

⧗

NICHOLAS SOAMES, the colourful Conservative MP, recently joked: 'I do not know what detox is. But, whatever it is, I am not doing it.'

⧗

FORMER MP and left-wing Labour maverick Bob Marshall-Andrews was never afraid to speak his mind. Commenting on his own party's PM, Gordon Brown, in 2008, he said dismissively: 'Gordon Brown is a tragic Shakespearean hero. He has the jealousy of Othello, the indecision of Hamlet, the futile rage of Lear and, like Brutus, he goes to the wrong people for advice.'

⧗

CONSERVATIVE DEPUTY SPEAKER Nigel Evans on himself: 'I am used to being unpopular. I am a Conservative and I'm from Wales.'

⚝

FORMER DEMOCRATIC UNIONIST MP the Reverend Ian Paisley was a good House of Commons speaker and well worth listening to. Mind you, his voice was so loud that if you were in the same room as him, you had no choice!

Commenting on former Sinn Fein MP Gerry Adams, he quipped: 'He should get himself a shave because he's not just a liar – he's a barefaced one.'

On the Good Friday Anglo-Irish Agreement: 'A Humpty Dumpty which cannot be put together again by the spin wizardry of Tony Blair and his bobbin boy David Trimble.'

And when someone suggested that he should 'build bridges' with the Nationalist community in Northern Ireland, he replied: 'I must warn you that bridges and traitors have one thing in common. They both go over to the other side.'

⚝

CONSERVATIVE MP Keith Simpson on Labour minister Jim Murphy MP: 'He looks like an understudy for *Wallace and Gromit*.'

⚝

LIB DEM heavyweight David Heath on life in politics: 'Some MPs do not want to get involved in semantics. Well, I am sorry because that is what the House of Commons is about.'

Later Heath raised an eyebrow or two when he said: 'Longevity is just something we have to live with.'

⚝

CONSERVATIVE BACKBENCHER Nadine Dorries MP, who is divorced, recently told a journalist: 'There is a rumour circulating that I am about to flat-share with three male MPs. The minute I heard the word "ironing", the rumour became untrue.'

⊠

LABOUR'S HAZEL BLEARS on Conservative London Mayor Boris Johnson: 'His policy statements appear to be "the only way forward is backwards."'

⊠

CONSERVATIVE MP for Harwich Douglas Carswell on the last Labour government led by Gordon Brown: 'The trouble is they insisted on treating young children as adults and adults as young children.'

⊠

ITALIAN PRIME MINISTER Silvio Berlusconi has had his fair share of bad publicity as a womanising man-about-town. He gave his critics further grist to the mill in 2009 when he appeared at a youth rally in Rome. Berlusconi was asked to say a few words and astonished the crowd by telling his audience: 'I will take questions from the guys but from the girls I want telephone numbers.'

Berlusconi has also provoked further criticism for describing US President Barack Obama as 'young, handsome, and also tanned'. He made the remarks after a meeting with the Russian president in Moscow. Opposition politicians in Italy said Mr Berlusconi's remarks about the then US president-elect were at worst racist and at best undiplomatic. Characteristically, Berlusconi did not apologise but called his critics 'humourless imbeciles'.

⊠

NIGEL FARAGE MEP, who is the leader of the UKIP group in the European Parliament, said in a debate early in 2010 that he did not want to be rude to the President of the European Council, Herman Van Rompuy – but then went on to be just that, describing him as having 'the charisma of a damp rag and the appearance of a low-grade bank clerk'.

⧗

TORY GRANDEE Michael (the Earl of) Ancram, aka the Marquess of Lothian, aka Michael Andrew Foster Jude Kerr, and, since 2010, also known as the life peer Baron Kerr of Monteviot, is often referred to by his parliamentary colleagues rather less ceremoniously as simply 'Crumb'.

This insulting nickname is attributed to a party he once attended, when on arrival he introduced himself as 'Lord Ancram' but due to the party hubbub this was misheard and he was duly announced as 'Norman Crumb'. Between 1998 and 2001 he served as Chairman of the Conservative Party.

He once acutely observed: 'Elections change governments but they cannot change truths.'

Amongst his other utterances, the following are worthy of note:

'Sometimes conflict is necessary in the short term to achieve peace through the threat of aggression, and sometimes it is the threat of conflict which can establish peace.'

On those who advocated a policy of shared control of Gibraltar: 'Shared sovereignty doesn't work, because sovereignty depends on being able to exercise authority.'

⧗

THE MP for Cardiff West is the ebullient Labour member Kevin Brennan, who is not only a good debater but is an excellent singer/songwriter.

In July 2011 he won the 'Best Labour Thorn in the side'

award, from *Total Politics* magazine for asking Commons
Leader Sir George Young if he would reform Prime Minister's
Questions. Brennan quipped: 'If there was a hooter at the
clerk's desk that sounded every time the Prime Minister
made a factual error that might help to prevent the patronising of people who are just putting him straight with
the facts.'

When Caroline Spelman did a U-turn on plans to sell off
British forests, she began to praise her own candour, saying,
'It is a good example of how humility is a valuable quality in
a politician.' 'Even if I say so myself!' interjected Brennan, to
loud laughter.

On another occasion Brennan asked: 'Can we have a debate
about the poor quality of the teaching of history in our so-called
great public schools? What else could explain the Deputy Prime
Minister's [Nick Clegg] comment that his reforms represent the
most important reforms since the Great Reform Act of 1832,
including universal suffrage, apart perhaps from his innate
tendency towards sanctimonious hyperbole?'

⧗

CONSERVATIVE LORD (Michael) Dobbs on modern day memorial
services: 'Memorials have become anodyne, over-regulated
and standardised. Dying isn't what it used to be.'

⧗

FORMER LABOUR MP Martin O'Neill had to take back his
description of the Tory Angela Browning as 'a second-rate
Miss Marple', as the Speaker ruled that the phrase was
un-parliamentary.

⧗

IN 2010, shortly after the general election, one of the 227 new

MPs publicly apologised for being drunk in the House of Commons and missing a vote on the Budget.

Kent MP Mark Reckless said he did not feel it was appropriate to take part in a vote in the early hours because of the amount he had drunk. The Conservative MP for Rochester and Stroud told the BBC: 'I made a mistake. I'm really sorry about it.'

His brave public admission of being drunk did not go down well with his parliamentary colleagues, with one saying he was 'Clueless rather than Reckless' and another suggesting that he should change his name from Reckless to 'Legless'.

⧗

LABOUR MP Shaun Woodward was first elected as a Conservative MP but later crossed the floor of the House to become a Labour member. As he is extremely wealthy, this led to some Conservatives teasing some old Labour MPs that they now had a colleague who was so rich he had a butler at his home. Woodward objected to this and retorted: 'We haven't got a butler. We just have three people who look after the house.'

⧗

HARRIET HARMAN was for a time Labour's deputy leader. Although she made a shaky start as a minister, she subsequently did rather well. In 2007 Ms Harman was appointed Secretary of State for Equalities – bringing up to five the number of government and party posts she then held. She was already Leader of the Commons, Deputy Labour Party leader, Party Chair and Minister for Women. Before the announcement, Conservatives had nicknamed her 'Four Hats Harman' for having to juggle her new roles under Gordon Brown. This then changed to 'Five Hats Harriet'.

But early in her career Tory MPs called her 'Hapless Harriet'.

After the 2010 general election, she was forced to apologise for branding a senior coalition minister a 'ginger rodent'.

Ms Harman later admitted she had been 'wrong' to use the description about Liberal Democrat Chief Treasury Secretary Danny Alexander in a speech.

The jibe was the most personal of a number aimed at political opponents in Mrs Harman's address to the Scottish Labour Party Conference.

'Many of us in the Labour Party are conservationists and we all love the red squirrel,' she said, 'But there's one ginger rodent we never want to see in the highlands of Scotland – Danny Alexander.'

⧖

CONTROVERSIAL CONSERVATIVE MP Philip Davies has never been one to hesitate to speak his mind. Like his father, the current Mayor of Doncaster, he will unhesitatingly say what he thinks.

This no nonsense approach has won him many friends, particularly amongst the Tory grassroots, but also some enemies too.

He was once referred to as a 'backwoodsman' by Labour MP Barbara Keeley and even called 'a troglodyte' by his then fellow Conservative MP John Bercow, before he became Speaker.

In 2011 he upset disability campaigners, and some members of his own party too, when in a debate about the minimum wage, he said: 'The people who are most disadvantaged by the national minimum wage are the most vulnerable in society. My concern about it is it prevents those people from being given the opportunity to get on the first rung on the employment ladder.'

When a member of the public complained to Davies about his remarks, Davies told him he would not be responding in detail because he was sure the man 'wouldn't want to let the facts get in the way of a good rant'.

He gleefully thanked another complainer 'for the revealing email, highlighting how intolerant you are to anyone who happens to hold a different view to you'.

⧖

LABOUR MP Tony Lloyd on Tory backbench MP Christopher Chope: 'He has an almost unique parliamentary role. I am never quite sure whether he is like an interesting piece of baroque architecture – delightful to look at, although I am not absolutely certain what the real purpose is – or whether he is at the dangerous end of the Conservative party, dragging it back to where it feels most comfortable. I feel he is the latter.'

And on Tory MP Philip Davies: 'He represents a significant body of opinion, not in the nation generally, but in the Conservative party. That ought regularly to be put on record to remind my own constituents and, for example, his own, just what a rotten, nasty party the Conservative party can be.'

⧗

CLAIRE PERRY is the Conservative MP for Devizes, having been first elected to Parliament in 2010 to replace the outgoing MP Michael (now Lord) Ancram.

Tall, attractive, highly articulate and referred to by some as 'the Duchess of Devizes', she is one of a number of the new intake of Conservative MPs who is likely to be promoted before too long.

However, soon after her arrival at Westminster she shocked fellow MPs with her language during an intemperate outburst in the Commons Tea Room. Perry, apparently boiling with rage at Speaker John Bercow's failure to call her take part in a debate, stormed in and shouted: 'What have I got to do to be called by the Speaker? Give him a blow job?'

Several MPs said they were shocked by her language but the incident is unlikely to do Ms Perry any harm at Westminster.

However, some senior Tories are outraged at what happened – but not at Ms Perry. They are furious that the long-held custom that Commons Tea Room talk is treated as confidential has been breached – not by Ms Perry but by those who blabbed to the press about her colourful outburst!

❖

LIB DEM Peer Lord Oakeshott hit the mark when he said: 'A tax haven can be described as a sunny place for shady people.'

❖

LIKEABLE LABOUR MP Tom Watson was rebuked recently for his attack on Education Secretary Michael Gove, calling him a 'miserable pipsqueak'. Mr Watson's insult – hurled across the chamber – earned him a ticking-off from Speaker John Bercow who ordered him to apologise.

❖

FOOTBALL PUNDIT, classical music buff and former National Heritage Secretary David Mellor received loud cheers from both the Tory and Labour benches when he said of the Lib Dems: 'None of their MPs are household names – not even in their own homes.'

Mellor also once silenced a heckler with the barb: 'I can see that the noisy gentleman is well past his yell-by date.'

❖

FORMER LABOUR MP Brian Sedgemore showed that he had little time for the 1997 intake of New Labour women MPs who he regarded as mere lobby fodder. Early in 1998 he surprised those attending a meeting at the Tate Gallery with the gibe: 'These new Labour women MPs are like the Stepford Wives with a chip inserted into their brain to keep them on message.'

However, at least one of Labour's women MPs proved herself a good match for Mr Sedgemore. Labour whip Bridget Prentice approached him when he indicated he was going to vote against his own party on single-parent benefits and cooed: 'If I thought you had goolies, I'd crush them.'

⌧

FORMER TORY MP Richard Ryder (now Lord Ryder of Wensum) hit the mark when he said of those MPs who insist on speaking in the Commons at a late hour: 'MPs who speak after ten o'clock at night do not win arguments, they just lose friends.'

⌧

THE LATE Richard Reader Harris MP on economists: 'An economist is someone who, in order to save his two-guinea shoes takes long strides... and splits his three-guinea trousers.'

⌧

FORMER CONSERVATIVE minister Steven Norris on the benefits of a peerage: 'It is like a vasectomy – you can have all of the fun without any of the responsibility.'

⌧

AND FINALLY, Lib Dem MP Don Foster on politicians: 'A politician is like a nappy – they need to be changed regularly, and for the same reason.'

ACERBIC AMERICA

As the political system in the United States of America is based on the British model, it is not surprising that its elected members spend a similar amount of time trading insults.

Certainly the American public seem to hold their politicians in the same low esteem. It was the American wit Mark Twain who wrote: 'Suppose you were an idiot and suppose you were a member of Congress – but I repeat myself.'

American humourist Will Rogers, a somewhat gentler observer, described politicians as 'a never-ending source of amusement, amazement and discouragement'. He went on to add: 'Congress has promised the country that it will adjourn next Tuesday. Let's hope we can depend on it. If they do, it will be the first promise they have kept.'

However, grumbles from the public, whinges from journalists and cracks from comedians pale into insignificance compared with the vitriol American politicians use against each other.

⊠

THE FIRST women to become members of Congress in the USA were regarded as something of a curiosity. In the 1920s Speaker Longworth called them 'gentlewomen'. They were, however, subject to much teasing. On one occasion when a female member of Congress tried to intervene in a debate, she was dismissed by the congressman who held the floor with 'Not now – it's not often that a man is in a position to make a woman sit down and keep quiet.'

No one could keep Alice Roosevelt Longworth quiet for

long. Commenting on politician Thomas Dewey in 1948 she lamented: 'You can't make a soufflé rise twice.'

And on Warren Harding she observed: 'He was not a bad man – he was just a slob.'

Clare Boothe Luce was vitriolic about former US Governor George Wallace of whom she said: 'What he calls his global thinking is, no matter how you slice it, still "globaloney".'

⧗

AMERICA'S SECOND President was John Adams. Attacking those who were at the time attempting to find a 'third way' in politics, he succinctly dismissed the idea, saying: 'In politics the middle way is none at all.'

Amongst his other comments, the following are the most memorable:

'Fear is the founder of most governments.'

'Democracy never lasts long. It soon wastes, exhausts and murders itself.'

⧗

JENKIN LLOYD JONES gave some advice which many politicians today would do well to heed. On a political oration he said: 'It is a solemn responsibility. The man who makes a bad 30-minute speech to 200 people wastes only half an hour of his own time. But he wastes 100 hours of the audience's time – more than 4 days – which should be a hanging offence.'

⧗

IN 1811 Kentucky representative Henry Clay silenced Virginia congressman John Randolph who had said Clay wasn't paying any attention to his speeches. Clay shot back: 'You are mistaken. I will wager that I can repeat as many of your speeches as you can.' This silenced Randolph for the rest of the week.

During one particular debate, North Carolina's Senator Robert Reynolds, who was known for his long-windedness, was rambling on about the fascinating places he had visited around the world. The leader of the Senate, Mr Barkley, was anxious to conclude the business and sat there listening impatiently. Eventually Reynolds moved on to the beauties on the Far West and started describing the islands in the Pacific. At this point Barkley interrupted him and said: 'Senator, please, let us off when you get to Changhai.'

On another occasion Senator Barkley was asked what made a wise Senator. He replied: 'To have good judgement. Good judgement comes from experience,' whereupon a student in the audience asked him what experience came from. Barkley's response: 'Well, that comes from bad judgement'.

Over the decades a number of congressmen have had a drinking problem. During one particularly boozy Congress where many of the elected representatives drank heavily, one politician posed a congressional riddle, namely: 'What is the difference between a discussion and a fight?' The answer: 'Six bourbons.'

⌖

A VIRGINIA senator called William Archer became the source of amusement to many of his colleagues for his preference for long-winded vocabulary. He was not a particularly good orator and for effect his used obscure long words. The result of this was that his speeches were almost incomprehensible.

Daniel Webster's style was completely opposite, as he realised that a good orator had to be understood by even the slowest of audiences. A colleague from South Carolina called Preston one day asked Webster what he thought of Senator Archer. 'He's too fond of grandiloquence,' Webster said. 'What precisely do you mean?' Preston asked. 'Well I dined with Archer today and I think he is a preposterous aggregation of heterogeneous paradoxes and perdurable peremptorences!'

⧗

ALEXANDER SMYTH was a long-winded bore. In the middle of
one his long speeches he noticed fellow congressman Henry
Clay getting restless and said: 'You may speak for the present
generation, but I speak for posterity.' To which Clay replied:
'Yes, and you seem resolved to continue speaking until your
audience arrives.'

⧗

IN 1984 Congressman O'Neill from Missouri was interrupted
during a speech and he was so furious he snapped back: 'If the
gall which you have in your heart could be poured into your
stomach, you'd die instantly of the black vomit.'

⧗

FORMER SENATOR John Randolph who served Congress in the
ninenteenth century was a mudslinger. During one debate he
called President John Quincy Adams 'a traitor', then he called
Daniel Webster 'a vile slanderer', and referred to John Holmes
as 'a dangerous fool'. He called another colleague 'the most
contemptible and degraded of beings, who no man ought to
touch, unless with a pair of tongs'.

However, Randolph did get his comeuppance. He had
rather a high-pitched voice, which caused Congressman
Burges to snipe: 'He is impotent of everything but malevolence
of purpose.'

Sometimes Randolph could be amusing. Of two congressional colleagues, Robert Wright and John Rae, he said: 'The
House exhibits two anomalies – a Wright always wrong, and
a Rae without light.'

And he effectively insulted Congressman Samuel Dexter, a
politician who had shifted his views on a number of issues:
'Mr Ambi-Dexter.'

On power he said: 'Power alone can limit power.'

On being in politics: 'It gives us that most delicious of all privileges – spending other people's money.'

He also said: 'Time is at once the most valuable and the most perishable of all our possessions.'

Randolph coined a number of *bons mots*, amongst which the following are the most memorable:

'Asking the United States to surrender part of her sovereignty is like asking a lady to surrender part of her chastity.'

'We all have two educations – one which we receive from others and another – and the most valuable – which we give ourselves.'

Former Massachusetts Congressman Ben Butler was extremely long-winded and would usually fill his speeches with references to his military exploits during the American Civil War. This led to one of his colleagues saying: 'Every time Ben Butler opens his mouth, he puts his feats in it.

⧗

SOME INSULTS can be unintentional. Benjamin Tillman used to represent South Carolina in the Senate. His most striking distinguishing feature was that he had a very bad cast in his left eye. One day he asked a new Senate page boy the name of a recently elected senator sitting on the Republican side of the chamber. Unfortunately the page boy not only didn't know who the Republican senator was, he did not know Tillman either. The page boy left Tillman and went over to the Senate clerk and asked: 'Who is the man with one eye?' Without looking up, the clerk replied: 'Cyclops'. The page boy rushed back to Tillman and said: 'Now, Senator Cyclops, I will go and find out the other senator's name.' For once Tillman was speechless.

⧗

I ADMIRE the nerve of former Republican Congressman Fred Schwengel. This Iowa politician received many letters from his constituents on the subject of alcohol prohibition in the United States.

His problem, however, was that his electors were equally divided on the issue. He therefore devised a brilliant way of dealing with the conflicting views expressed in his postbag. Whenever he was asked what his views were, he would send the following letter:

Dear Elector,

I had not intended to discuss this controversial subject at present. However, I want you to know that I do not run away from a controversy. I will take a stand on any issue at any time regardless of how controversial it may be. You have asked me how I feel about whisky and I will tell you.

If when you say 'whisky' you mean the devil's brew, the poison scourge, the bloody monster that defiles innocence, dethrones reason, destroys the home, creates misery and poverty, literally takes the bread from the mouths of little children; if you mean the evil drink that topples Christian men and women from the pinnacles of righteous, gracious living into the bottomless pit of degradation and despair, shame, helplessness and hopelessness – then certainly I am against it with all of my power.

But if, when you say 'whisky', you mean the oil of conversation, the philosophic wine, the ale that is consumed when good fellows get together, that puts a song in their hearts and laughter on their lips and the warm glow of contentment in their eyes; if you mean the drink that enables the man to magnify his joy and his happiness and to forget, if only for a little while, life's great tragedies, heartbreaks and sorrows; if you mean the drink, the same which pours into out treasuries untold millions of dollars to provide tender care for our little crippled children, our blind, our deaf, our dumb, our aged and infirm, and allows us to build highways, hospitals and schools – then certainly, I am in favour of it.

This is my view and I will not compromise.

　　　　　　　　　　⌛

DURING ONE particular election in Oklahoma, Democratic Senator Robert Kerr was faced with a Republican opponent who was a preacher. They had agreed to a joint debate and the preacher went first, telling the audience, 'I became a candidate for the Senate only after I spent the night wrestling in prayer with the Lord and being told by Him that it was my duty to run for office.'

When replying Kerr said: 'It is true that a senator holds a most important office and he can do much good for God and country. I can, therefore, concede of the possibility that the Almighty might urge an individual to run for Senate.' He paused for a moment and then continued: 'It is inconceivable, however, that the Almighty would tell anyone to run for the Senate on the Republican ticket.' Kerr won the election.

　　　　　　　　　　⌛

AMERICAN POLITICAL campaigner Edgar Watson Howe coined a number of *bons mots* and the following are among his best:

'Some people never have anything except ideals.'

'He belongs to so many benevolent societies that he is destitute.'

'If you think before you speak, the other fellow gets in his joke first.'

'No man's credit is as good as his money.'

'One of the difficult tasks in this world is to convince a woman that even a bargain costs money.'

'The most natural man in a play is the villain.'

'Financial sense is knowing that certain men will promise to do certain things, and fail.'

'Express a mean opinion of yourself occasionally; it will show your friends that you know how to tell the truth.'

'A modest man is usually admired – if people ever hear of him.'

'Many a man is saved from being a thief by finding everything locked up.'

'The way out of trouble is never as simple as the way in.'

⌛

BEN BUTLER was a Republican candidate for Congress in the 1860s. During a political rally in New York he encountered much heckling which threatened to disrupt his speech. Suddenly an apple was thrown in his direction and hit him on the head. Butler at once pulled out a knife and some of the people in the front row were frightened that he was going to start slashing out at the demonstrators near the stage. Instead, he bent over, picked up the apple, peeled it and began eating it. The crowd became quiet and Butler commented: 'Mmm, not a bad apple that.' He was cheered and then continued his speech in perfect silence.

⌛

AMERICAN PRESIDENT Abraham Lincoln, who was assassinated in 1865, is well known as a civil rights campaigner. However, he also had a barbed tongue. Of a colleague he remarked: 'He can compress the most words into the smallest idea better than any man I ever met.'

On slavery: 'What kills a skunk is the publicity it gives itself.'

And, in replying to an admirer who sent him a copy of a first edition, he gave the delightfully equivocal reply: 'Be sure that I shall lose no time in reading the book which you have sent me.'

In 1858, when Lincoln was standing for the Senate against Stephen Douglas, he said of his opponent: 'When I was a boy

I spent considerable time sitting by the river. An old steam boat came by, the boiler of which was so small that when they blew the whistle, there wasn't enough steam to turn the paddle wheel. When the paddle wheel went around, they couldn't blow the whistle. My opponent, Mr Douglas, reminds me of that old steam boat, for it is evident that when he talks he can't think and when he thinks he can't talk.'

During that election Douglas and Lincoln held a number of debates in various parts of Illinois. In the course of one of them Douglas made continual references to Lincoln's lowly origins, and in one particular speech he said that the first time he'd met Lincoln was across the counter of a general store where Lincoln was selling whisky. Realising that there were temperance people in the audience, Douglas added: 'And he was an excellent bar tender too.' Thinking he'd got the better of his opponent, he sat down. Lincoln rose to his feet and capped Douglas's comments with this reply: 'What my opponent says is true. I did keep a general store and sometimes sold whisky. I particularly remember Mr Douglas as he was a very good customer. Many a time I have been on one side of the counter selling whisky to Mr Douglas who was on the other side. But now, here's the difference between us – I have left my side of the counter, but he sticks to his.'

Although he won the argument that night, Lincoln lost the election. When the result was declared, he said he felt 'like the boy who stubbed his toe', adding: 'I am too big to cry, and too badly hurt to laugh.'

When his host mentioned a local historian and enthused: 'I doubt whether any many of our generation has plunged more deeply into the sacred fount of learning.' Lincoln, who was not impressed, snapped: 'Yes, or come up drier.'

Asked by a journalist who his grandfather was, he snapped back: 'I don't know who my grandfather was. I am much more concerned to know what his grandson will be.'

On one occasion he ignored a snide remark by a colleague and actually went out of his way to be polite. Later a friend asked why he had not dispatched the political foe and Lincoln explained: 'Am I not destroying an enemy when I make a friend of him?'

He later developed this philosophy further, adding: 'A drop of honey catches more flies than a gallon of gall. So with men. If you would win a man to your cause, first convince him that you are his sincere friend. Therein is a drop of honey which catches his heart, which, say what he will, is the high road to his reason.'

He did not think much of the refreshment provided on Capitol Hill. To one of the waiters he barked: 'If this is coffee, please bring me some tea; but if this is tea, please bring me some coffee.'

On his electorate: 'It has been my experience that people who have no vices have very few virtues.'

On being accused of breaking an election pledge: 'Bad promises are better broken than kept.'

When he was asked to comment on the weight of his adversary Stephen Douglas's argument, he said: 'It is thin as the homeopathic soup that was made by boiling the shadow of a pigeon that had starved to death.'

On later being called a 'two-faced politician' by the said Mr Douglas, he replied: 'I leave the answer to my audience – if I had another face to wear, do you think I would wear this one?'

On a political colleague: 'He reminds me of the man who murdered both his parents and then, when sentence was about to be pronounced, pleaded for mercy on the grounds that he was an orphan.'

On being asked how long he held a grudge: 'I choose always to make my statute of limitations a short one.'

On women: 'A woman is the only thing I am afraid of that I know will not hurt me.'

On political tact: 'The ability to describe others as they see themselves.'

Among his other sayings, the following are the best:

'No man has a good enough memory to make a successful liar.'

'I don't think much of a man who is not wiser today than he was yesterday.'

'I can make a Brigadier-General in five minutes, but it is not easy to replace a hundred and ten horses.'

'The best thing about the future is that is comes only one day at a time.'

'Nearly all men can stand adversity, but if you want to test a man's character, give him power.'

'No man is good enough to govern another man without that other's consent.'

His rebuttal of socialism has stood the test of time, being frequently quoted to great effect by President Reagan in the 1980s: 'You cannot strengthen the weak by weakening the strong. You cannot help the wage earner by pulling down the wage payer. You cannot help the poor by destroying the rich. You cannot help men permanently by doing for them what they could and should do for themselves.'

When attacked for being a 'Conservative', he replied: 'Well, what is conservatism? Is not adherence to the old and tried against the new and untried?'

During the Civil War Pennsylvania Congressman Thaddeus Stevens said that he thought that the War Minister Simon Cameron was a 'consummate scoundrel'. When his friend queried what he meant, saying, 'Surely you don't think that Cameron would steal?' Stevens thought about the matter and replied: 'Well, I don't think he would steal a red hot stove.' President Lincoln came to hear of the gibe, liked it, and repeated it himself on several occasions.

⌛

SOMETIMES AN INSULT can be used by a politician to get himself out of a highly embarrassing situation. Once, when Washington Democrat Senator Henry Jackson was campaigning, he fell through a rotten stage floor and the audience started laughing at his predicament. He turned the situation to his advantage by quickly clambering back to the microphone and quipping: 'I was obviously standing on one of the planks from the Republican platform.'

It is not only bile and venom that over the years have threatened the good order of debate. In the nineteenth century Massachusetts Senator Daniel Webster often imbibed too freely before making a speech. On one occasion he was in such a bad state as he was due to speak that a friend sitting behind him agreed to help him through the ordeal. As Webster stood wavering after his opening remarks, the senator sitting behind him whispered 'tariff'. It seemed to do the trick and Webster gathered his thoughts and proceeded to speak for a couple of minutes on the subject. Then he began to sway and nod. 'National debt' prompted his friend again. Again, Webster was able to continue: 'Gentleman, then there's the national debt – it should be paid.' At this point loud cheers broke out in the chamber which roused Webster. 'Yes, gentlemen,' he repeated himself. 'It should be paid.' This produced even louder cheers, at which point Webster seemed to have forgotten what he was talking about. 'And I'll be damned,' he said, taking out his cheque book, 'I'll pay it myself. How much is it?' At this, any bad temper that his drunken ramblings were arousing completely dissolved into loud laughter as Webster was always broke. He then collapsed into his chair and promptly fell asleep.

However, this amusing but rather disgraceful episode appears to have been the exception as far as Webster was concerned. Many contemporaries have commented that Webster was one of the few politicians who could speak effectively even when completely drunk. Indeed, many a young politician concluded that Webster did his best work 'whilst under the influence' and some of them drank to excess in the hope of becoming as fluent. In 1920s Britain, the Conservative F. E. Smith had a similar capacity, often amazing friends and colleagues with his witty speeches delivered when he was three sheets to the wind.

⬚

FORMER US PRESIDENT Thomas Jefferson was right on the button when commenting about his office: 'No man shall ever bring out of the Presidency the reputation which carries him into it.'

One-time Virginia Senator John Randolph was, in his day, one of the most striking figures to appear in Congress. He used to ride to Capitol Hill and enter the chamber with riding whip in hand and a small cap on his head. He was unpredictable – and usually very insulting.

On one occasion a man who had met him at a dinner a couple of days earlier saw him walking to the Capitol, rushed over to him and said: 'Good morning, Mr Randolph – how do you do?' 'Good morning,' Randolph replied without stopping or looking up. The man continued, 'You walk very fast, Mr Randolph, and I have great difficulty in keeping up with you.' Randolph snapped back, 'In that case, I'll increase the difficulty,' and hurried off.

He was an ardent supporter of President Jefferson for most of his career, but he thought President John Quincy Adams was useless. He once met an Adams supporter on a narrow pavement. The man stopped in front of Randolph, completely blocking his way and said to him belligerently, 'I never step out of my way for puppies!' 'Oh, I always do,' said Randolph as he stepped aside. 'Please pass.'

⬚

IN 1824 Henry Clay threw his support behind John Quincy Adams in the election of that year. After Adams's victory, he was made Secretary of State. Incensed, Randolph spoke of a 'corrupt bargain' between the two and, addressing the House in 1826 talked about 'the alliance – offensive and defensive' between the two men, later referring to their friendship as a deal between 'a puritan and a blackleg'. Clay deeply resented being called a blackleg, which meant a crooked gambler, and actually challenged Randolph to a duel. This incident, however, ended happily as when they fired their shots in the duel, both missed, and then made up their quarrel.

Towards the end of his life, he became somewhat senile, frequently tearing up his papers in sudden outbursts of anger. He directed that when he died he was to be buried facing west so that he could keep an eye on Henry Clay whose nationalist views he detested.

⧗

IN DECEMBER 1889 Maine's representative Thomas Reed became Speaker of the House and soon came to be respected for his forceful but firm rulings.

One day when his integrity was questioned by Richard Townsend, the congressman from Illinois, Reed announced to the House: 'There are only two sets of people whose opinions I respect, my constituents, who know me, and the House, who knows Townsend. It is hardly necessary to say, therefore, that I stand vindicated before both.'

Reed also showed that he had a sense of humour. He once sent a telegram to members of the House demanding their presence for a sitting as he was concerned to see that a quorum was achieved. One congressman who was held up by a flood which had washed away half of the railway line telegraphed back: 'Washout on the line. Can't come.' Reed immediately sent a telegram back: 'Buy a new shirt and come at once.'

When Reed was in conversation with one of the oldest congressmen in the House and he asked him to what he attributed his long life, the elderly politician replied: 'I always have a slug of liquor every afternoon and I vote a straight Democratic ticket.' Reed, who was a teetotaller, as well as being a fervent

Republican, replied: 'Well that explains it – one poison offsets the other.'

Among the most memorable of Speaker Reed's sayings are the following:

'A statesman is a politician who is dead.'

'All the wisdom of the world consists of shouting with the majority.'

On President Theodore Roosevelt: 'If there is one thing more than any other for which I admire him, it is his original discovery of the Ten Commandments.'

On two fellow congressmen of whom he did not have a high opinion: 'They can never open their mouths without subtracting from the sum total of human knowledge.'

And, on a member of the opposition: 'The volume of his voice is equalled only by the volume of what he does not know.'

When William Springer, a Democrat, rose to his feet to ask for permission to make an apology for an incorrect attack he'd made on the Republican party, Reed exclaimed: 'No correction is needed – the House didn't believe you in the first place.'

On another occasion Congressman Lewis, who was rather good looking, raised a point of personal privilege when a tabloid newspaper referred to him as 'a thing of beauty and a joy forever'. Reed at first appeared to agree with him, saying it was a valid point, but then added, 'The newspaper should have said "a thing of beauty and a jaw forever".'

On the Senate: 'It is the little house – a close communion of old grannies and tabby cats; a place where good representatives go when they die.'

On those who specialise too much: 'If a man studies finance intimately, and continues his study long enough, it disqualifies him from talking intelligently upon any other subject. If he continues his studies still longer, it eventually disqualifies him from talking intelligently upon that!'

When Reed was campaigning in Maine during one presidential contest, a Democrat sat in the front row to heckle him.

The Democrat kept asking impertinent and rude questions, which Reed answered courteously.

It soon became obvious that the Democrat wanted to goad Reed into losing his temper, but Reed kept his cool. Finally, realising that his ruse was not working, after a particularly polite and detailed answer to one of his questions, the heckler bawled: 'Oh, go to hell.' Reed immediately responded: 'I have travelled in many parts of the State and have spoken at many meetings, but this is the first time I have received an invitation to the Democratic headquarters.'

When a particular congressman who was in favour of war told Reed that it was the duty of the United States to 'take freedom to the Philippines', he shot back: 'Yes, canned freedom.'

The Republican Reed Smoot, one-time Senator of Utah, used to tell of the incident when one of his pompous colleagues was in a Washington hotel being shaved by an old black barber who had seen many senators come and go through the years. The pompous politician said to the barber: 'You must have had many of my distinguished predecessors in your chair.'

'Yes,' answered the barber. 'I've known most of them and you remind me of Daniel Webster.'

The politician beamed with pride. 'Is it my profile or my speeches that remind you of him?' he inquired.

'Neither,' said the barber. 'It's your bad breath.'

⧗

CHURCH MINISTER Edward Hale became chaplain of the Senate in the United States in 1903. After he had been opening their sessions with a prayer for several weeks, a member of the public approached him in the street and said: 'Oh, I think I know you. Are you the man for prays for the senators?'

'No,' Dr Hale snapped. 'I am the man who looks at the senators and prays for the country.'

⧗

WHEN NORTH CAROLINA Senator Robert Strange was on his death bed, he called for his son and said: 'On my tombstone I want the inscription "Here lies an honest Congressman."'

His son interjected: 'And then your name?'

'No,' said Strange, 'that won't be necessary. People who read it will say, "That's strange!"'

☒

IN 1919 President Wilson of the USA suffered a stroke. Senator Fall, who had opposed some of Wilson's policies, called to see him and said: 'Mr President, we have all been praying for you.' Wilson snapped: 'Ah, but which way?'

☒

ALL GOOD orators have an off day. Senator Robert La Follette from Wisconsin, normally an excellent speaker, was making a speech in February 1912 to the Periodical Publishers Association and, ignoring the late hour, he went on somewhat at length discussing the evils of corporate control of American newspapers. After he had been speaking for about an hour and a half on the same subject, he posed a rhetorical question to his audience and asked, 'Is there a way out?' At which some wag got to his feet and shouted 'We hope so' and headed for the exit. Not only did this destroy the rest of La Follette's speech, but it effectively killed off his campaign for the Republican nomination for President that year!

Of course, not every time a member of the audience scores against the platform speaker is it intentional. At one political gathering Congressman Hancock of New York was due to address the audience at a meeting which started with some band music. After the orchestra had played a couple of numbers the chairman inadvertently insulted the guest speaker by asking: 'Do you want to speak now, or shall we let the audience enjoy themselves a little longer?'

Senator Claude Swanson of Virginia *was* deliberately insulted by an old dear in the audience after he had made a long and rambling speech. 'I liked your speech fine, Senator,' she said, but then added, 'but it seems to me you missed several excellent opportunities.' The senator was puzzled. 'Several opportunities for what?' he inquired. 'To quit,' she snapped.

Louisiana Senator Huey Long, elected in 1930, was regarded as a formidable opponent. He compared Herbert Hoover to a 'hoot owl' and Franklin D. Roosevelt to a 'scrootch owl'. Explaining himself, he said: 'A hoot owl bangs into the nest and knocks the hen clean off and catches her whilst she's falling. But a scrootch owl slips into the roost and scrootches up to the hen and talks softly to her. And then the hen just falls in love with him and the next thing you know, there ain't no hen.'

His name, Long, suited him. In 1935 he filibustered non-stop for fifteen and a half hours – one of the longest political speeches ever – against FDR's New Deal Bill. During the course of his speech he read to the Senate the complete constitution of the United States, which caused satirist Will Rogers to remark: 'Most of the senators thought he was reviewing a new book.'

He hit the nail on the head when talking about effective political tactics: 'In a political fight, if there is nothing in favour of your own side, start a row in the opposition camp.'

Long aroused the ire of Senator Glass who, after one of Long's speeches, announced that Long's electorate had outdone Caligula: 'Where Caligula made his horse a consul, Long's constituents have made the posterior of a horse a US senator.'

Were he alive today, he would probably have been frequently suspended from the chamber for his bad language. With hindsight Long would probably have welcomed this to the alternative: on 8 September 1935, after making a particularly vicious speech, he was shot as his left the chamber. He died two days later.

WILLIAM H. TAFT, upon losing the presidential race to Woodrow Wilson, made the best fist of, for him, an appalling result by quipping 'I have one consolation. No candidate was elected ex-President by such a large majority.'

Anonymous on President Harry S. Truman: 'Among President Truman's many weaknesses was his utter inability to discriminate between history and histrionics.'

⧗

US PRESIDENT Theodore Roosevelt, who became President just after the turn of the twentieth century, was a master of the political barb. He once called President Castro of Venezuela 'an unspeakably villainous little monkey'.

On an American judge: 'He is an amiable old fuzzy-wuzzy with sweetbread brains.'

On politician John Tyler: 'He's been called a mediocre man – but this is unwarranted flattery. He was a politician of monumental littleness.'

On his successor Woodrow Wilson: 'He is a Byzantine logothete.'

On some demonstrators campaigning against blood sports: 'They are logical vegetarians of the flabbiest Hindoo type.'

On William Jennings Bryan: 'He represents that type of farmer whose gate hangs on one hinge, whose old hat supplies the place of the missing window pane and who is more likely to be found at the crossroad grocery store than behind the plough.'

Roosevelt was also responsible for a number of new phrases entering the vocabulary. Among his many utterances he coined the sayings 'the lunatic fringe', 'weazel words' and 'pussyfooting'.

Franklin D. Roosevelt said of his own career: 'I ask you to judge me by the enemies I have made.'

⧗

DURING THE 1940s Senator Wherry of Nebraska made quite a
name for himself as a malapropist. In virtually every speech he
would get something wrong. On one occasion he referred to
'Indigo China'. He later called the Chinese Nationalist leader
Chiang Kai-Shek 'Shanghai Jack'.

He also once said: 'The issue is clear and indistinct to me.'

And speaking of the Defense Department joint chiefs of
staff he alluded to 'the chief joints of staff'. However, those
he insulted knew that he couldn't help it and he came to be
affectionately known as 'the Sam Goldwyn of Capitol Hill'.

⧖

TEXAS REPRESENTATIVE Sam Rayburn became Speaker of the House
of Representatives in 1940. He prided himself in telling the truth
as he saw it, even if this meant upsetting his friends. His local
preacher criticised Rayburn's support for President Truman's
sacking of General MacArthur and added: 'If your constituents
elect you to office again, they will be deaf, dumb and ignorant.'
Rayburn turned to the preacher and said: 'Being a believer in
God and his word, which was "and on earth, peace and goodwill to all men", I fear that your conduct will not be conducive
to carrying out these things. In other words, God travelling with
you would be in poor company.' Then he walked off.

Among his many quips, insults and sayings the following
are the best:

'Any man who becomes conceited and arrogant isn't big
enough for the job.'

'Anyone who will cheat for you, will cheat against you.'

'There is a time to fish and a time to mend nets.'

'If there is anything I hate more than an old fogey, it's a
young fogey.'

'No one has a finer command of language than the person
who keeps his mouth shut.'

'Always tell the truth then you'll never have to remember
what you said the last time.'

He snapped back at a critic who didn't think he was being partisan enough: 'Remember, number one: we're Americans first and Democrats second. And number two: we're builders not obstructionists. Any jackass can kick down the barn door, but it takes a carpenter to build one.'

And taking a swipe at a colleague who criticised the United States overseas: 'Politics should stop at the water's edge – when it comes to foreign policy you support your country.'

◧

US PRESIDENT Woodrow Wilson was the twenty-eighth President of the United States, being first elected to office in 1911. Unusually for a man with many liberal traits, he glorified the rise of the Ku Klux Klan, commenting at the time that 'the white men were roused by a mere instinct of self-preservation'.

His administration instituted segregation in the US federal government for the first time since Abraham Lincoln began de-segregation in 1863. Wilson also regarded mixed race Americans with suspicion, calling them 'hyphenated Americans' (Irish-Americans, German-Americans etc.). He once snapped: 'Any man who carries a hyphen about with him carries a dagger that he is ready to plunge into the vitals of our Republic whenever he gets ready.'

On the subject of making speeches, he once famously – and accurately – remarked: 'If I am to speak for ten minutes, I need a week for preparation; if fifteen minutes, three days; if half an hour, two days; and if an hour, I am ready now!'

◧

DURING 1939 on the eve of the Second World War, the British King and Queen visited Washington to secure further help from the US towards Britain's war effort.

The royal family were insulted – though not intentionally – by the behaviour of Congressman Joe Martin. He was a member of the committee deputed to welcome the royal couple and, like the other committee members, he was expected to wear a morning coat and silk top hat for the occasion.

The day before the trip Texas Congressman Sam Rayburn told Joe Martin that he didn't have a top hat and wasn't going to get one. He indicated that he was just going to wear a bowler hat. Martin did have a top hat, but since Rayburn didn't, he decided to give moral support to his old friend and wear his bowler hat also.

When he got to Capitol Hill the next day, however, he was amazed to find Rayburn wearing a shiny silk hat which someone had lent him at the last minute.

Martin had no alternative but to attend the reception wearing his bowler hat whilst everyone else was properly attired. Local newspapers made much of the 'snub' and there was considerable criticism from other congressmen.

Whether or not the royal couple noticed is not recorded, but clearly Martin's colleagues and the press thought it was a deliberate insult. Worried about the reaction of his constituents, in view of all of the publicity, Martin was amazed to find that on his return to Massachusetts he was regarded as a hero. Constituency mail poured into his office praising his 'plucky performance'. Local party workers patted him on the back and said they were glad he had the gumption to stand up to the King of England rather than crawl to him in a high hat as others had done, which just goes to show that, in politics, public reaction is always unpredictable.

☒

PAT HARRISON, a Mississippi senator, did not have much time for Theodore Bilbo, a Senator from the same state, of whom he said: 'When Bilbo dies the epitaph on his gravestone should read: "Here lies Bilbo, deep in the dirt he loved so well."'

Once when John Allen of Mississippi was standing for Congress, he agreed to debate with his opponent, one W. B.

Walker. Walker spoke first and said to the audience: 'Ladies and gentlemen, I want you to notice my opponent Mr Allen. Just look at him sitting over there, big and fat. He's literally pregnant on other people's money, he has been in Congress so long.' When Allen's time came to speak he patted his large stomach and said: 'What Mr Walker said is true about me being pregnant. If it's a girl I will name it Martha Washington. If it's a boy, I will name it George Washington, and if it's a jackass, I will name it W. B. Walker.'

For all candidates, most election campaigns have their difficulties. The reason is simple. It is impossible for a politician to express his opinion on the issues of the day without alienating some of his voters. The most successful constituency members are those who never talk politics in their own area, but confine themselves to issues where there is a broad consensus – such as improving the road network in the area, having the pavements resurfaced or, perhaps, campaigning for increased pensions. However, the general election public meeting is one occasion when a politician cannot avoid controversy, quite simply because he is certain to be asked a question on a current contentious issue. Texas Senator Tom Connally had a deft way of deflecting these questions. Once when he was in east Texas he was addressing an open-air crowd and his speech went down quite well. He was then asked a question by a farmer in the audience who said: 'How do you stand on the cotton issue?' Without a moment's hesitation Connally replied: 'I am OK on that one. Are there any other questions?'

⧗

AMERICAN PRESIDENT Calvin Coolidge was widely regarded as dull and inactive. Indeed, he even pleaded the case for political inaction when he said: 'In politics, if you see ten troubles coming down the road, you can be sure that nine of them will run into the ditch before they reach you.'

Not at all handsome, one opponent of Coolidge quipped that he 'looked as if he had been weaned on a pickle'.

When told that Coolidge had died, the wit Dorothy Parker asked: 'Well, how can you tell?'

On one occasion whilst serving as President, Coolidge visited a farm with his wife and they were given separate tours of the establishment. During her tour, Mrs Coolidge asked her host whether the cockerels copulated more than once a day. When she was told 'Yes, dozens of times' she remarked: 'Well, tell that to my husband.'

Upon being told of his wife's remark, the President asked: 'And is this with the same hen every time?'

'No, Mr President,' the farmer replied, 'it's with a different one each time.'

'Then,' said Coolidge, 'make sure you tell *that* to my wife.'

⬛

DURING A RAMBLING and almost incoherent speech made by a colleague in the Senate, Senator Eugene Millikin interrupted: 'If the distinguished Senator will allow me, I will try to extricate him from his thoughts.'

⬛

TAKING THE BLAME for an unfortunate decision by a subordinate, former American Present Harry S. Truman coined the phrase: 'The buck stops here.'

On trying to control children: 'I have found that the best way to give advice to your children, is to find out what they want and then advise them to do it.'

On himself: 'I am not sure that I managed it, but I did learn that a great leader is a man who has the ability to get other people to do what they don't want to do – and like it.'

'Men make history and not the other way round.'

Insulting himself: 'Well, my speech seems to have been a hit according to all the newspapers. It shows you never can tell. I thought it was rotten.'

Among his other comments, the following are worthy of note:

'Don't talk about rope in the house of somebody who has been hanged.'

'Whenever an elector tells me he's non-partisan, I know that he's going to vote against me.'

'Statesmen are more expendable than soldiers.'

Slapping down a journalist who was disparaging Truman's poor family background, Truman retorted: 'My father was not a failure. After all, he was the father of a President of the United States.'

To another journalist he barked: 'If you want to ask me an impudent question, that's all right. I will give you an impudent answer.'

On Richard Nixon's first attempt to become president: 'You don't send a fox to watch the chickens just because he has had a lot of experience in the hen house.'

Towards the end of the war he said: 'If we see that Germany is winning the war, we ought to help Russia, and if Russia is winning, we ought to help Germany, and in that way let them kill as many as possible.'

On his successor: 'Some of the newspapers are making snide remarks about Mrs Eisenhower saying she has a drinking problem. It wouldn't surprise me if she did because look what that poor woman has to put up with. She's married to a no-good son of a bitch.'

Accurately summing up the loneliness of the world's most powerful job: 'If you really want a friend in Washington, get a dog.'

Famous American cartoonist Al Capp, who created the character Li'l Abner, was attending a party when he was introduced by the hostess to Present Truman: 'Mr President, I'd like you to meet the famous comic strip cartoonist, Al Capp.' To which the President inquired: 'Which comic strip?'

The hostess turned to Mr Capp and said to him: 'I'd like to introduce you to President Truman.' To which Capp replied: 'Which country?'

☒

FORMER KENTUCKY SENATOR Alben Barkley, who was Harry Truman's Vice President, had been happily married for many years when he was asked what his formula was for a successful marriage. He replied: 'My wife and I have an agreement that she makes all the small decisions and I make all the big ones.' 'And have you ever argued?' a journalist asked. 'Never,' he replied, later adding: 'But then, we have never had to make a big decision.'

The Chairman of the Aluminum Association of America was not a Barkley fan and he found an effective way of deflating the Vice President after Barkley had made a prepared speech to the Association. Barkley thought he had done quite well but the Chairman rose from his seat and told the audience, 'I have three criticisms. In the first place, you read your speech. In the second place, you read it poorly. And in the third place, it wasn't worth reading,' before disappearing out of the door.

☒

DWIGHT D. EISENHOWER was US President between 1952 and 1960. A Second World War hero, the Republican leader became universally known as 'Ike' during his incumbency.

In his first address as President he said: 'A people that values its privileges above its principles soon loses both.'

On leadership: 'You do not lead by hitting people over the head – that's assault not leadership. Humility must always be the portion of any man who receives acclaim earned in the blood of his followers and the sacrifices of his friends.'

Amongst his other sayings the following are the best:

'The world moves and ideas that were good once are not always good.'

'Every gun that is made, every warship launched, every rocket fired signifies, in the final sense, a theft from those who hunger and are not fed, those who are cold and are not clothed.'

'The only way to win World War III is to prevent it.'

☒

DURING THE 1950s Republican Senator Wayne Morse decided to leave the Republican Party and join the Democrats. Clare Boothe Luce silenced him with the barb: 'Whenever a Republican joins the Democrats, it raises the intelligence quotient of both parties.'

Senator Smoot of Utah did not think much of British author D. H. Lawrence. Having read *Lady Chatterley's Lover*, he described Lawrence as 'a man with a soul so black that he would even obscure the darkness of hell'.

However, Smoot's aim to continue the ban on the book he regarded as obscene failed, causing a more liberal senator to remark: 'The United States has been officially lifted out of the infant class.'

During a particularly amusing debate in Congress, members of the public in the gallery started laughing so loud that it disrupted the proceedings. The presiding officer threatened to clear the galleries if the noise didn't cease, when Senator Barkley rose apparently to plead on behalf of the public, saying: 'I do not think that the Chair ought to be too hard on the galleries. When people go to a circus, they ought to be allowed to laugh at the monkey.'

This not only caused more laughter, but was quite a clever way of throwing an insult towards Senator Huey Long, who was speaking at the time.

☒

REPUBLICAN BARRY GOLDWATER was regarded by the majority of Americans as unelectable because of his extremist views. However, he did have the ability to encapsulate his arguments succinctly. He said: 'Minority groups now speak much more loudly than do majority groups which I classify as the forgotten American... the man who pays his taxes, prays, behaves himself, stays out of trouble and works for his government.'

Tired of being attacked as an 'extremist' by his opponents, who had claimed to be 'moderates', he said: 'May I remind you that extremism in the defence of liberty is no vice. And let me tell you that moderation in the pursuit of justice is not a virtue.'

During the early 1960s Goldwater came into confrontation with the Democratic Senator Hubert Humphrey. Humphrey of course regarded Goldwater as extremely right-wing and a reactionary. They met at a reception given in Hollywood for a movie company and Humphrey quipped: 'Senator Goldwater would have been a great success in the movies – working for Eighteenth Century Fox.'

Goldwater soon got his own back. Of Humphrey he remarked: 'He talks so fast that listening to him is like trying to read *Playboy* with your wife turning the pages.'

On Democratic President Lyndon B. Johnson: 'He fiddled while Detroit burned and he faddled while men died [in Vietnam].'

On state interference and 'big government': 'A government that is big enough to give you all you want is big enough to take it all away.'

⋈

HUBERT HUMPHREY is perhaps better remembered not as a Senator but as a failed presidential candidate. After his ambitions to enter the White House had been destroyed, he gave some good advice to losers: 'If you can't cry a bit in politics, the only other thing you'll have is hate.'

⧖

PRESIDENT JOHN F. KENNEDY may have been right when he claimed, 'Mothers all want their sons to grow up to be President – but they don't want them to become politicians in the process.'

And on Senator Everett Dirksen: 'The Wizard of Ooze.'

⧖

FORMER DEMOCRATIC President Lyndon Johnson did not think much of Jack Kennedy before Kennedy became President, saying of him: 'He's just a flash in the pan. The boy has no record of substance.'

And of former Kennedy aide Bob Griffin he thought even less: 'He's not going anywhere. That elongated son of a bitch looks down his nose at me like I'm shit. Every time I see him I almost go through the roof.'

In 1948, before Johnson had aspirations to become President, he stood for election to the United States Senate. He won, but by such a narrow margin that some of his opponents alleged that he had rigged the ballot. They referred to him sarcastically as 'Landslide Lyndon'.

These allegations led some Republicans to tell the story of a man who came across a small Mexican boy who was crying his heart out. 'Why are you crying?' asked the man. The Mexican lad replied, 'My daddy doesn't love me.' The man was rather amazed by this response as he knew the boy's father had been dead for some time. 'But your daddy is dead,' the man replied. 'Yes,' cried the lad, 'but he came back to vote for Lyndon Johnson and he didn't come to see me.'

Johnson was a ruthless politician. Before he became President, he ran into difficulties when fighting a primary election. It was in a state that was distant from his home and where he was not well known and he was fighting against a worthy opponent who was a church-going, respected pillar of society. Johnson, who was not making much impact, discussed with his campaign manager what he should do. During the meeting, Johnson suggested that they should leak the news to the press that their distinguished opponent had been guilty of vile sexual practices. His team were aghast and unanimous that it should not be done. 'It's not true,' an aide protested.

'No,' said Johnson, 'it's not, but I just want to hear him deny it.'

On Republican President Gerald Ford: 'He is a nice guy, but he played too much football with his helmet off.'

On when to trust colleagues: 'I never trust a man unless I've got his pecker in my pocket.'

On what life was like in the Oval Office: 'Being President is like being a jackass in a hailstorm. There's nothing to do but stand there and take it.'

On a speech by Republican Richard Nixon: 'I may not know much but I know chicken shit from chicken salad.'

On foreigners: 'They ain't like the folk you were reared with.'

On conquest: 'The best fertiliser for a piece of land is the footprints of its owner.'

⧗

WHEN SENATOR Robert Kennedy was standing in the Democratic presidential primaries in 1968 he was due to address a meeting of farmers. He arrived rather early and walked in to the back of the room, where he was unnoticed at first. He overheard some of the farmers grumbling about what a drain it would be on the budget 'if those nine or ten Kennedy children get into the White House'. Announcing his arrival, he then added: 'Yes, I've got ten kids and they all drink milk. Tell me anyone else who is doing that much for the farmer.'

Kennedy also quipped: 'One fifth of the people are against everything all the time.'

⧗

JAMES MICHAEL CURLEY, four times Mayor of Boston in the United States, was something of a rascal who didn't mind bending the rules to get his own way. His motto used to be: 'Do unto others as they wish to do unto you – but do it first.' One opponent whom Curley did it to first started to refer to him as 'old cabbage ears', and the name stuck.

His methods were unorthodox, but usually effective. Once, when his office was owed a large amount of money, he realised that he was unable to pay all of the city employees on time. He personally telephoned the chairman of the company who owed the debt and said: 'I have a nice picture of you at home and a nice picture of the beautiful house you have in the country. If I don't get the money for my payroll by this evening, I am going to print both these pictures in the local newspaper. Under your picture it will say "This is the man who is responsible for city employees not being paid", and under the picture of your house it will say "And this is where he lives".' He then put down the phone. The ruse worked and Curley got his money on time.

His view of Tip O'Neill was extremely basic: 'He's a fat bastard.'

⧗

SENATOR EUGENE MCCARTHY on being a successful politician: 'It is like being a football coach. You have to be smart enough to understand the game and dumb enough to think it's important.'

⧗

FORMER US PRESIDENT Richard Nixon was always a controversial figure. On politics he remarked: 'There is one thing solid and fundamental in politics – the law of change. What's "up" today is "down" tomorrow.'

His advice to young politicians was: 'Always remember

others may hate you but those who hate you don't win unless you hate them. And then you destroy yourself.'

And his maxim for political success: 'To be popular in office, you need an enemy. Reagan had the USSR and Congress. Clinton, as yet, has not found one.'

His thumbnail assessment of former Russian President Boris Yeltsin: 'He burns all his candles at both ends and he is compulsive. I give him only slightly more than a 50 per cent chance of success. But he's got guts.'

To an aide: 'Use all the rhetoric, so long as it doesn't cost money.'

And: 'Voters quickly forget what a man says.'

Harry Truman disliked Nixon, calling him a 'no-good lying bastard' and adding for good measure: 'He can lie out of both sides of his mouth at the same time, and even if he caught himself telling the truth, he'd lie just to keep his hand in.'

Despite a landslide re-election victory Nixon never completed his second term, being forced to resign in disgrace following the Watergate hearings. Shortly before his death, showing that he still had a sense of humour, he said: 'I hear that whenever anyone in the White House tells a lie, I get a royalty.'

On political speeches: 'I have often said that the best political speech is poetry. Jesse Jackson is a poet but Michael Dukakis[*] is a word-processor.'

American car sticker in 1960, when J. F. Kennedy was the Democratic candidate and Richard Nixon was standing for the Republicans: 'Thank God only one of them can win!'

At the time of Nixon's troubles over Watergate, graffiti seen on a wall in Washington read: 'Where is Lee Harvey Oswald now that his country needs him?'[†]

On his predecessor: 'People said that my language was bad, but Jesus, you should have heard LBJ.'

---

[*]   Democratic presidential contender in 1988 who lost to George Bush Sr.
[†]   President Kennedy's assassin.

Silencing a heckler: 'The jaw-bone of an ass is just as dangerous a weapon today as in Samson's time.'

Amongst Nixon's best quips are the following:

'Never strike a king unless you kill him. In politics you shouldn't hit your opponent unless you knock him out.'

'The successful leader does not talk down to people. He lifts them up.'

'A man is not finished when he is defeated. He is finished when he quits.'

'A good politician knows not only how to count votes but how to make his vote count.'

And amongst the best from anonymous commentators on Nixon:

'He's the kind of guy who would call in phoney reprieves to death row.'

'Nixon has one simple political principle: if two wrongs don't make a right – try a third.'

'Nixon told us he was going to take crime off the streets. He did. He took it into the White House.'

'Nixon impeached himself – he gave us Ford as his revenge.'

Richard Nixon should have heeded the words of John G. Diefenbaker, former Prime Minister of Canada, who said 'Freedom is the right to be wrong, not the right to do wrong.'

During the term of office of President Nixon, a Republican Senator wanted Congress to appropriate $600 million to help bring the nation's sewage disposal system up to date. He knew that President Nixon was opposed to the measure and, therefore, he prepared a well-argued and detailed speech on the subject, in which he discussed household effluent and the waste-disposal systems in some detail.

When he finished his address, New Hampshire Senator Norris Cotton approached him and said: 'I never realised until now what you're an expert on, but now I know.' 'What's that, Norris?' asked the Senator. Cotton responded tersely: 'Shit.' The senator was nonplussed for a moment and then recovered the situation with his response: 'Norris, can you think of anything more important to be an expert on in the Senate than that?'

⧗

AMERICAN PRESIDENT Gerald Ford was frequently ridiculed in satire shows for his clumsiness. However, occasionally he put his detractors in their place. He once said: 'A bronco is something that kicks and bucks, twists and turns, and very seldom goes in one direction. We have one of those things here in Washington – it's called the Congress.'

One story told in Washington was how when President Ford was due to take a trip on Air Force One, he couldn't remember the number of the flight.

It was also said of him: 'Gerald Ford was unknown throughout America until he became President. Now he's unknown throughout the world.'

Ford was not, however, without wit himself. He once said of Senator and presidential hopeful Hubert Humphrey: 'I can still remember the first time I ever heard him speak. He was in the second hour of a five-minute talk.'

Ford served in Congress before achieving his country's highest office. Once, when Hubert Humphrey was making a lengthy speech, Ford, who had just entered the chamber, asked his neighbour: 'What follows Humphrey?' He received the riposte: 'Christmas.'

Humphrey acknowledged that he was often long-winded, remarking to one colleague: 'I can't even clear my throat in less than three minutes.'

⧗

RICHARD NIXON'S Vice President Spiro Agnew must have sounded somewhat like Leonard Sachs of TV's *The Good Old*

Days when he said his opponents in Congress were 'pusillanimous pussyfooters', adding for good measure: 'They are nattering nabobs of negativism.'

※

IN 1973 beef prices in America were soaring. In order to try to protect the consumer, Congressman Frank Annunzio from Chicago introduced an amendment in committee to freeze the price of beef. Somewhat to his surprise the amendment was passed.

Afterwards he was interviewed by the *Wall Street Journal* and he expressed his pleasure at the successful amendment adding, 'This is a victory for the American people.'

However, as is often the case in politics, his victory was short-lived. Overnight, beef farmers went into action and started lobbying politicians. They were so successful that the next day the committee voted to reconsider Annunzio's amendment and decided to reject it.

The same reporter from the *Wall Street Journal* sought out the Chicago congressman and asked him again for his reaction now that his amendment had been rejected. Rather tersely Annunzio stated: 'The American people got fucked.' The shocked reporter protested: 'I can't use that quote – this is a family newspaper.' Turning to leave, Annunzio snapped, 'In that case, tell them the American *family* got fucked,' and walked off.

※

THE USE of the insult during an election campaign can backfire, particularly if the public perceive that the gibe is unfair or just downright nasty. Governor Pat Brown of California, when challenged at the polls by Ronald Reagan, ran a series of insulting television adverts that opened with the line 'I am running against an actor... and you know who killed Abraham

Lincoln, don't you?'. This backfired badly and Reagan won the subsequent election by a landslide.

Reagan's more restrained retort to Pat Brown was: 'He is one of those liberals* who thinks that all the world's problems can be solved by throwing taxpayers' money at them.'

Reagan was known as 'The Great Communicator' due to his consummate skill on television, and also, on Capitol Hill, as 'The Great Persuader' because of his ability to persuade a number of Democrats, who controlled Congress, to agree to his programme. Despite the fact that he never had a majority in the House, Reagan managed to push through most of his manifesto by splitting the opposition.

His popularity was – and is – undoubtedly due to the fact that he came over on television as 'a nice guy' – someone totally free of malice. However, when he thought the occasion demanded it, he was not afraid to use invective to make his point. Before the collapse of Communism he caused a furore when he referred to the USSR as 'the evil empire'. Liberal opinion was similarly outraged in 1986 when he referred to Iran as 'Murder Incorporated'.

His view of Gaddafi's regime in Libya is similarly robust: 'We are not going to tolerate these attacks from states run by the strangest collection of misfits, loony tunes, and squalid criminals since the advent of the Third Reich.' He later said of Gaddafi: 'Not only a barbarian but flaky.'

During his time as Governor of California, Reagan was faced with a delegation of students who took over his office. Some were barefooted, several were wearing torn T-shirts and when the Governor entered the room, no one stood up. The ringleader said to Reagan: 'We want to talk to you but we think it's impossible for you to understand us. You weren't raised in a time of instant communications or satellites and

---

* The word 'liberal' has a different connotation in USA politics to its UK meaning. Reagan was being derogatory. Our equivalent description would be 'left-winger'.

computers, solving problems in seconds. We now live in an age of space travel and journeys to the moon, of jet travel and high speed electronics. You didn't have those things when you were young...'

At this point Reagan interrupted the student spokesman and said: 'No, we didn't have those things when we were your age – we invented them.' Not only did Reagan silence the students but he let it be known that his only policy would be that they should 'obey the rules or get out'.

Just before he became President, Reagan made a devastating attack on his predecessor, telling a crowd: 'A depression is when you're out of work. A recession is when your neighbour is out of work. And a recovery is when Jimmy Carter is out of work.'

Amongst his one-liners, the following are the best:

'Nothing lasts longer than a temporary government programme.'

'Government does not generate revenue, it merely consumes it.'

'Origins matter less than our destination. That is what democracy is all about.'

'Government is just like a big baby – a big appetite at one end and no responsibility at the other.'

'A friend of mine was invited to a fancy dress ball recently. He slapped some egg on his face and went as a left-wing economist.'

During his presidency Reagan maintained his friendships with the world of show business. Once, at a White House banquet, he found himself talking to old friend Bob Hope, a golf fanatic. Hope inquired whether Reagan had any time for golf and asked the President: 'What's your handicap?' Reagan shot back: 'Congress.'

On former Speaker of the House Tip O'Neill: 'He could be sincere and friendly when he wanted to be, but he could also turn off his charm and friendship like a light-switch and become as blood-thirsty as a piranha.'

On his former Secretary of State Alexander Haig: 'He could pound the table and seemed ready to explode. He was insecure. I thought he was seeing shadows in a mirror.'

During the 1984 presidential race, when Reagan was seeking re-election, his opponent Walter Mondale jibed: 'I don't like to attack Ronald Reagan as being too old for the job, but I remember that in his first movie Gabby Hayes got the girl.'

These jokes about Reagan's age backfired however. During the televised presidential debate, a journalist asked Reagan outright, 'Will age be an issue in this election?' Reagan gently replied: 'I am not prepared, for party political advantage, to make reference to the "youth" and "inexperience" of my opponent.' Even his rival Mondale could not help laughing at this response and from then on the 'age' issue was never mentioned again in the campaign.

During his period as President and before the Berlin Wall was pulled down, one of Reagan's favourite stories was of Leonid Brezhnev on his death bed giving advice to his successor Andropov. Raising himself on one arm Brezhnev said: 'Let me give you one piece of advice. When you take over from me, make sure in whatever you do that the Soviet people follow you.' At which point Andropov replied to the dying Brezhnev: 'Don't worry. If they don't follow me, I'll make sure that they follow you.'

On the USSR before the Berlin Wall came down: 'I think at last President Gorbachev realised he was head of an economic basket case.'

In the 1988 American presidential race, responding to a journalist's reference to his young age for such high office, Dan Quayle, then candidate for the vice-presidency, pointed out that John Kennedy was of a similar age when he stood for the presidency. This led the Democratic Vice Presidential candidate Lloyd Benstsen to say, 'I knew President Kennedy, and Senator you're no Jack Kennedy.' The insult hurt but it was not until four years later that a Republican politician turned the insult back upon the Democrats. On the opening day of the Republican convention in 1992, Reagan referred to Bill Clinton's claim that he was the new Thomas Jefferson, and added: 'I knew Thomas Jefferson. He was a friend of mine – and Governor Clinton, you ain't no Thomas Jefferson.'

Early in his presidency even his opponents were impressed by Reagan's first televised budget speech, in which he used a handful of small change to illustrate the effects of inflation on the value of the dollar. A Democratic rival observed: 'Carter would have emphasised all the wrong words. Ford would have fumbled and dropped the cash – and Nixon would have pocketed it.'

On the problems he faced in office: 'In this present crisis government is not the solution to our problems. Government is the problem.'

On his political opponents: 'The leaders of the Democratic Party have gone so far left, they've left the country.'

After Bill Clinton had admitted that he smoked pot whilst a student, though he claimed he had not inhaled, Reagan gave some advice to his supporters on the Democratic candidate's election promises: 'When you hear all of that smoky rhetoric billowing out of Clinton's headquarters, take the advice of their nominee – don't inhale.'

Once more giving his views of government: 'Governments tend not to solve problems, only rearrange them.'

One quality Reagan possessed in abundance was his sense of humour. Asked his view on the abortion issue, he quipped: 'I notice that everyone who is for abortion has already been born.'

And, commenting on the bid, ultimately successful, by actor Clint Eastwood to become Mayor of the California town of Carmel: 'What makes him think that a middle-aged actor who's played with a chimp could possibly have a future in politics?'

Former Labour minister Denis (now Lord) Healey was not impressed with Reagan's economic record, saying: 'He has done for monetarism what the Boston Strangler did for door-to-door salesmen.'

Veteran Republican Barry Goldwater was similarly unimpressed: 'He can't decide whether he was born in a log cabin or a manger.'

Reagan was disarming, amiable and approachable both before during and after he served as US President. He showed none of the petulance that is sometimes associated with those who achieve high office. Once, when a lowly TV cameraman asked for a photograph with the President, his colleague had a problem focusing the camera and became embarrassed for keeping Reagan waiting. 'Don't worry about it,' Reagan smiled, 'everybody's got to make a dollar.'

Reagan's popularity continues to rise around the world and since his death in 2004 many former critics are now prepared to admit that he was indeed one of America's great presidents. In 2011 a statue was erected in London to mark the centenary of his birth.

⧗

FORMER PRESIDENT George Bush Senior had a vicious line on his Democratic opponent during the 1992 election: 'I consulted with John Major and other leaders on foreign policy issues – Bill Clinton took advice from Boy George.'

In a similar vein, again on Clinton: 'While I bit the bullet, he bit his nails. His policy can be summed on by a road sign he's probably seen: "Slippery when wet". He says he's for one thing and then comes out for another. He's like that on a lot of issues – first one side then the other. He's been spotted in more places than Elvis Presley.'

During his first election campaign in 1988: 'My opponent has a problem. He won't get elected unless things get worse – and things won't get worse unless he gets elected.'

On Andrew Young: 'He is a loose cannon on a rolling deck.'

On Clinton's policies: 'He says he wants to tax the rich, but he defines rich as anyone who has a job. You've heard of the separation of powers. Well Bill Clinton practices a different theory – the power of separations. His government would have the power to separate you from your wallet.'

And returning to his Presley theme: 'Clinton's plan for America really is 'Elvis economics' – the country will be checking into the Heartbreak Hotel!'

On talking to the press: 'Never answer a hypothetical question – it gets you to beyond where you want to be.'

On his US defence policy: 'Giving peace a chance does not mean taking a chance with peace.'

During the 1992 presidential election, Bush called the Democratic team 'a couple of bozos', which led to the retort from President Clinton: 'All I can say is a bozo makes people laugh and Bush makes people cry... and America is going to be laughing on election night.'

His comments before polling day on the way the Clinton campaign was conducted could with hindsight be applied to his own performance. He unwisely remarked: 'It reminds me of the old conman's advice to the new kid when he said, "Son, if you're being run out of town, just get in front and make it look like a parade."'

The penchant of a free press to exaggerate bad news is well-known. Lord Tombs, former Rolls Royce boss, once startled a group of reporters by announcing: 'Gentleman, I have a problem for you. We have just won a massive order which secures hundreds of jobs. As I therefore have only *good* news to announce, you won't have a typeface small enough for the story.'

After months of gloomy news reports, just before his failed re-election bid, Bush, in a similar vein, remarked: 'When the Berlin Wall fell, I half expected to see a headline "Wall falls, three border guards lose jobs".'

It was once said of President George Bush Sr by an opponent that he was: 'All hat and no cattle.'

FORMER AMERICAN Vice President Dan Quayle has often been the butt-end of press criticism and political sniping from the Democrats.

However, it is Quayle himself who has generally given his detractors the ammunition. During the early stages of the 1992 presidential election, he misspelt potato as 'potatoe'. This led to howls of derision from his opponents, which Quayle tried to turn back against the Democrats by quipping: 'If Bill Clinton is a moderate, then I am a world-champion speller.'

This was a good come-back line but even his own supporters began to despair of him after the following gaffes:

'There's a lot of uncharted waters in space.'

'If we do not succeed, then we run the risk of failure.'

And on visiting Latin America, he astonished the press by saying: 'The only regret I have was that I didn't study Latin harder in school so I could converse with these people.'

⧗

THOMAS 'TIP' O'NEILL, former Speaker of the House of Representatives, was for many years one of America's most colourful public figures. He retired in 1986 having served for thirty-four years as a member of Congress, ten of those as Speaker – the longest continuous term in the United States.

On Christian Herter, a former politician from Massachusetts: 'He was extremely partisan. The rules, as he understood them said "screw the Democrats".'

On John F. Kennedy: 'The first time I met Jack Kennedy I couldn't believe this skinny pasty-looking kid was a candidate for anything! He had absolutely no political experience. Although he was a Democrat, looking back I'd say he was only nominally a Democrat. He was a Kennedy, which was more than a family affiliation. It quickly developed into an entire political party. He certainly knew how to charm the ladies and he always made a point of appealing to what he called "womanpower" – the untapped resource.'

On Bobby Kennedy: 'He was a self-important upstart and a know-it-all. Jack Kennedy had not grown up in the school of hard knocks. He was used to people loving him and if somebody said something mean about him and it got back to him, he would wonder why they didn't like him. But with Bobby... when Bobby hated you, you stayed hated.'

On former Congressman Howard Smith of Virginia: 'A taciturn, arrogant son of a bitch who was no more a Democrat than the man in the moon. As far as he was concerned, the civil war was still going on.'

On former President Lyndon Johnson: 'As a professional politician he had the right idea but he was crude about it. His political style was overwhelming and there was nothing subtle about it.'

On the Kennedy–Johnson relationship: 'The Vice-Presidency is never an easy office to occupy but it rankled Johnson that this young, rich upstart was in the White House while he, who had come up the hard way, was the all-but-forgotten number two man.'

On former presidential hopeful Eugene McCarthy: 'He was a whimsical fellow with a meanness in his heart. He was lazy and a bit of a dreamer. He had the support of all the way-out flaky Liberals in the country.'

On Wayne Hayes, a former congressman: 'He was an excellent orator but had a mean streak and was often abusive to people he didn't agree with. Even when he praised you he did it with a nasty twist. When he resigned from Congress most of us were delighted to see him go.'

On the American news reporting team of Evans and Novak: 'They ought to be called "Errors and No facts".'

On politics: 'Power is never given – it is only taken.'

On former President Richard Nixon: 'He was brilliant but he had a quirk in his personality that made him suspicious of everybody – including members of his own cabinet. He was a leery and nervous president.'

On former President Gerald Ford: 'Although he was wrong most of the time, he was decently wrong.'

On former presidential hopeful George McGovern: 'His nomination was a disaster. He never should have been selected as the Democratic candidate but he was chosen by the cast of *Hair*. I was absolutely shocked when the young people in the party picked him as their champion. The party has an occasional suicidal tendency and you didn't need to be a pollster like Harris to see that McGovern was going to get creamed. In the eyes of many Americans, George McGovern was so far to the left he was off the map.'

On former President Jimmy Carter: 'He came in young and vigorous but left a tired man. When it came to the politics of Washington, he never really understood how the system worked – he didn't want to learn about it either. He rode into town like a knight on a white horse, but while the gentleman leading the charge was capable, too many of the troops he brought with him were amateurs. But that didn't prevent them from being arrogant. Too many of his aides – especially his Chief of Staff Hamilton Jordan – came to Washington with a chip on their shoulder and never changed. Those guys came in like a bunch of jerks and went out the same way.'

And warming to his main target, Mr Jordan: 'He is a son of a bitch. As far as he is concerned, the House Speaker is something you bought on sale at Radio Shack. I prefer to call him Hannibal Jerken.'

When O'Neill became Speaker of the United States House of Representatives, a young congressman asked him why he was not being included in the decision making. O'Neill shot back: 'Although I take you seriously, you must remember that when a storm comes along, I don't want to grab on to a young sapling that sways in the wind. In difficult times, I prefer to go along with the sturdy old oak.'

On the difference between the two houses in the US Congress: 'Congressmen are the workhorses while senators are the show horses.'

On political lobbying: 'I believe that public protest is more effective than a silent majority. I am convinced that the squeaky wheel gets the grease.'

And expanding his views on the subject: 'When someone asks me why the Greeks in America always get a hearing for their side, and the Turks can't get anywhere, I will say: "That's because nobody knows a Turk, but everybody knows the people who run all those restaurants." It's the same with the Arab–Israeli conflict. The experts can come up with a dozen reasons to explain why America supports Israel, usually that Israel is the only true democracy in the Middle East or that the Soviet Union used to provide huge arms shipments to Israel's enemies. That might be true enough, but to the average American it often boils down to something more basic – the fact that some of his friends and neighbours happen to be Jewish. The answer is simple. All politics is local.'

Amongst his other comments the following are worthy of note:

'The press, in its cynical way, loves to portray just about every congressional trip as a junket.'

'Money is the mother's milk of politics.'

On the office of President: 'What Jimmy Carter failed to understand is that the American people want a magisterial air in the White House which explains why the Kennedys and the Reagans were far more popular than the Carters and the Lyndon Johnsons – most people prefer a little pomp in their Presidents.'

On former President Ronald Reagan: 'The press saw Lyndon Johnson as crude, Richard Nixon as a liar, Gerald Ford as a bumbler, Jimmy Carter as incompetent, but they were certainly rooting for Ronald Reagan. Reagan has enormous personal appeal and he quickly became a folk hero. He performed so beautifully on the tube that he could sell anything but he has been a rich man's President. He has shown no care or compassion for the poor, but when it comes to giving money to the Pentagon or tax breaks to the wealthy, Reagan has a heart of gold. He is Herbert Hoover with a smile. He is a cheerleader for selfishness.'

Continuing his attack on Reagan, he did concede the former President's strengths: 'In 1986 he started singing that familiar song that those Americans who were out of work could get jobs if they really wanted to. I couldn't believe he was still spouting this nonsense. This was Ronald Reagan at his worst, but later that same day I saw the President at his best. After our first meeting the space shuttle *Challenger* exploded after take-off and that evening the President went on television. He made a masterly speech and as I listened to him, I had a tear in my eye and a lump in my throat. Ronald Reagan may have lacked some of the management skills that a President needs, but he's the best public speaker ever and in this respect he dwarfs both Roosevelt and Kennedy.'

On his own philosophy: 'I'm against any deal I'm not in on.'

On the congressmen elected on the coat-tails of President Reagan's popularity: 'They were nothing – just Reagan Robots.'

Television can be deceptive. As Margaret Thatcher once said: 'Selective seeing is believing.' After the United States Congress admitted television cameras, a number of representatives would take advantage of the 'Special Orders' procedure to attack their opponents. This is a part of the day in Congress which is similar to the adjournment debate in the British House of Commons. It is a period at the end of the day's business where any member is entitled to take the floor and to speak for up to an hour (in the British House of Commons it is usually limited to thirty minutes) on any subject of his choosing. On most occasions the House chamber is empty and Special Orders speeches are usually made for consumption back in the constituency. On one occasion Robert Walker, a Congressman from Pennsylvania, used his speech to attack another Congressman whom he knew had left the building. He attacked his colleague's voting record and generally criticised him. Under the rules of Congress, the television camera was focused only on Walker, so anyone watching TV at home would assume that not only was the House full, but that also the politician being insulted was sitting, inert, just listening to the diatribe. To encourage this perception, Walker would pause from time to time as if to give his opponent the chance to reply. The inference drawn by the viewer was that the man being slagged off was actually accepting by his silence the criticism being levelled.

Walker might have got away with this but for the fact that Tip O'Neill, then House Speaker, was watching the perform-ance from the television monitor in his office. O'Neill called the director of television and told him to pan the cameras around the entire chamber. He did so and the television viewer then saw that the chamber was empty. Walker's tactics, there-fore, backfired badly, although he and his fellow Republicans did lodge a complaint against O'Neill for altering the rules of transmission. O'Neill had the last word by publicly rebuking Walker and his colleague, Congressman Gingrich, for attempt-ing to deceive the public.

⧗

FORMER CONGRESSMAN John Le Boutillier had a sharp tongue for nearly everyone. Commenting on Harvard University he said: 'The University is filled with hypocritical, bleeding-heart Leftists.'

At the time of his election in 1980 Le Boutillier, who was only twenty-seven, was the youngest member of Congress but that didn't stop him from insulting some senior US politicians. He referred to President Carter as a 'complete bird-brain', Democratic presidential hopeful George McGovern was dismissed as 'scum', and he called Speaker Tip O'Neill 'big, fat, and out of control – just like the Federal Government'.

He even went to the unusual lengths of campaigning against the Speaker's re-election using the slogan 'Repeal O'Neill'. Despite this O'Neill was comfortably re-elected.

⧗

THE FIRST female mayor of Ottowa, Charlotte Whitton, commenting on what it is like being a woman in politics, said: 'Whatever women do they must do twice as well as men to be thought half as good. Luckily, this is not difficult.'

⧗

AUTHOR PHILIP STERN caused a furore in 1998 with his book *The Best Congress Money Can Buy*. To attempt to make his point he put a one-dollar note inside 509 copies of his book and posted them to all members of Congress.

A few of the dollars were returned with brief notes from the congressmen concerned saying that they could not accept cash, some congressmen kept the money and the book, but Stern was surprised with the letter he received from Jerry Lewis, the Californian Republican representative who returned the dollar note wrapped in toilet paper. In an accompanying letter Lewis wrote: 'Anyone who presumes that people who seek to serve in public affairs can have their principles purchased by one dollar, or one thousand dollars, should look into the mirror and carefully measure their own character.' Senator Jesse Helms went one better. He kept the dollar and wrote back: 'I don't resent your implication that Congress can be "bought" because I am willing to assume that you have some exceptions in mind and that I am one of the exceptions.'

⧗

A MISSISSIPPI CONGRESSMAN, Robert Roberts, was once assailed by a constituent who complained that he took little part in debates in the House of Representatives while other congressmen made many speeches and attracted a lot of national attention. Roberts took his constituent to task, replying: 'When I was a young man, I used to ride a horse and whenever I came to the bank of a stream, I put my ear to the ground and ascertained whether water made a noise. At that place, I always marched in – it was sure to be the shallowest place.' And with that he walked off.

⧗

ALTHOUGH MOST politicians are adept at the art of the putdown, sometimes they receive their comeuppance from a most unusual quarter. In 1987 Senator Bill Bradley was having a meal and asked the waiter for more butter. He was duly given an extra pat. Later on he asked the same waiter if he could have yet more butter, to which the waiter replied: 'Sorry, but I have already given you two portions.' Bradley turned upon the waiter and said: 'I don't think you know who I am. I am Bill Bradley the Rhodes scholar, ex-professional basketball player, a world champion, and now United States Senator.' Without batting an eyelid the waiter replied: 'Well, perhaps you don't know who I am.' Bradley exploded: 'Well, I don't. Who are you?' To which the waiter replied, 'Well, I'm the man who's in charge of the butter,' before disappearing out of the dining-room.

⧗

THE OFFICE of Vice President of the United States of America is perhaps the most maligned position in any democracy. Franklin D. Roosevelt said that the job was 'the spare tyre in the US government'.

Roosevelt's Vice President was John Nance Garner, who said that 'a great man may be a vice president, but he can't be a great vice president because the office in itself is unimportant'.

President Kennedy summed up why the post can be an unrewarding one: 'The vice-presidency is the worst of both worlds. You don't have any power and the Secret Service is always on your tail.'

Lyndon Johnson had practical experience of the job. He was VP to Kennedy before becoming President himself following Kennedy's assassination. He thought even less of the number two job saying that it 'wasn't worth a pitcher of warm piss'.

Earlier, John Adams, the first US Vice President, said: 'My country has in its wisdom contrived for me the most insignificant office that has ever been conceived by the imagination of man.'

Referring to the Vice President's duty of having to preside over sittings of the Senate, Adams continued: 'It is a punishment to have to hear other men talk five hours every day and not be at liberty to talk at all oneself.'

Harry Truman, who was Franklin D. Roosevelt's third Vice President, had a similar turn of phrase to Johnson, though marginally less crude: 'They are about as useful as a cow's fifth teat.'

Roosevelt appeared to share these sentiments. Once, when a tinkling chandelier in the White House disturbed his slumbers, he ordered the staff to remove it. When he was asked what should be done with the offending item he said: 'Take it to the Vice President – he needs something to keep him awake.'

Walter Mondale, whose challenge for the presidency against Ronald Reagan ended in disaster, had previously served as Vice President. He shared the views previously expressed about the office. He often told the story about a man who lived near Three Mile Island who had been assured by an expert that the area was safe from radioactivity 'because the President had visited the area'. When the man questioned this and asked: 'What makes you think that that proves it is safe?' He received the response: 'If it wasn't safe, they would have sent the Vice President.'

⧖

A CANDIDATE for a North Carolina constituency called Frank Grist was furious when the local paper wrote an article which concluded: 'Frank Grist is not qualified to be a dog catcher.' On the advice of his lawyer he sent a telegram to the newspaper threatening to sue for libel unless it retracted its comments. The paper duly obliged and in the next edition carried the following: 'Frank Grist is fit to be a dog catcher, but instead of running for that office, he is seeking the post of United States Senator.

⌛

TAKING A SWIPE at education wets, Republican Representative John Ashbrook said: 'A Harvard professor is an educator who thinks that the American eagle has two left wings.'

⌛

THE FORMER United States Senator for Ohio, Stephen Young, once received a letter saying: 'You are a stupid fool for favouring gun control. I am sure you could walk upright under a snake's tail with your hat on and have plenty of headroom.' The constituent also gave his address and telephone number and said: 'I would welcome the opportunity to have intercourse with you.'

Young rose to this insult and replied: 'Sir, I am in receipt of your most insulting letter, and I note your offer in the final paragraph where you welcome the opportunity of me having intercourse with you. No, indeed. You go ahead and have intercourse with yourself.'

Young also said to a local lawyer who insisted on giving him some advice as to how he should vote: 'Don't give me any more of this unsolicited advice. I know it costs nothing, but that is exactly what it's worth.'

Summing up his own philosophy he said: 'Sarcasm is the sour cream of wit.'

⌛

A STORY is told in the lower house of a Congressman and his wife who were fast asleep in bed when a noise from downstairs woke her. Waking the Congressman from his slumbers, she said, 'Darling, I think there's a thief in the house.'

Ignoring her and turning over he said: 'Maybe in the Senate, my dear, but certainly not the House.'

⧗

FORMER REPUBLICAN SENATOR and one-time presidential candidate Bob Dole was a formidable politician. I met him on a number of occasions and found him both impressive and witty; however, he has a vicious tongue which spares no one. Not even himself! This has led to him earning the nickname 'Hatchet man'.

When Dole was the running-mate of President Gerald Ford in 1976, he unintentionally damaged his own chances during a debate with his opponent Walter Mondale, when he snapped: 'If we added up all those killed and wounded in Democrat wars in this century, it would be about 1.6 million Americans – enough to fill the City of Detroit.' The description of several world conflicts as 'Democrat' wars didn't hurt Mondale, it hurt Dole – and he knew it. He later admitted: 'I was supposed to go for the jugular and I did – my own.'

In 1972, he was chairman of the Republican National Committee when the Watergate scandal broke. Asked what he knew about it he quipped: 'I don't know, I was pulling a job in Chicago that night.' He later went on: 'Well, we got the burglar vote.' Shortly after this he was dismissed by President Nixon and the role of Chairman was given to George Bush.

Facing Senate re-election in 1974, Dole was worried that the fall-out from Watergate might affect his chance of re-election. His Democratic opponent was Dr Bill Roy, a Roman Catholic who not only supported abortion but who, as a doctor of medicine, had performed a number of abortions as well. During the campaign when Dole spoke at Roman

Catholic Schools, he would say to the children, 'When you go home, ask your mother if she knows how many abortions Dr Roy has performed.' Dole won the election.

On the US Congress: 'The first month I was there, I wondered how I ever got in. And ever since I've been wondering how the rest of them got in.'

When Dole ran for his party's presidential nomination against George Bush Sr, some party members were concerned that his virulent attacks on Bush would damage the chances of both men. Answering this criticism Dole snapped: 'I will stop telling the truth about Bush, if he stops telling lies about me.'

After a meeting between three ex-presidents Dole commented: 'At a party a few weeks ago, I saw Carter, Ford and Nixon – See No Evil, Hear No Evil and Evil.'

When it was revealed that Richard Nixon had taped all of his White House conversations, Dole joked: 'Thank goodness whenever I was in the Oval Office I only nodded.'

And when President Carter blocked grain sales to the Soviet Union after it had invaded Afghanistan, Dole barked: 'Carter took a poke at the Soviet bear and knocked out the American farmer.'

On fellow Republican, former President George Bush Sr: 'He's never had to do a day's work in his life.'

And, again on Bush the first: 'He never leaves any footprints, wherever he goes.'

During the Gulf War, he slammed the Democrats: 'The Republican strategy is to get Saddam Hussein out of Kuwait. Some of the Democrats' strategy appears to be to get Bush out of the White House.'

On the Clinton administration's changes of direction: 'Clinton's policies need to be checked hourly.'

Amongst his best remarks are the following:

On one of his own rather lacklustre and subdued performances: 'I was heavily sedated. It was my night to be nice to everybody.'

'The life jacket of one generation can become the strait-jacket of the next.'

On the diminutive Senator John Tower: 'I got a standing ovation from him once and I didn't know the difference.'

And a similarly size-ist remark on Senator Howard Baker, who was one of his rivals for the 1980 Republican Presidential nomination until Baker dropped out of the race: 'He can always open up a tall men's clothing store – in Japan.'

'Shame is a powerful weapon.'

On President Jimmy Carter: 'Southern fried McGovern.'[*]

Dole later said: 'I take back calling Jimmy Carter "Chicken-fried McGovern"... because I've come to respect McGovern.'

On Carter's administration: 'We've had the New Deal, the Fair Deal and now Carter wants to give us a fast deal... that will surely end in an ordeal.'

'Good news is, a bus full of supply-siders went over the cliff. Bad news is, there were three empty seats.'

Dole had a long-running verbal feud with the high profile Democrat Senator Edward Kennedy, calling him 'a phoney, a limousine liberal, a big spender raised on a silver spoon'.

On another occasion he sniped: 'Ted Kennedy thinks "The Chins Syndrome" is what you get after eating too much chop suey.'

Alluding to Kennedy's high-profile difficulties, in various outbursts, he famously said the following of him:

'He needs a bridge over troubled waters.'

'He always tries to make a big splash.'

'Ted Kennedy is a candidate with a deliberate, thoroughly worked out game plan for winning the Democratic nomination – for whatever that nomination is worth. His plan calls for [other] Democratic presidential candidates to exhaust each other's resources in an inconclusive series of primary battles, so they'll turn to a man who wouldn't get his feet wet. In

---

[*] A reference to the extremely left-wing democrat George McGovern.

short what we want from him is a little less profile and a little more courage.'

On Democrat Attorney-General Ramsey Clark: 'A left-leaning marshmallow.'

On what to do about fat-cat business supporters: 'Take their money and screw 'em.'

On President Clinton's plan to balance the American budget in ten years: 'There are two ways to get to the top of an oak tree. One is to climb. The other is to find an acorn and sit on it.'

Of course, over the years Dole has made enemies, some of them in his own party. A fellow Republican who was asked to define Dole's views said: 'Oh, that's easy. Bob just waits to see which way the wind is blowing.' Dole himself once appeared to agree with this verdict, commenting, 'If you're looking for ideology – there's Ronald Reagan.'

Finally, Dole on politics: 'You've got to make hard choices if you're going to be a leader. But if you just want to be a politician you vote no against all the hard things and you vote yes for all the easy things and then you go out and make speeches about how tough you are.'

⧗

USA SENATOR Phil Gramm on balancing the state books: 'Balancing the budget is like going to heaven. Everybody wants to do it, but nobody wants to do what you have to do to get there.'

⧗

FORMER CALIFORNIA Governor Republican Pete Wilson on his Democratic opponents: 'They can kiss my rear end – if they can leap that high.'

⧗

FORMER PRESIDENT Bill Clinton was, during his term of office, perpetually dogged by allegations of impropriety, both sexual and financial. It was perhaps not surprising therefore that he was dubbed 'The Prince of Sleaze' and 'Slick Willie'.

Although the Paula Jones sexual harassment case against Clinton was thrown out by the US courts in April 1998, no sooner had this occurred than the Monica Lewinsky scandal took off.

On the political dinner circuit a regular and popular joke at the time was: 'Gallup pollsters interviewed 100 women and asked them if they would sleep with Bill Clinton if it would enhance their career – and 98 replied "Never again".'

In summer 1998, after the allegations were made that Clinton had had an affair with White House aide Monica Lewinsky, some were saying that the affair, if proved, could turn out to be 'Clinton's Watergate'. This led to one Republican to dub the incident 'Zippergate'. When the press later revealed that Miss Lewinsky was only twenty-one years of age, another referred to the incident as 'Jailbaitgate', adding 'in this case the smoking gun is in Mr Clinton's trousers'.

The Lewinsky story broke in America during the 'Unabomber' terrorist trial, leading one wag to call Clinton's scandal 'Unibanger'.

During the 1996 presidential election, the third candidate, the independent Ross Perot said: 'Nobody likes to be called a liar, but to be called a liar by Bill Clinton is really a unique experience.'

And a Republican view of Clinton's foreign policy expertise was provided by Republican Pat Buchanan: 'Bill Clinton's foreign policy experience stems mainly from having breakfast at the International House of Pancakes.'

Some Republicans used to tell the story that Bill Clinton, during his time in the White House, despairing of his domestic troubles over sexual impropriety, went for a midnight jog around Washington to think and seek inspiration for what he should do.

He stopped at the statue of George Washington, looked up and heard a voice say, 'You must be honest like me – I never told a lie.' Clinton thought, 'Well, it's too late for me to do that now!' So he continued jogging and reached the statue of Thomas Jefferson. He looked up and heard a voice say, 'Abide by the rules of the Constitution – I should know I wrote it – and you will inspire the American people.'

'Well,' he thought, 'it's too late for me to do that now!' So he turned back to the White House and made a final stop at the statue of the great Republican President Abraham Lincoln. He looked up and said, 'You were a truly great President, even though you were a Republican. Tell me do you have any suggestions about what I should do?' And he heard a voice say, 'Have you ever thought of going to the theatre?'

Overheard at a Democratic Party meeting: 'I think Clinton's got vision, determination and tremendous leadership qualities. It's such a pity she's married to that slob Bill.'

A Congressman overheard during a particularly volatile day on the stock market: 'The Dow Jones has been up and down more often than Clinton's pants.'

Overheard in Washington, on why Hillary Clinton has stayed loyal to husband Bill: 'Hillary only weighs ninety-five pounds. The rest is thick skin.'

Dismissing Clinton's claims that allegations against him were just part of a right-wing conspiracy, one Republican said: 'He's just Arkan-sore.'

Graffiti seen in Washington during the Clinton years: 'Monica Lewinsky now votes Republican. She says the Democrats have left a bad taste in her mouth.'

Even today, over ten years since he left office, the gags against Clinton still abound. Recently, in Canada, a black comedian opened his act by saying that he 'misses Bill Clinton', adding: 'Yep, that's right – I miss Bill Clinton! He was the closest thing we ever got to having a black man as President. Number one – he played the sax. Number two – he smoked weed. Number three – he had his way with ugly white women.

Even now, look at him... His wife works, and he don't! And, he gets a cheque from the government every month.'

Other recently heard Clinton quips are:

'Manufacturers announced today that they will be stocking America's shelves this week with "Clinton Soup", in honour of one of the nation's most distinguished men. It consists primarily of a weenie in hot water.'

'Chrysler Corporation is adding a new car to its line: to honour Bill Clinton, the Dodge Drafter will be built in Canada.'

'When asked what he thought about foreign affairs, Clinton replied, 'I don't know, I never had one.'

'The Clinton revised judicial oath: 'I solemnly swear to tell the truth as I know it, the whole truth as I believe it to be, and nothing but what I think you need to know.'

'Clinton will be recorded in history as the only President to do Hanky Panky between the Bushes.'

Clinton, like others before him, has found life after the Presidency not to be too bad. Although he left office under various clouds, last year he made nearly $10 million in after-dinner speeches and appearances and his 2004 autobiography is also believed to have earned him a $10 million advance. Little wonder therefore that he has been nicknamed 'Dollar Bill'.

⧗

ON THE 1992 American presidential election, when voters were faced with a choice of either George Bush, Bill Clinton or Ross Perot, one politician commented: 'Choosing between those three was like needing clean underwear but being forced to decide between three dirty pairs.'

⧗

ANONYMOUS ON former Vice President Al Gore: 'He is in danger of becoming all things to no people.'

⧗

AMERICAN REPUBLICAN Newt Gingrich commenting on too much government: 'Bureaucratic rules cannot take the place of common sense.'

And on today's problems: 'No society can survive, no civilisation can survive, with having twelve-year-olds having babies, with fifteen-year-olds killing each other, with seventeen-year-olds dying of AIDS, with eighteen-year-olds getting diplomas they can't read.'

⧗

GEORGE W. BUSH was elected US President in 2000 by the narrowest of margins. It is reported that when he entered the White House grounds for the first time, he saw a sign which read: 'Keep off the grass.' Bush jested: 'Was that put there for Clinton?'[*]

In 2003, most Londoners were either entertained or angered by the antics of American illusionist David Blaine who spent weeks in a glass box suspended above the river Thames as a publicity stunt. Shortly after his ordeal ended, Bush paid a historic state visit and upon arriving joked: 'It was pointed out to me that the last noted American to visit London stayed in a glass box dangling over the Thames. A few might have been happy to provide similar arrangement for me.'

Many of the insults directed at George W. Bush arise out of his own sometimes sloppy use of language. Some of the most notorious examples of his verbal blunders and tortured syntax are as follows:

'Let me put it to you this way, they misunderestimated me.'

'We want to make America a literate country and a hopefuller country.'

---

[*]   Bill Clinton admitted taking cannabis when he was a student.

'Well, I think that if you say you're going to do something and don't do it, that's trustworthiness.'

'Being President is like running a cemetery: you've got a lot of people under you and nobody's listening.'

'I have a different vision of leadership. A leadership is someone who brings people together.'

'It isn't pollution that's harming the environment. It's the impurities in our air and water that are doing it.'

'Rarely is the questions asked: is our children learning.'

Admitting his tendency to mangle his sentences sometimes, in 2004 he admitted: 'I have a few flaws – people sometimes have to correct my English – I knew I had a problem when Arnold Schwarzenegger had to do it.'

Showing increasing confidence three years into his presidential term, he self-deprecatingly joked: 'The thing about the Presidency is that whatever shortcomings you have people are going to notice them.'

He has also said of himself: 'Some folks attack me for a certain swagger, which in Texas we call "walking".'

When someone asked him how he expected his hour and a half debate with Democrat challenger John Kerry to go, he replied: 'He could spend the ninety minutes debating himself.'

Amongst his other remarks, the most memorable are:

'My opponent is running on a platform of increasing taxes – and that's the sort of promise most politicians usually keep.'

'I support the institution of marriage against activist judges.'

'Millions of people in the Middle East plead in silence for their liberty.'

When a secular study argued that bad economic times can actually be good for you because people tend to exercise more and eat better, one politician sniped: 'This is now not to be called a recession, this is the Bush Health Care Plan.'

When President Bush, was on a European tour, one wag in Congress quipped: 'He's on a four-day trip to Belgium, Slovakia, Belarus and several other places he cannot pronounce.'

And, recalling Bush's successful re-election campaign, a commentator joked: 'There was just one awkward moment where a black man stood up to ask a question and out of habit, Bush said, "Clemency denied".'

In 2004, following the Bush administration's invasion of Iraq, some graffiti appeared, referring to the reaction in Europe to the conflict. It read: 'Thousands of Germans have taken to the streets to protest at the US invasion of Iraq. That's when you know you've really accomplished something – when the Germans think you're invading too much!'

⧗

CAR BUMPER STICKER seen during the 2004 presidential election: 'Bush–Cheney – Four More Wars.'

And, in a similar vein: 'Vote John Kerry – Bring complete sentences back to the White House.'

⧗

THE VICE PRESIDENT to George W. Bush was Dick Cheney, who is reckoned to be cursed – bad things happen to all those who hire him.

Cheney got his first political job from Richard Nixon, who was then forced from office. He was then given a job by Nixon's successor Gerald Ford who, with Cheney's help, lost the 1976 election to Jimmy Carter. Then, George Bush's father George H. W. Bush made Cheney his Secretary of State for Defense before promptly being defeated by Bill Clinton in 1992. Some Republicans suggested that Cheney should have volunteered to work for Democrat Barack Obama in 2009!

⧗

ANONYMOUS ON one particular Senator: 'They just called him the town drunk. However, he lived in New York at the time.'

⧖

FORMER US Secretary of Defense Donald Rumsfeld has shown himself to be the master of the bamboozling answer. When faced with a hostile question from the press about Iraq, he once memorably responded: 'Reports that say something hasn't happened are always interesting to me because, as we know, there are known knowns; there are things that we know we know. We also know that there are known unknowns; that is to say that we know there are some things that we don't know; but there are also unknown unknowns, the ones we don't know.' Follow that!

⧖

FORMER DEMOCRAT presidential hopeful John Kerry has the distinction of having married two heiresses, first Julia Thorne and then his current wife Teresa Heinz. This has led some Republicans to make capital out of his relationships. One Senator has recently called him 'John Gigolo Kerry', whilst another wisecracked: 'He lives off other men's money by marrying their wives and daughters.'

Perhaps more damaging to his 2004 presidential campaign were accusations of his constant policy changes or 'flip-flops'. One anti-Kerry TV ad starts by stating 'He flip-flopped on his marriage of eighteen years...' and then goes on to itemise his 'flip-flops' on policy – to the theme tune from the film about a dolphin called Flipper!

Former Vice President Dick Cheney, attacking Kerry on his inconsistency, wryly said: 'He spends some time wrestling with the problems of today, but he spends most of his time wrestling with himself.'

Anonymous on John Kerry: 'His hobby is windsurfing. Most appropriate as he always faces whichever way the wind blows.'

Kerry himself has rather fuelled accusations of 'flip-flops'

by saying: 'You might "be certain" but wrong. Certainty can
sometimes get you into trouble.'

⧖

WHEN ARNOLD SCHWARZENEGGER was inaugurated as Governor
of California, an opponent said that the oath of office should
be changed to: 'Raise your right hand and butcher the English
language after me.'

⧖

SEEN PINNED on the wall in a Democrat's office during the first
presidential term of George W. Bush:

Warning!
    The Centre for Disease Control has issued a warning
about a virulent new strain of Sexually Transmitted Infection.
The infection is contracted through dangerous and high-
risk behaviour. The infection is called Gonorrhea Lectim
[pronounced 'gonna re-elect him'].
    Many victims contracted it in 2004, after having been
screwed for four years. Cognitive characteristics of individuals infected include: anti-social personality disorders, delusions of grandeur with messianic overtones, extreme cognitive dissonance, inability to incorporate new information,
pronounced xenophobia and paranoia, inability to accept
responsibility for one's own actions, cowardice masked by
misplaced bravado, uncontrolled facial smirking, ignorance
of geography and history, tendencies towards evangelical
theocracy, and categorical all-or-nothing behaviour.
    This destructive infection originated only a few years ago
from a bush found in Texas.

⧖

RECENTLY OVERHEARD on Capitol Hill:

'In South Africa, most politicians seem to spend a lot of time in jail before they are elected. Here in the USA it's the other way around.'

On one heavy-drinking Congressman: 'He drinks so much, he's been officially declared a beverage.'

On an independent politician: 'He's half Republican and half Democrat. He eats like an elephant and looks like a jackass.'[*]

⧗

REPUBLICAN HOPEFUL Mike Huckabee enlivened one 2008 primary speech he was making, about the growing cost of healthcare as America's baby-boomer generation reaches retirement age, by remarking: 'Imagine what it's going to cost when all the hippies realise they can get free drugs.'

⧗

FORMER PRESIDENT Bill Clinton hit the campaign trail again in 2008, but this time to support his wife Hillary in her presidential ambitions. Asked about the campaign of her main rival, fellow Democrat Barack Obama, he jibed: 'The biggest fairytale I have ever seen.'

Hillary herself accused fellow Democrat Barack Obama of political plagiarism: 'If your candidacy is going to be about words then they should be your own words. Lifting whole passages from someone else's speeches is not change you can believe in; it's change you can Xerox.'

Barack Obama, meanwhile, said of himself: 'I am so overexposed, I am making Paris Hilton look like a recluse.'

---

[*]   The emblem of the Republican Party is an elephant and that of the Democrats is a donkey.

One Republican supporter, speaking after an oration by the Democrat victor Obama, declared: 'He ought to be called Barack O'Blah-blah.'

⌛

DURING THE 2008 presidential primaries, veteran Republican John McCain was on good form. He asked: 'What is the difference between a lawyer and a catfish?' Answering his own question, he quickly replied: 'One is a scum-sucking bottom feeder and the other is a fish.'

At a rally in South Carolina McCain illustrated his battle to cut profligate congressional spending with two more wise-cracks. He told a 1,000-strong crowd: 'Ronald Reagan used to say "Congress spends money like a drunken sailor", but I never met a sailor with the imagination of congress.' He continued: 'This is a true story: about six months ago I got an email from a guy who wrote: "As a former drunken sailor, I resent being compared to Congress."'

At another rally, maintaining his attack on federal spending, McCain said: 'Congress recently spent $3 million for a programme to study the DNA of bears in Montana. Now, I don't know if this was a criminal issue or a paternity issue.'

⌛

MCCAIN CAUSED a few raised eyebrows when he picked the unknown Alaskan Sarah Palin as his running mate during the summer of 2008.

Mother of five, Mrs Palin immediately showed that she was no wimp by describing herself as 'a pit bull in lipstick', before savaging Democrat Barack Obama and his calls for 'change' by declaring: 'In politics, there are some candidates who use change to promote their careers. And then there are those, like John McCain, who use their careers to promote change.'

Obama was to continue to be a rich source for Palin:

'A man who has authored two memoirs but not a single major law or reform – not even in the state senate.'

'This is a man who can give an entire speech about the wars America is fighting, and never use the word "victory" except when he's talking about his own campaign.'

Palin herself has not escaped criticism from her opponents, being called 'Sarah Barracuda' by her detractors.

⌛

EDWARD KENNEDY, who died in 2009, commenting a few years before on not getting the top job in US politics, said: 'I don't mind not being President. I just mind that someone else is.'

⌛

BARACK OBAMA is the forty-fourth President of the United States of America and is the first African-American to hold such office. He previously served as US Senator for Illinois, from January 2005 until he resigned following his success in the 2008 election.

Before his election victory, he was insulted by his opponents frequently and the insults often contained racial overtones. His rival, Senator Joe Biden – before later becoming his Vice President – called Obama 'clean' and 'articulate' in an interview with a New York weekly, days before he launched his own campaign. The words were taken to be racially charged and Biden spent the first day of his campaign apologising.

But Obama gained support when, unprompted, he came to Biden's aide, saying: 'I've worked with Joe Biden, I've seen his leadership, I have absolutely no doubt about what is in his heart and the commitment that he's made with respect to racial equality in this country, so I will provide some testimony, as they say in church.'

Later, the Hillary Clinton campaign was forced to make its first official apology, after South Carolina State Senator

Robert Ford said Obama wouldn't be able to win the White House because he is black.

Another apology loomed after Bill Shaheen, a Hillary Clinton campaign co-chairman, had told the *Washington Post* that Republicans would ask Obama, 'Did you sell [drugs] to anyone?' Shortly afterwards, Hillary Clinton herself had to apologise to Obama.

However, Obama has shown he himself is not averse to employing a bit of choice language when attacking opponents. During the 2008 election, he poked fun at opponent McCain and his running-mate Palin's mantra for 'change'. Of their plans he said: 'You can put lipstick on a pig, but it's still a pig.' As the crowd of his supporters cheered, he added: 'You can wrap an old fish in a piece of paper called change, but it's still gonna stink.'

Many observers took the 'lipstick' line as a reference to Sarah Palin, who had said when describing herself that the difference between a hockey mom and a pit bull was a single word: 'lipstick'. (See above.) This attack led the McCain campaign to claim Obama called Palin a pig, which he did not (quite).

Other Barack Obama quotes worthy of note are:

'I think it is important for Europe to understand that even though I am President and George Bush is not now President, al Qaeda is still a threat.'

'My job is not to represent Washington to you, but to represent you to Washington.'

'If you're walking down the right path and you're willing to keep walking, eventually you'll make progress.'

'One of the great strengths of the United States is we have a very large Christian population – but we do not consider ourselves a Christian nation or a Jewish nation or a Muslim nation. We consider ourselves a nation of citizens who are bound by ideals and a set of values.'

'I think when you spread the wealth around it's good for everybody.'

'The fact that my fifteen minutes of fame has extended a little longer than fifteen minutes is somewhat surprising to me and completely baffling to my wife.'

'My faith is one that admits some doubt.'

On his fellow countrymen: 'Americans still believe in an America where anything's possible – they just don't think their leaders do.'

And on himself: 'I miss being anonymous.'

After his decisive election win, Obama was asked whether he thought that the vitriolic reaction to his health care plans was driven partly by racism. The question was fuelled by former US President Jimmy Carter saying he thought that racism *was* a factor. President Obama, calmly dismissing these suggestions, replied: 'I think it's important to realise that I was actually black before the election.'

⌛

DEMOCRATIC VICE PRESIDENT Joe Biden first stood for President of the US in 1987. His disastrous campaign collapsed, however, due mainly to an act of plagiarism when he borrowed the words of another politician, Britain's Neil Kinnock.

Unfortunately, he borrowed Kinnock's life story too, by claiming that he was 'the first Biden to go to university' and that his ancestors 'had worked down a coal mine'. Both these assertions were untrue and Biden's presidential campaign spectacularly collapsed.

It was surprising that anyone should copy a speech of Kinnock, who only ever managed to lead the Labour Party to defeat. But Biden perhaps felt an affinity for Neil Kinnock because Biden too is regarded as a notorious windbag who loves nothing more than the sound of his own voice.

It therefore came as a surprise to many that Barack Obama should choose Biden as his Vice Presidential running mate in 2008. As expected, Biden's run on the 2008 ticket did not come without mistakes. It was only a few weeks before he was chosen that he was proclaiming that Obama was 'too inexperienced for the top job', whilst proclaiming that he would be 'honoured to run with or against' Obama's rival, the Republican John McCain.

As mentioned above, Biden also embarrassingly once described Barack Obama as 'the first mainstream African-American who is articulate and bright and clean and a nice looking guy'.

⌛

FORMER SENATOR and current US Secretary of State Hillary Clinton on the US–UK relationship: 'If there were any closer alignment, we would worry about each other.'

⌛

ACCORDING TO one disillusioned US politician, the reason the President has an Oval office is so that 'in reality, the buck won't stop anywhere'.

WHO SAID THAT?

During the seventeenth century, John Tillotson had a dim view of those politicians who defamed others: 'Slanderers are like flies; they leap over a man's good parts to light upon his sores.'

Defamatory bile is remembered, more often than not, even if the circumstances and the names of the perpetrators become lost in the mists of time. MPs will often recollect a good put -down not because they are interested in the circumstances of its use but because they may wish to re-use it in future themselves!

Although Hansard records for posterity what is said in both Houses, it is the barbs thrown outside the Chamber, unrestricted by narrow rules of order, that are usually the most insulting, the more amusing and chiefly dishonourable. The trouble is that these can soon be lost to posterity with the passage of time, unless they are recorded somewhere.

In this section, although mud slung has been recorded, the culprits are not known.

⧗

A TORY MP on Caroline Spelman MP, after her policy U-turn on the sale of forests in 2011: 'I worship the quicksand she walks in.'

And another: 'She is so religious she wears stained-glass contact lenses.'

⧗

ON FORMER Lib Dem Leader Menzies Campbell:
'I have seen better-looking faces on pirate flags.'

'You know that organisation that freezes bodies – well he is a founder member.'

⧗

ON FORMER Labour minister and MP, the tall red-headed Vera Baird: 'The Towering Inferno'.

⧗

ON A PARTICULAR New Labour MP: 'She has been in more beds than a packet of seeds.'

⧗

DISENCHANTED LABOUR MP on his party's current leader and shadow Chancellor: 'Ed Balls and Ed Miliband ought to be on TV on one of those food programmes. Balls has been cooking the books for years and Ed is clearly a chef – he makes a meal out of everything he does.'

⧗

ON THE Lib Dems' Nick Clegg:

'There are two sides to every question – and he always takes both.'

'Whenever he gets an idea in his head it's a stowaway.'

'Calamity Clegg.'

During a speech by Clegg, an MP was heard to mutter: 'I am full of admiration.' When a colleague replied that Clegg's speech was 'not that good', the MP snapped: 'I know. I am full of admiration for the audience for listening to this twaddle.'

⧗

ON THE LATE Eric Forth MP: 'He looked like a Victorian under-taker dressed for a day at the races.'

✕

ON DENNIS SKINNER:

'He was an unwanted child. When they gave him a rattle it was still attached to the snake.'

'Did you know when Dennis Skinner was only three months old he was left on a doorstep for three days and three nights in a little basket and nobody picked him up... so his mother and father took him in again.'

✕

ON ANDREW MITCHELL MP: 'He was always willing to lend a help-ing hand to the one above him.'

✕

TORY MPS on Labour's Stephen Timms:

'He's the only politician who could appear live on *Spitting Image*.'

'He is so thin, the crease in his trousers is him.'

'He looks like one of the comic characters from the Bash Street Kids.'

✕

LABOUR MP on Conservative peer Lord (David) Maclean: 'He's nothing but a Thatcher knicker-washer.'

✕

OVERHEARD IN the Commons Tea Room:

MP 1: 'I predict that Matt Hancock will be the first

MP from the 2010 intake to be made a minister and given high office.'

MP 2: 'Oh, he is very good then?'

MP 1: 'I have no idea – but he IS a friend of George Osborne.'

※

A LABOUR MP commenting on a particularly pompous Tory member: 'He is so 'up himself' that he has to view life out of his belly button.'

※

TORY ON Tony Blair: 'He was extremely brave, fearlessly exchanging a quip or two with vicious interviewers like Des O'Connor.'

※

ON LABOUR MP Meg Munn: 'I think she has her hair done at Interflora.'

※

ON LABOUR's Barry Sheerman: 'Barry? – I love every bone in his head.'

※

ON TORY David Liddington MP: 'When he speaks he doesn't know what to do with his hands. It's a pity he doesn't put them over his mouth.'

※

ON BOURNEMOUTH, one MP was heard to remark: 'So many retired people live there, all the shop windows are bifocal.'

✖

ON SOUTH YORKSHIRE: 'At the height of the output from their coal mines even the birds woke up coughing.'

✖

ON ED MILIBAND:

'He's got a terrible inferiority complex – and he's right.'

'Ed Miliband says he will be Prime Minister one day – and I think one day will be quite long enough.'

Backbench MP on Labour's Ed Miliband: 'His open mind should be closed for repairs.'

'I heard Ed Miliband's speech under very unfortunate circumstances – my seat faced the platform.'

✖

ON FORMER Labour minister Vernon Coaker: 'The difference between Vernon Coaker and yoghurt is that yoghurt has real culture.'

✖

ON CONSERVATIVE Daniel Kawczynski, who is the tallest MP in the House:

'It's amazing how even at six feet eight inches tall, so much still goes over his head.'

'He's so tall, he has to have his passport photo taken by satellite.'

✖

ON LIB DEM Simon Hughes:

'He has nothing to say but you have to listen a long time to find that out.'

'He's always me-deep in conversation.'

⧗

ON BOB NEALE MP: 'A lovely guy but he is so small he has turn ups on his beach shorts.'

⧗

A TORY WHIP on a fallen colleague: 'If the end result is profit, there is always a temptation to break the law.'

⧗

ON LABOUR'S Steve McCabe MP: 'He would make a great distant relative.'

⧗

LABOUR MP commenting in 2009: 'What is brown all over and makes a mess of everything it touches?... Gordon, our leader.'

⧗

ON FORMER Conservative leader Michael Howard MP: 'He looks like an Italian fullback about to cut your legs away.'

⧗

ON THE LATE Sir Angus Maude: 'He had so many cavities he spoke with an echo.'

⧗

TORY MPS on Glenda Jackson:
'She has a face that would fade flowers.'

'She's "pushing thirty-five" so long it's pleated.'

☒

ON NEW Tory MP Claire Perry: 'Claire is to politics what perry is to champagne.'

☒

ON ONE female MP who was given a make-over: 'Putting lipstick on the pig may make it look better but you still don't want to kiss it.

☒

ON ONE particularly unctuous Tory Cabinet minister: 'Mr Slimeball'.

☒

ON TORY MP Simon Burns: 'Simon Burns doesn't know much about foreign affairs. He thinks the Gaza Strip is Paul Gascoigne's football shirt.'

☒

ON TORY MP Nicholas Soames: 'He can trace his ancestors back to royalty – King Kong.'

☒

ON A FORMER Labour MP who was invariably inebriated: 'She's joined Alcoholics Anonymous. She still drinks but under an assumed name.'

☒

ON FORMER London Mayor Ken Livingstone: 'If you only want to read about his sensible policies, it won't take long. You could write them on the back of a postage stamp.'

⊠

ON CONSERVATIVE MP Peter Bone:
  'The way he finds fault, you'd think there was a reward.'
  'Peter Bone doesn't suffer from insanity. He enjoys every minute of it.'

⊠

LABOUR MP on former Labour minister Charles Clark: 'The trouble with Charles is that he's an over-educated Philistine.'

⊠

ON VETERAN MP Frank Dobson: 'If he got lost in thought it would only be because it is unfamiliar territory.'

⊠

ON FORMER Tory whip Tim Wood, who used to work in computers before entering politics: 'He knows all there is to know about state-of-the-ark computers and trailing-edge technology.'

⊠

TORY MP on the Conservative–Lib Dem coalition and its policies: 'I thought it would be a case of open-necked shirts and sandals – but the reality is a succession of flip-flops.'

⊠

ON ENVIRONMENTAL CAMPAIGNER and extremely wealthy Conservative MP Zac Goldsmith:

'He thinks he is a very green, important, politician but in reality he is just impotent and very green *as* a politician.'

'The only person I know who puts Perrier water in his bath.'

'He's so rich, when he catches a plane he has to check in his wallet.'

'He made his money the old-fashioned way. He inherited it.'

⧗

ON THE LATE Labour MP Jo Richardson: 'She was such a bad driver her driving licence had a picture of St Christopher in it and her car was insured with Lloyds of Oops.'

⧗

MP'S DEFINITION of the 'First Rule of Journalism': 'All journalists follow this simple rule – first simplify, then exaggerate.'

And again on journalism: 'Most journalists I know work eight hours a day and sleep eight hours a day. The trouble is they're the same eight hours.'

⧗

TORY MP on former Respect Party MP George Galloway: 'George can come and live next door to me anytime – my house is next to a cemetery.'

⧗

ON DAVID CAMERON:

'I won't say he's conceited but if you asked him to name the Seven Wonders of the World, he would probably mention himself twice!'

'He reminds me of some cutlery. He was born with a silver spoon in his mouth, speaks with a forked tongue and knifes his colleagues in the back.'

'Proof that no shirt is too young to be stuffed.'

Lib Dem dissident on Cameron: 'He's the Karaoke Kid – he'd sing anything to get re-elected.'

And a former Conservative MP on the Prime Minister: 'Never trust a man with a woman's mouth.'

⧗

AN MP on former Tory leadership contender Michael Portillo: 'He has child-bearing lips.'

⧗

ON LABOUR MP Keith Vaz: 'I won't say he is slimy but he ought to be named vasoline.'

⧗

ON LABOUR'S former MP James Wray: 'He doesn't hold a conversation – he strangles it.'

⧗

ON TORY MP Sir Peter Tapsell:

'He has more crust than a pie factory.'

'I don't know how old he is but when he was young the Dead Sea was still alive!'

'Sir Peter Tapsell MP doesn't have an enemy in the World... he's outlived them.'

⧗

ON ED BALLS MP:

'He is about as much use as a ribless umbrella.'
'He's just embarked on a boast-to-boast tour.'
'Whenever he enters a room, he gets a cringing ovation.'

⌧

ON LABOUR'S Alan Johnson MP: 'Living proof that not all con men in Britain are selling second-hand cars.'

⌧

ON ONE former Tory MP, who during his last parliament ran into financial problems: 'He has a black belt in borrowing.'

⌧

ON TORY MP Andrew Selous: 'He's so tall his shadow has a hinge.'

⌧

GOVERNMENT WHIP to backbencher: 'Listen to me. I did not say you were going on a trip to South Korea. What I said was your career is going south.'

⌧

ON ONE particular MP, usually found in one of the Commons bars: 'The only diet he believes in is the alcohol diet. In his case it sometimes works – just this month he has already lost three days.'

⌧

ON JOHN MAJOR: 'John Major was an eternal optimist – even in 1995 he still believed that Donald Campbell was just missing.'

※

SOMETIMES THE insulting banter takes on a life of its own. Commenting on former Tory minister Steve Norris, who was a candidate for London's first Lord Mayor, and who, according to the press, once had five mistresses, one Tory colleague said: 'A case of too much Dick and not enough Whittington.'

This caused another politician to allude to Mr Norris's former position as a junior transport minister and riposte: 'Well you can't blame him really. Sex is rather like the problems he encountered with transport. You wait a long while and then five come along at once.'

Another colleague accepted this explanation, adding: 'Well, I suppose there is always room for another one on top.'

※

ON JAMES MORRIS MP: 'He doesn't have his hair cut, he goes for an oil change.'

※

FORMER ATTORNEY GENERAL Sir Reginald Manningham-Buller was often insultingly referred to as 'Sir Reginald Bullying-Manner' by his opponents.

※

'DOUGLAS ALEXANDER is doing the best he can. There, that's scared you.'

※

ON FORMER MP Ann Widdecombe: 'She has the body of a twenty-year-old... a twenty-year-old Skoda.'

⧗

ON HAZEL BLEARS MP: 'She's so short, when she sits she's taller.'
Again on Ms Blears: 'When it rains she's the last to know.'
And again: 'The ginger chipmunk.'

⧗

ON TORY David Davis MP:
  "David Davis has never ever been guilty of discrimination.
He'll kick anyone in the groin.'
  'He has knifed more people than a surgeon.'
  'He always sees germs in the milk of human kindness.'
  'He never hits a man when he's down. He kicks him.'

⧗

ON LABOUR's Geoffrey Robinson MP: 'He's so rich, he has
bookcases for his bankbooks.'

⧗

ON TORY Tim Yeo MP: 'To him a game of golf isn't a matter of
life and death – it's more important than that.'

⧗

ON THE Strangers' Cafeteria: 'It's the only place where you say
grace over grease.'

⧗

ACCORDING TO one Labour MP, the definition of 'confusion' is
Fathers' Day at a Tribune Meeting.

⧗

A TORY MP who now sits in the Cabinet, on seeing David Cameron and George Osborne walking down a Commons corridor together, joshed: 'Here come Bill and Ben.'

And again on Cameron and Osborne: 'They are the Ant and Dec of British politics.'

⧗

WHEN THE House returned from its summer break, one Tory MP quipped: 'During the summer recess, whilst touring Europe, I got through two Louise Bagshawe novels. I must remember to take enough lavatory paper next time.'

⧗

ON LABOUR veteran David Winnick MP:

'He is so old that on his birthday his family open a magnum of Wincarnis.'

'He was born in the Year of Our Lord only knows.'

⧗

TORY MP overheard discussing his travel arrangements: 'I never travel on the London Underground because I suffer from Riff-Raff-obia.'

⧗

ON TORY MP Howard Flight when he was deselected by the then Tory leader Michael Howard: 'A combination of a Stuffed Shirt and a Hooray Henry – but currently completely stuffed.'

⧗

'SILENCE IS a long conversation with Lord Ryder of Wensum.'

⌛

YOUNG TORY on a female Labour MP: 'She has the looks that turn heads.'

Tory whip: '... and stomachs too.'

⌛

TORY MP on UK minority parties: 'They make no real contribution to our parliamentary process. They play at it. Most of them probably think that tactics are a type of peppermint.'

⌛

ON LABOUR's Chris Bryant MP:
'He thinks "pause" is a disease.'
'He speaks at 120 words a minute – with gusts up to 150.'
'He's a born-again cretin.'

⌛

ON FORMER Labour MP Barbara Follett:
'In her house the antique furniture is just stuff from her first marriage.'
'She's so rich, the bags under her eyes are Gucci.'

⌛

ON LORD BILSTON: 'He has a great voice... unfortunately it's in someone else's throat.'

⌛

ON NEW Conservative MP Richard Fuller: 'He looks like Neville Chamberlain's grandson.'

⧗

ON MARGARET HODGE MP: 'She should leave and let live.'

⧗

ON GEOFFREY COX QC MP: 'His way of being right is to be wrong at the top of his voice.'

⧗

ON LABOUR'S Gordon Brown: 'When Gordon Brown was Chancellor of the Exchequer, the difference between a taxidermist and the taxman is that the taxidermist leaves the skin.'

⧗

ON FORMER Labour minister Fiona Mactaggart MP: 'She has a new form of exercise – aerobic nagging.'

⧗

ON ONE of Labour's female MPs elected in 1997: 'She's had so much bridge work done in her mouth, if you kiss her you have to pay a toll.'

⧗

TORY MP on the difference between Tony Blair and Gordon Brown: 'Blair was "Teflon man" – nothing stuck to him, not even his own mistakes. Gordon Brown on the other hand is "Velcro Man" – he gets the stick for everything.'

⧗

ON ONE new female Labour MP: 'When she has one drink, she can't feel it. When she has two drinks, she can feel it. After her third drink, anybody can feel it.'

⊠

ON ONE particular female MP 'Some women have faces that can stop a clock. She could stop Switzerland!'

⊠

ON THE late Sir Nicholas Fairbairn: 'A chain drinker.'

And again on Sir Nicholas: 'He never drinks unless he's alone or with someone.'

⊠

ON HARRIET HARMAN MP: 'She's really moving but that's because she's going downhill.'

⊠

ON DAVID MILIBAND MP: 'He would make a perfect stranger.'

⊠

ON ONE particular MP: 'He was descended from a long line his mother fell for.'

⊠

TORY WHIP commenting on former minister Nicholas Scott: 'He has a good head on his shoulders – a different one each night.'

⊠

ON ONE particular MP: 'He drinks so much, when he sweats he's a fire hazard.'

⧗

ON ONE MP who is notorious for not buying a round of drinks when his turn arrives: 'He would make an excellent employee of MI5. He is too mean to give himself away.'

⧗

ON CONSERVATIVE Henry Bellingham MP: 'The closest he'll come to a brainstorm is a slow drizzle.'

⧗

ON PETER HAIN MP: 'He's nobody's fool. He freelances.'

⧗

TORY COMMENTING on accident-prone former Labour defence minister Lord Malloch-Brown: 'He should be named Lord Bollock-Brown.'

⧗

LABOUR MP: 'In my constituency, if you pay the rent on time, they arrest you for robbery.'

⧗

ON LIB DEM MP Danny Alexander: 'An unknown amongst unknowns.'

⧗

LIB DEM MP Vincent Cable on PM Gordon Brown: 'A twitching corpse.'

🗙

ON ONE new Labour woman MP, known for flirting: 'She used to live in all the best hotels... one hour at a time.'

🗙

'I THINK William Hague is just like Winston Churchill. Both look like new-born babies.'

🗙

ON THE late Gwyneth Dunwoody MP: 'She has an unlisted dress size.'

🗙

ON LABOUR's Barry Gardiner MP: 'Some people say he's a pain in the back. Others have a lower opinion of him.'

🗙

ON CHRIS HUHNE MP: 'For years he was an unknown failure. Now he is a known failure.'

🗙

ON A FORMER MINISTER: 'She talks so much she's listed in the Guinness Book of Broken Records.'

🗙

ON ONE particular female MP: 'I don't know what's eating her – but it's going to get indigestion.'

⧗

ON MARK PRITCHARD MP: 'He's got a good sense of rumour.'

⧗

ON THE chefs in Westminster: 'At least the Commons Dining room is consistent – they serve steak, coffee and ice cream, all at the same temperature.'

⧗

ON MP and minister Shaun Woodward: 'He's got about as many friends as an alarm clock.'

⧗

ON TORY MP Alistair Burt: 'He claims to speak to the Lord – on a one-to-one basis.'

⧗

ON CONSERVATIVE Gary Streeter MP 'He's so religious, he has all his papers marked "Top Sacred".'

⧗

'I'M ALL in favour of women MPs. It's better having them in the House than outside driving cars.'

⧗

ON FORMER Conservative Leader, Michael Howard: 'He is living proof that there is life after death.'

And on former Lib Dem Leader Menzies Campbell: 'Clear proof that there isn't.'

⊠

ON TORY MP Neil Parrish: 'He puts the rust into rustic.'

⊠

WHEN THE Tory leadership election in 2005 led to a run off between David Davis MP and David Cameron MP, one Conservative MP quipped: 'It's a choice between one of the Bash Street Kids or Little Lord Fauntleroy.'

⊠

MP OVERHEARD on Northern Ireland: 'Put two Ulster MPs on a desert island and within a week there would be three churches.'

⊠

ON CLEMENT ATTLEE MP: 'Self-effacing to the point of extinction.'

⊠

ALLUDING TO the practice of voter impersonation, one MP claimed to have heard an election report from Ireland which stated: 'With three cemeteries still to be heard from, the election is too close to call.'

⊠

OVERHEARD IN Strangers' Bar: 'I hit John Prescott yesterday. I will probably be charged with "Fair Play".'

⊠

ON CIVIL servants: 'To err is human, to shrug is civil service.'

⧓

A TORY MP, told he was putting on weight: 'I have started exercising. I am keeping in shape by jogging three times a day around Eric Pickles.'

⧓

SOMETIMES AN MP can contribute to his own bad publicity unwittingly. One December, a politician was informed by his secretary that the political editor of his regional paper had telephoned and wanted to know what the MP wanted for Christmas.

Flattered, the MP told her to phone him back. 'Tell them I am not expecting anything,' he said. 'But a large bottle of whisky for me and a box of mints for the wife would be nice.'

On Christmas Eve the paper carried a seasonal story on its centre pages: 'Prime Minister David Cameron wants world peace this Christmas; Ed Miliband wants the elimination of world poverty, but your local MP says that all he wants is a large bottle of whisky and a box of mints.'

⧓

TWO POLITICIANS were talking about the Bill Clinton–Monica Lewinsky scandal, one an American Democrat and the other a British Conservative. The Democrat, clearly embarrassed, tried to change the subject and started criticising Britain's regal pomp and ceremony. He argued that President Clinton did not have to take part in ostentatious routines when he was on official duties. The British Tory silenced him with the curt reply: 'Oh, in Britain it's not so bad. In our country young students meeting our head of state are only expected to drop down on one knee!'

⧗

UPON SEEING an Iranian and Spanish politician talking, a whip remarked: 'There's Oil of Olé.'

⧗

AN MP explaining why he had fallen out with one of his own party's whips: 'It was just a clash of personalities. I had one and he didn't.'

⧗

Labour MP on Conservative minister Michael Gove: 'He is the Terminal 5 of British politics.'[*]

⧗

COLLEAGUE COMMENTING on junior culture minister Ed Vaizey: 'He ought to be renamed Dead Lazy.'

⧗

NEWS BROKE in 2011 that new Tory MP Louise Bagshawe, known since her marriage as Louise Mensch, may have taken drugs before she entered politics, an assertion which Mrs Mensch did not deny.

A year after her election to Parliament, she made a number of accusations against TV presenter Piers Morgan on the subject of phone-hacking, before withdrawing them and apologising to him.

---

[*] The opening of Terminal 5 at Heathrow Airport in London in 2008 was a national disaster, with hundreds of flights being cancelled and thousands of bags being lost or delayed.

This led one Tory wag to comment: 'Louise is certainly going places: from just 'high', to 'high-politics' then 'high-handed' in a very short space of time.'

WAGS, WITS AND WORDS OF ADVICE

Good writers borrow and great writers steal. And it's no different with politicians. Jokes are overheard, recycled and enlessly reinvented. And some of those jokers in the Tea Room are not so careful about who overhears their latest sallies...

☒

JOKERS OVERHEARD in the Commons Tea Room...

Four surgeons were taking a coffee break and discussing their work.

The first said, 'I think accountants are the easiest to operate on. You open them up and everything inside is numbered.'

The second said, 'I think librarians are the easiest to operate on. You open them up and everything inside is in alphabetical order.'

The third said, 'I like to operate on electricians. You open them up and everything inside is colour coded.'

The fourth one said, 'I prefer to operate on New Labour MPs. They're heartless, spineless, gutless and their heads and behinds are interchangeable.'

☒

MP 1: 'Under David Cameron's premiership, what is the difference between a city businessman and a pigeon?'
MP 2: 'Don't know.'
MP 1: 'These days only the pigeon can still put a deposit on a new BMW.'

⧖

TWO MPS on an overseas trip to Canada, one of them Labour, one of then a Tory. Trekking through the woods they get lost and suddenly find themselves confronted by a 500-pound grizzly bear. The Labour MP stoops down and pulls a pair of running shoes out of his rucksack and puts them on. Noticing this, the Tory MP starts laughing. 'Goodness me, you Labour chaps don't know anything about wildlife or the countryside do you. You stupid duffer. You'll never outrun a grizzly bear, old boy.' Turning on his heels, the Labour MP shouts back: 'I don't have to outrun the grizzly – I just have to outrun you!'

⧖

'WHAT HAS five heads, ten legs and three teeth?' Answer: 'The front row at a Fabian meeting.'

⧖

MP 1: 'I've heard that Nick Clegg hasn't got life insurance.'
MP 2: 'Why?'
MP 1: 'Nobody knows his policy.'

⧖

WHEN LEAVING the Commons one night Ed Miliband fell into the Thames and got into difficulty. Hearing his cries for help as he left, the Prime Minister dived in and fished him out. Rather embarrassed, Miliband thanked Cameron for his rescue but said nervously, 'Please don't leak it to the Press that I can't swim.' Cameron looked at him equally nervously: 'All right,' he agreed, 'provided also that you don't leak it to the press that I can't walk on water.'

⧖

MP 1: 'What's the difference between Hugh Grant and President Clinton?'

MP 2: 'Well, one is a second-rate actor whose career nosedived after it was revealed a woman gave him oral sex – and the other is the star of the film *Four Weddings and a Funeral*.'

☒

ALTHOUGH IT is no longer fashionable to talk ill of our European partners, during the Second World War things were different. Then the gossip at Westminster was whether you had 'heard the one about the Italian soldier who deserted his regiment and stood his ground'. But the most popular quip at the time was about the Italian soldier who 'drew his sword... and cut up a side street'.

One wag even described the Italian flag as 'a white cross on a white background'.

In these Europhile times, surprisingly things are not all that different. One MP was recently explaining that when Europeans die they all go to heaven or hell: 'The difference is that in Heaven the English are the police, the French the cooks, the Germans the mechanics, the Italians the lovers and the Swiss organise everything. Whereas, in hell, the Germans are the police, the English the cooks, the French the mechanics, the Swiss the lovers and the Italians organise everything.'

☒

IN THE 1980s, after the Falklands War, the question then was 'Why does the new Argentinian navy have glass-bottom boats?'

'To see the *old* Argentinian navy.'

☒

'THE IRA leaders have told their men to equip themselves for germ warfare – so their supporters have all bought themselves septic tanks.'

⧗

A MAN DIED and went to heaven. As he stood in front of St Peter at the Pearly Gates, he saw a huge wall of clocks behind him.

He asked, 'What are all those clocks?'

St Peter answered, 'Those are Lie-Clocks. Everyone on Earth has a Lie-Clock. Every time you lie the hands on your clock will move.'

'Oh,' said the man, 'Whose clock is that?'

'That's Mother Teresa's. The hands have never moved, indicating that she never told a lie.'

'Incredible,' said the man. 'And whose clock is that one?'

St Peter responded, 'That's Abraham Lincoln's clock. The hands have moved twice, telling us that Abe told only two lies in his entire life.'

'Where's Gordon Brown's?' asked the man.

'Gordon's clock is in Jesus' office. He's using it as a ceiling fan.'

⧗

AN UNEMPLOYED constituent demands of his MP: 'Give me £10 till payday.' The MP replies: 'When's payday?' The constituent says: 'I don't know! You're the one that's working!'

⧗

AFTER HAVING their tenth child, a Liverpool couple decided that was enough, as the social wouldn't buy them a bigger bed and they weren't strong enough to nick one. The husband went to his MP and told him that he and his wife didn't want to have any more children.

The MP told him there was a procedure called a vasectomy that would fix the problem but due to NHS waiting lists, the only option was to go private and this was expensive. A less costly alternative, the MP explained, was to go home, get a firework, light it, put it in a beer can, then hold the can up to his ear and count to ten.

The Scouser said to the MP, 'I may not be the smartest bloke in the world, but I don't see how putting a firework in a beer can next to my ear is going to help me.'

'Trust me, it will do the job', said the Member of Parliament.

So the man went home, lit a banger and put it in a beer can. He held the can up to his ear and began to count 'one, two, three, four, five,' at which point he paused, placed the beer can between his legs so he could continue counting on his other hand.

This procedure also works in parts of Essex, Luton and anywhere in Ireland!

⊠

AND ELSEWHERE...

Frank Maguire, the late Independent MP for Fermanagh and South Tyrone, on hearing a buxom young girl at a tube station say 'Maida Vale, single', stepped forward and said: 'Frank Maguire, married but willing.'

⊠

WHEN A heckler declared, 'I was born Labour, I have lived as a Labour man and I'm going to die Labour,' the Tory candidate said, 'So much for your ambition.'

⊠

A LABOUR MP tried to motivate his staff and put up signs in his office which said 'THINK'. Upon returning early from a period of parliamentary recess, he noticed that some wag had written 'OR THWIM' on one of them.

⧗

ON TELLING an old joke, a heckler shouted at the MP, 'That joke was your father's.'

The MP shot back: 'And you were your mother's.'

⧗

ONE ELDERLY MP attending a Christmas dinner was already the worse for wear before the meal had started. Upon being asked to say Grace, he stumbled to his feet and in his stupor managed to conjoin two different ecclesiastical phrases, telling the astonished diners: 'For what we are about to receive... may the Lord have mercy upon our souls.'

⧗

OVER THE YEARS, former Chipping Barnet MP Sir Sydney Chapman had to suffer more than his fair share of long boring speeches from visiting politicians. He had a rather unique way of dealing with the problem. Whenever he was asked to say Grace, he used to recite:

'Oh Lord please bless this food and wine,
And those here present about to dine,
But if long speeches we must endure,
Pray God they serve a good liqueur.'

⧗

PARLIAMENTARY PUTDOWNS:

'He has the manners of a gentleman – I knew they couldn't belong to him.'

'You're obviously not yourself today. Enjoy it whilst you can.'

'I'm told men drink to your face – they'd have to.'

'Brains aren't everything. In your case, they're nothing.'

'Don't worry. There is a good reason for you to have that stupid look on your face. You are stupid.'

'Well, I'd like to leave a thought with you – but where would you put it?'

'You know, you are so dull, you can't even entertain a doubt.'

'I have nothing but confidence in you – and not a lot of that.'

'Sir, it's a good thing for you that mirrors can't laugh.'

'He has no equals – only superiors.'

'I am sure you use your head – mostly for a rock garden.'

'If I had a lower IQ, I'm sure I'd enjoy your company.'

'She's a legend in her own mouth.'

'Why don't you go home now? Your cage has been cleaned.'

'I am sure you're kind to your inferiors... but where do you find them?'

'You're about as useful as a one-legged man trying to put out a grass fire.'

'I can see you started at the bottom... and sank.'

'I wish my future was as bright as your suit.'

'I've seen better arguments in a bowl of alphabet soup.'

'I may not agree with what you say but I'll defend to the death your right to shut up.'

'Look at him, living proof that care in the community doesn't work.'

'I can hardly contain my indifference.'

'There are two theories on how to successfully argue with women politicians. Neither one works.'

'I'm trying to imagine you with personality.'

'I never forget a face and I can remember both of yours.'

'He's an unlucky politician – when he got 24-hour flu even that lasted three weeks!'

'If I said anything to offend it was purely intentional.'

'A diplomat is someone who can tell you to go to hell in such a way that you will look forward to the trip.'

'Of course I don't look busy – I did it right the first time.'

'He's multi-talented: He can talk and annoy you at the same time.'

'How can I miss you if you won't go away?'

'Sorry if I looked interested – I'm not.'

'The National Lottery is just a tax on people who are bad at maths.'

'Please keep talking – I need the sleep.'

'I can see your point, but I still think you're full of it.'

'I like you, you remind me of when I was young and stupid.'

'You see… you should never drink on an empty head.'

'It is clearly not only the wall that's plastered.'

'I can see with you ignorance is a religion.'

'You're depriving a village somewhere of an idiot.'

'He's not paranoid, everyone does hate him.'

'Her face bears the imprint of the last man who sat on it.'

'You're taking a long time making your pointless.'

'Do you ever suffer delusions of adequacy?'

'You would be out of your depth in a puddle.'

'Your point has been received, understood and ignored.'

'Ninety-nine per cent of politicians give the rest a bad name.'

'If I need a worthless opinion, I'll ask.'

⌛

MOTTOS FOR POLITICIANS:

'Never mess up an apology with an excuse'.

'Never test the depth of the water with both feet.'

'Never underestimate the power of stupid people in large groups.'

'Success in politics is about being in the right place at the right time. Always try to stay at the table.'

'Diplomacy is about surviving until the next century. Politics is about surviving until Friday afternoon.'

'Diplomacy is the art of letting someone else get your way.'

'Diplomacy is the art of saying "good doggie" while looking for a bigger stick.'

'Don't steal. The government hates competition.'

'Diplomacy is about surviving until the next century. Politics is about surviving until Friday afternoon.'

'A political culture that has no time for lunch is no culture at all.'

'We will never have great leaders as long as we mistake education for intelligence, ambition for ability and lack of transgression for integrity.'

⧖

FOR WHIPS:

'In politics, a backbencher must learn to rise above principle.'

'If you are nice – you lose.'

'Silence is not only golden... it is never misquoted by the tabloids.'

⧖

AND, FINALLY, for the general public:

'A politician is a person with an infinite capacity for taking praise.'

'A statesman is a politician who didn't get caught.'

'The House of Commons is a rather odd place: an MP gets up to speak – and says nothing. Nobody listens – and then everybody disagrees.'

'The House of Commons is a pool of humanity which exercises democratic power. However, unlike other pools, when leaks occur, the leaks generally come from the top.'

'If you ever see a politician who pleases everybody, he will be neither sitting on the left, nor standing on the right. He will be lying flat and there will be a lot of flowers around him.'

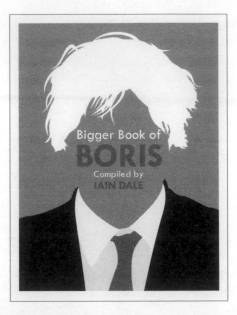